Henry Parry Liddon

## Advent in St. Paul's

Sermons bearing chiefly on the two comings of Our Lord. Vol. 2

Henry Parry Liddon

**Advent in St. Paul's**
*Sermons bearing chiefly on the two comings of Our Lord. Vol. 2*

ISBN/EAN: 9783337264710

Printed in Europe, USA, Canada, Australia, Japan

Cover: Foto ©Lupo / pixelio.de

More available books at **www.hansebooks.com**

# Advent in St. Paul's

# Advent in St. Paul's

*SERMONS*

BEARING CHIEFLY ON THE TWO COMINGS OF

## OUR LORD

By H. P. LIDDON, D.D., D.C.L.

CANON AND CHANCELLOR OF ST. PAUL'S

*IN TWO VOLUMES*

VOL. II.

*Nox præcessit: dies autem appropinquavit.    Alleluia*

RIVINGTONS

*WATERLOO PLACE, LONDON*

MDCCCLXXXIX

# CONTENTS.

# SERMON XLII.

## THE DAY OF JUDGMENT AND MORAL COURAGE.

### St. Luke ix. 26.

# SERMON XLIII.

## THE MYSTERIES OF GOD.

### I Cor. iv. 1.

# SERMON XLIV.

## THE END.

### Rev. xxi. 6.

# SERMON XLV.

## PREMATURE JUDGMENTS.

### I Cor. iv. 5.

# SERMON XXVI.

## PREPARATION FOR CHRIST'S COMING.

### I. THE COUNSELS OF PRUDENCE.

(ADVENT SUNDAY.)

Amos iv. 12.

*Prepare to meet thy God, O Israel.*

IF you wish to master a moral truth—so said a man who knew much of human nature—depend upon it, sooner or later, you must give a good deal of time to the work. The reason, he added, why so many men make so little of life, is that they do not know how to concentrate attention. They interest themselves in everything; they possess themselves of nothing. This has always been more or less true; but it is especially true in a busy age like ours, when more facts and thoughts press upon the minds of civilized men than at any earlier time in the world's history. And if it is true now of men generally, it is true as nowhere else in a city like this in which the thoughts as well as the countenances of all the peoples of the earth continually meet, in which the energy and the resource and the many-sidedness of human life is seen as perhaps nowhere else on the surface of the globe.

The Egyptian solitaries of the fourth century of our era were in many respects unlike us Londoners of to-day; but, at least, they understood the value of concentrating the mind on a moral truth which you wish to make your own. They may have done less than justice to the practical demands of human life, but they knew what was due from the human mind to the majesty and the depth of Truth. One of these men would take with him to his cell in the desert a single verse of Scripture— only one—to be thought over, prayed over, struggled over, for an entire day, for a week, for a month. No daily paper placed him in contact with the outer world; no human voice broke in, at distant hours, upon the solemn monotony of that sustained meditation; he sternly denied himself any such variety of occupation as might give a new direction to his thoughts; he lived from hour to hour, from sunrise to sunset, in sunshine and in rain, by day, and almost throughout the night, in steady, un-broken, unflagging contemplation of the one precept or truth on which he had decided to fix his thought. And, at the end, what had happened? Had he penetrated it? had he even compassed it? No; if he could have used modern words he would say that he was still an infant crying for the light; that he was on the surface of truth, not within it; that he was on the ocean, in a frail bark, but only better able to understand how measureless were the spaces around him. Yes! that is what is gained by such concentration as this; not comprehension, but some sort of apprehension of what there is to comprehend; not insight and mastery, but some approach to perceiving what the conditions of insight and mastery may possibly be. For each utterance of the Infinite Being has in it something of His own Infinity; and while we men cannot hope, by any devotion of time or toil, to penetrate the impenetrable, to exhaust the inexhaustible, we may do a great deal towards finding out what is really possible here and now; what we may hope for as possible in a higher and a more illuminated life.

There is a dry proverb, probably Eastern, which says that, after all, the sun is larger than it looks. What is implied is that the mass of human beings think of the sun as being as large as it looks and no larger. They give it now and then a passing glance on a bright day; they are not prepared to contradict what is known about its real size, for they do not think at all on the subject. Of that slow and patient toil whereby astronomy has climbed to ascertain the sun's distance from our earth, to appraise its magnitude, and even to speculate on the secrets of its brilliancy, they are content, or condemned to be ignorant; anyhow, they are ignorant. And as with the sun, so it has fared with some of the simplest and most familiar Christian truths which present themselves, in those new heavens upon which faith gazes, to the eyes of Christendom. If they are to be more to us than meaningless commonplaces, we must not think it enough to bestow on them, at distant intervals, a passing notice. We must, on the contrary, look hard at them; we must find out what has been thought about them by those who have preceded us; we must, so to say, go round and round them; we must take account of their different bearings and aspects, or, at least, of some of them; we must, if we can, place ourselves in a condition to understand, with respect to them, that, after all, "the sun *is* something greater than it seems to be." At the end we may well find that what we know is very little; but, at least, we shall be far better off than we should have been had no effort whatever been made. We shall know thus much; that there are worlds of truth above, around, beneath us, which we cannot as yet, but may some day, hope to make our own.

It is on this general principle that we may do well, on this and the three following Sundays in Advent Season, to place ourselves under the guidance and inspiration of the words of the shepherd-prophet Amos: "Prepare to meet thy God, O Israel." Certainly, when Christmas Day comes, we shall be as far as possible from feeling that we have got to the bottom of this solemn and momentous warning. Four short half-hours on four successive Sunday afternoons will not do for us what a month of uninterrupted meditation failed to do for the old Egyptian recluses. But it is, at least, possible that we may, some of us, see some new flash of light passing across the surface, the text, the sound, of very familiar words which have lost, if for us they ever had, their true meaning. It is possible that, by God's grace, some of us may date from this Advent our setting about a work which has as yet been neglected or quite forgotten ; the work of pre-paring to meet our God.

## I.

A warning like this appeals to a great deal in human character; it touches us on many sides of thought and life. To-day let me begin by, and confine myself to, observing that it appeals with particular force to our sense of prudence.

Prudence,—what is it? Why need I ask the question? Looked at from our everyday and popular point of view, prudence is, perhaps, the first of the virtues; the most needed for the well-being of human life. Prudence in man is not unlike the higher forms of instinct in animals;

only human prudence knows better what it is about than
animal instinct; it is too deliberate to be mere instinct.
Prudence in man does two things; it thinks and it acts,
or it decides to refrain from action. It looks beyond the
present moment; it is mainly concerned, not with what
is, but with what is coming; it almost lives in the future,
whether immediate or remote, but with a view to present
action. Forecast without action is mere dreaminess;
action without forecast is always folly. Prudence is foresight with a practical object; we all of us know it by
sight when we meet it in the ordinary paths of life.
Prudence is the labouring man who reflects that he will
not be always strong and young, and who puts by something year by year, if he can manage to do so, for his old
age. Prudence is the parent who scans again and again
the character of his son, before he decides on his work in
life, or on the education which will best prepare him for
it. Prudence is the boy or young man who bethinks
himself that health, and high spirits, and older friends,
and opportunities for improvement will not always last,
and who betakes himself seriously to the task of improving his mind and character. Prudence sometimes
acts by deciding not to act, where action would be more
or less natural. The prudent man does not marry when
he has no prospects whatever of being able to support
a wife and family; nor does he put the savings of years
into the first investment that offers him a tempting rate
of interest, with the risk of waking some morning to find
that a gigantic deficit has to be made good out of his
remaining capital. Such is prudence in daily life; sometimes active, sometimes hesitating, but always thoughtful. And when prudence addresses itself to higher
matters, it is still, as before, of this twofold character;
only it commands a wider horizon. Its thought reaches

beyond the grave ; and it acts or hesitates with an eye
to Eternity.

Prudence, it must be admitted, has a bad name for a
virtue ; it often is tacitly associated with selfishness ;
it is contrasted to its disadvantage with disinterestedness.
Here, men say, is prudence taking thought for the
morrow ; but Divine Wisdom points to a perfection
which takes no thought for the morrow, since the morrow
will take thought for the things of itself, and sufficient
for the day is the evil thereof." And, in earthly matters,
we must admit that prudence is not always exactly
goodness ; it gets into bad company in this our fallen
human nature, and loses the lustre of its original form.
There is prudence and prudence in earthly matters ; a
prudence which is narrow, grasping, selfish, and a prudence which can be frank and open-handed. But in the
things of Heaven there is only one kind of prudence
possible. To take really wise forethought for the
spiritual self, and to act or refrain from action accordingly, is to be at the same time disinterested. In this rare
and bright atmosphere, the truest good of man, and the
glory of the Perfect Being, and the highest good of all
other beings, absolutely coincide. In seeking the one we
seek the other ; in doing what is spiritually best for self
we achieve disinterestedness. We take no thought for the
morrow in one sense, yet in another we never forget it.
How, indeed, could it be otherwise, if, as is the case,
prudence be in the human soul a shadow of that Attribute
of the Perfect Being, which touches us at every point
of our existence ? What is prudence in man is Providence
in God. Only God, being the All-sufficient, has not to
care for Himself, but only for His creatures ; and, being
the Eternal, He cannot, strictly speaking, look forward,

" St. Matt. vi. 34.

since to Him, what has been, and is, and is to be forms
an everlasting Now. Still, of this His all-penetrating
care, which, looked at from our human point of view,
seems like foresight or providence, human prudence,
which is really foresight, is a ray in the soul of man.
And human prudence is likest to the Pattern in the
Heavens when it is most disinterested. The artisan—let
me speak of a case within my personal knowledge—who
could anticipate for his son a life of conspicuous usefulness, and then work year after year for two guineas a
week, and save nearly one half for the schooling of the boy,
who thereby was able to achieve the highest honours at
the University;—what is this but a true ray in human life
of that Loving Providence Which gives us all, if we will,
the chance of mounting heavenward? And therefore, in
connection with the first and gravest of all subjects, our
Lord Jesus Christ continually, in His teaching, appeals
to the sense of prudence as that which, if exercised on
a sufficient field, will secure to man his truest happiness.
He points out the imprudence of becoming wealthy in
this world's goods without being rich towards God.[a] He
commends the unjust steward, not for his injustice, but
for his prudence in making friends of his lord's debtors
with a view to the future, adding sorrowfully that "the
children of this world are in their generation wiser than
the children of light."[b] He pathetically describes the man
who, in the midst of his plans for pulling down his barns
and building greater, heard the solemn summons, "Thou
fool, this night thy soul shall be required of thee."[c] He
bids His disciples, "Lay not up for yourselves treasures
upon the earth, where moth and rust doth corrupt, and
where thieves break through and steal; but lay up for
yourselves treasures in Heaven, where neither moth nor

[a] St. Luke xii. 21.      [b] *Ib.* xvi. 8.      [c] *Ib.* xii. 20.

rust doth corrupt, and where thieves do not break through and steal."[a]   He asks pointedly, "What man having to build a tower sitteth not down first, and counteth the cost, whether he shall be able to finish it ? . . . What king, before going to war with another king, considereth not whether he be able with ten thousand to meet him that cometh against him with twenty thousand; or else, while the other is a great way off, he sendeth an embassy, and demandeth conditions of peace?"[b]   The two disciples petition for thrones on His right and His left, and He asks in turn, "Can ye drink of the cup that I shall drink of, and be baptized with the baptism that I am baptized with?"[c]   He raises the all-including question, "What shall it profit a man, if he shall gain the whole world, and lose his own soul? or what shall a man give in exchange for his soul?"[d]

In these and many other sayings our Lord recognizes, endorses, consecrates the sense of prudence as an instrument for the attainment of the true end of man. And surely, if there be words that are not His, yet which appeal to our sense of prudence with peculiar force, they are those of the Prophet in the text, "Prepare to meet thy God."

## II.

And these words lose nothing of their force when we consider by whom they were uttered and under what circumstances.

Amos was a rude countryman, who spent his boyhood in tending sheep and goats, and in cultivating sycamore trees, in the upland village of Tekoah, in Judah. One day he was summoned to prophesy to Israel; how exactly

---

[a] St. Matt. vi. 19, 20.      [b] St. Luke xiv. 28-31.
[c] St. Mark x. 38.            [d] *Ib.* viii. 36, 37.

we are not told. He was, he says, no prophet, neither
was he a prophet's son.  He had not been trained in those
schools of the prophets which Samuel had founded up
and down the country, and by which the true religion
was to a certain extent kept alive in the midst of apostate Israel. He was like those clergymen among ourselves who are ordained without having been at a University; but for him, as for many of them, the light of
Heaven did more than could have been done by any
human teacher.  A walk of ten hours would have
brought him from his home in the south, and across the
frontier, to Bethel, where was the chief sanctuary of the
apostate tribes, and the altar which the man of God had
denounced in the days of the first Jeroboam.  Thence he
would have travelled northward to the capital; and, like
Hosea, he must have seen Samaria in the days of its
greatest prosperity.  For they were the days of Jeroboam
II., the most powerful of the kings who ruled the ten
tribes after the separation from Judah.  In those days
Israel was a state of much account in Western Asia; considerable additions had been made to its territory, and as
yet its people had not learnt to think of the dangers
which might threaten their independence from the valley
of the Euphrates.  In those days Samaria, as the capital
of a strong, confident, and prosperous power, was a city
of some outward splendour and pretension.  A simple
peasant, journeying from the south, as he crossed the
western spur of Mount Ebal which parts Samaria from the
vale of Shechem, may well have paused in silence and in
wonder, when first he beheld that royal hill, which, rising
from a fertile valley, and girded at its base by a triple
wall, was decked with every variety of public and private
building, up to the palace and, probably, the Baal-temple,
at its summit.  But as we read the prophecies which make

up his book, we see how little his eye was caught by that
which lay upon the surface; how keenly he observed all
that goes to make up the real life, whether of a man or a
people. In Samaria there were found side by side the
extremes of luxury and the extremes of want; the de-
bauchery and expenditure of a wealthy class, made possible by grinding oppression of the poor, by perversion
of justice, by extortion, by violence, by false weights and
measures, by all the machinery of social wrong. Amos
compares the ladies of Samaria, whose expenses were
supported out of the toil and sufferings of the poor, to the
fierce and unfeeling she-kine of Bashan that dwell on the
surrounding mountains; [a] he marks how in public courts
of justice " they sell the righteous for silver, and the poor
for a pair of sandals;" [b] how high officials " afflict the just,
and take a bribe, and turn aside the poor in the gate from
their right." [c]

Read through Amos and Hosea—they are not very long
books—before next Sunday, and observe how two religious
minds look, not with the same eyes, but with the same
general result, at the same society around them. Hosea
points to the root of Israel's evil, Amos sketches the
branches; Amos denounces the details of popular sins,
Hosea the animating principles. But we are in the same
atmosphere throughout as we read the two Prophets;
they are each looking hard at a society which had many
outward tokens of prosperity and splendour, but which
had ceased to take any real account of God.

Amos, throughout his book, is the prophet and apostle
of prudence. To Amos, a simple, pious soul, caring
chiefly, or rather exclusively, about questions of right and
wrong, and caring little, or rather not at all, about the
vulgar glitter of a God-forgetting civilization, it was clear

[a] Amos iv. 1.      [b] *Ib.* ii. 6.      [c] *Ib.* v. 12.

that the state of things in Samaria could not last. It would break up from within, or it would be broken up from without; it had not the strength of resistance, not even the strength of cohesion.

"Prepare to meet thy God, O Israel." Yes, Israel was to meet Him, in a few short years, here on this earth, in national disaster, national agony, national ruin. God looks nations, as He looks men, in the face, during temporal judgments. Certainly, at other seasons, He is here and to be met with by those who seek Him. He is the very atmosphere which we breathe; in which, whether we will or not, we move and are and have our being.[a] But He makes such creatures as, through sin, we are, feel His Presence rather in the storm than in the sunshine, rather in judgments than in blessings. And thus, while the sky was yet bright and the prospect fair, Amos hears the whispered mutterings of the yet distant tempest; he lifts his eyes to the hills which on these sides surround Samaria, and in which its people saw the natural defences of their city, and he summons an avenging host of heathen to behold from these very heights the wrong and oppression that was wrought within the walls; and he foretells a day when an adversary will bring down the strength of Israel, and its palaces would be spoiled.[b] There were past judgments to which he points as earnests of the future. The recent famine, when God gave to Israel "cleanness of teeth" in all his cities;[c] the drought, when "two or three cities wandered unto one city to drink water;"[d] the blasting and mildew, when the gardens and vineyards and orchards were smitten with death;[e] the plague, after the manner of Egypt; and, most of all, the recent earthquake—never a common visitation on the soil of Palestine, though very

[a] Acts xvii. 28.    [b] Amos iii. 11.
[c] *Ib.* iv. 6.    [d] *Ib.* 8.    [e] *Ib.* 9.

common in Northern Syria—the earthquake which brought
ruin and death to man, to civilization, to nature. These
were but heralds of some other judgment which he does
not name, but with reference to which he says, " Prepare
to meet thy God, O Israel." What had been might yet
be, would yet be—ay, and more also. It was an appeal to
prudence. And since prudence is action as well as forecast, Amos is ready with practical advice. He warns
Israel against the schismatic worship established since the
days of the first Jeroboam. "Thus saith the Lord unto
the house of Israel, Seek ye Me, and ye shall live: but
seek not Bethel, nor enter into Gilgal, and pass not to
Beersheba: for Gilgal shall go into captivity, and Bethel
shall come to nought."[a] Again, "Seek the Lord, and
ye shall live; lest He break out like fire in the house
of Joseph, and there be none to quench it in Bethel."[b]
Again, with an eye to the nature-worshippers, "Seek Him
that maketh the seven stars and Orion; that turneth the
shadow of death into the morning, and maketh the day
dark with night; that calleth for the waters of the sea,
and poureth them upon the face of the earth: The Lord is
His Name."[c] Again, as against the mockers at right and
wrong, "Seek good, and not evil, that ye may live: and
so the Lord, the God of Hosts, shall be with you. . . . Hate
evil, and love the good, and establish judgment in the
gate: it may be," he adds, "that the Lord will be gracious
unto the remnant of Joseph."[d] What was this but prudence in action; practical prudence; the prudence which
had looked forward into the future, and was to act accordingly? What are these but varying notes of the solemn
warning, "Prepare to meet thy God, O Israel"?

[a] Amos v. 4, 5.    [b] *Ib.* 6.    [c] *Ib.* 8.    [d] *Ib.* 14, 15.

# III.

To Israel the words of Amos meant, at any rate primarily, a judgment in the not distant future. To us Christians they may mean this and more. The faith of Jesus Christ illuminates the Old Testament with meanings which its first readers thought not of.

"Prepare to meet thy God." This may be God's message to a modern nation, as to Israel of old; He has not changed because some twenty-six centuries have passed since the days of Amos. Now, as of old, He meets the peoples of the world in the hour of temporal judgment. He meets them in social unsettlement, in depression of trade, in the transfer of the sources of wealth to other markets of the world, in the collapse of credit, and in the consequences which may then follow where wealth exists under highly artificial conditions, and much depends on confidence. Men set themselves to discover the sole cause of the calamity in the mismanagement of capital; in the misconduct or irritability of labour; in some fatalistic doctrine that commercial prosperity and depression move in recurrent and necessary cycles, and that we have happened just now upon a period of depression. But what if the real cause be at once simpler and deeper? What if He, Who is as much the Lord of commerce as He is the Lord of Revelation, so acts upon the minds and wills of men as to bring about a punishment for our past ingratitude? Certainly, it well may be that if, some few years ago, in days when the commercial prosperity of this country was at its height, each man of wealth had decided to give to God, according to the old Divine rule, one tenth of his income as a matter of duty,

and then as much more as he could as a tribute of love,
it might now have been otherwise with us than as it is.
God Himself, surely, meets us as a nation in this persistent
depression of trade ; He bids us ask ourselves whether we
have used our wealth and our opportunities as He would
have us use them ; He warns us that, if we turn a deaf
ear to present judgments, there may be something sterner
in store for us.    Ay, and He meets us as men, as sons,
as fathers, as wives, as mothers, as single human beings
on our trial ; He meets us in the many vicissitudes of
private fortune, in failure in work, in the alienation of
trusted friends, in the death of those we love, in the
stealthy approach of illness felt in our own bodily frame,
in permanent loss of health and spirits, in the never
knowing what it is to have a night's rest.    These things
do not, indeed, come to us by chance ; nor does He
merely send them to us and let them do their work.
They are the very instruments of His appeal to us ; the
chariot on which He rides, as He draws near to a sinful soul,
and looks it straight in the face, and asks it how far it
can bear His Eye.    And to prepare for these meetings
with God is the business of man, in days of health and
strength, of high spirits and buoyant hopes, when as yet
no cloud has risen above life's horizon, and nothing
threatens to disturb its placid harmonies.    God grant
those of us whom it concerns to do this while we may !

"Prepare to meet thy God, O Israel."    Every man
who believes that God exists, and that he himself has
a soul which does not perish with the body, knows that
a time must come when this meeting will be inevitable.
At the hour of death, whether in mercy or in displeasure,
God looks in the face of man, His creature, as never before.
The veils of sense, which long have hidden His counte-

nance, then are stripped away, and as spirit meets with
spirit, without the interposition of any fibres of matter,
so does man in death meet with God.  It is this which
makes death so exceedingly solemn.  Ere yet the last
breath has fairly passed from the body, or the failing
eyes have closed, the soul has partly entered upon a
world altogether new, magnificent, awful.  It has seen
beings, shapes, modes of existence, never imagined before.
But it has done more; it has met its God, as a disem-
bodied spirit can meet Him.  Surely, "Prepare—prepare
for death!" is the voice of prudence.  The one certain
thing about life is that we must leave it.  The one
certain thing about death is that we must die.  What
will happen first, we know not.  How much time will
pass before our hour comes, we know not.  What will
be the manner of our death, violence or disease, an
accident or what we call natural causes, we know not.
Where we shall die, at home or on a visit, in our beds
or in the street, or in a railway train, or in a sinking
steamboat,—this, too, we know not.  Under what circumstances we shall die, in solitude or among friends, with
the consolations of religion or without them, in spasms
of agony or softly, as if we were going to sleep, we know
not.  The time, the place, the manner, the circumstances
of death, are hidden from every one of us; but that which
stands out from all this ignorance, in absolute, unassailable, tragic certainty, is the fact itself that we must die,
all and each of us.  Scripture says, and experience
echoes, that "It is appointed."[a]

"Prepare to meet thy God" in death—this is the
second precept of prudence.  If there were any chance
of escaping death, or of somehow modifying it, or even
of postponing it; if science, which has done so much for

----

[a] Heb. ix. 27.

man, could keep the last enemy at bay until, at least, we
were ready and willing to encounter him; then it might
not be imprudent to defer our preparations for meeting
God. But if man, so powerful elsewhere, is powerless
here; if, with all our increasing mastery of nature, we
are individually just as little able to escape dissolution
as were our rudest forefathers; then, surely, "Prepare to
meet thy God!" should be a text written up in large
letters in every Christian bedroom, that each night as
we lie down to rest, and each morning as we arise from
sleep, we should be reminded, like the Macedonian
monarch, that we *must* die, and, like Christians, that
death means nothing less than meeting with the Author
and Redeemer of our life.

"Prepare to meet thy God." Death is not all that
awaits us. "It is appointed unto men once to die, but
after death the Judgment."[a] That which our moral sense
demands, God's Revelation in Christ proclaims. We
shall each of us be judged. "God hath appointed a day,
in which He will judge the world in righteousness by
that Man Whom He hath ordained; whereof He hath given
assurance unto all men, in that He hath raised Him from
the dead."[b] Towards that final, solemn, unimaginable
meeting with God, every human life, every national
history, all human movement, is moving steadily, inevitably forward; it will at last come, and then all will
enter, in this direction or in that, upon an endless future.
Of some of the prospects which are thus opened up we
may think another Sunday; to-day let us reflect that to
keep it steadily in view, and to act accordingly, is the aim
of every human life that is not wasted, because it is alive
to the first and last lesson of true human prudence.

[a] Heb. ix. 27.         [b] Acts xvii. 31.

# SERMON XXVII.

## PREPARATION FOR CHRIST'S COMING.

### II. THE SENSE OF JUSTICE.

#### (SECOND SUNDAY IN ADVENT.)

Amos iv. 12.

*Prepare to meet thy God, O Israel.*

LAST Sunday [a] we had under consideration the appeal of
the Prophet Amos in the text, as it addresses itself
to our sense of prudence. The vicissitudes and uncertainty of life on the one hand, and the certainty of death
and judgment on the other, appeared to invest the warning, "Prepare to meet thy God," with particular force
when considered by the practical faculty which looks as
far into the future as it can, and does the best that can
be done in view of what it foresees as coming. To-day
we will bring another sense or instinct of the human soul
into the presence of these solemn words. We have to ask
ourselves, What do they say when confronted with our
sense of justice?

## I.

Justice—the sense of justice—what is it? You may
well say, Why ask the question? Justice is, in truth, one

[a] See Sermon XXVI.

of the most elementary ideas in the soul of man; it is
part of that original stock of intuitions with which our
minds find themselves possessed at the outset of life, and
for the presence of which within us we can only account
by saying that our Creator has given it to us. The idea
of justice just as much belongs to the constitution of our
minds as does our apprehension of the first truths of
mathematics. As we cannot help understanding that
things which are equal to the same thing are equal to
one another, so we cannot help perceiving that there is
a difference between justice and injustice, even when we
are not agreed as to what is in detail just or what is
unjust. As to the true duties of justice, there is indeed
a very wide difference of opinion among those human
beings who do not receive God's Revelation of His Will
through Jesus Christ. The old historian, Herodotus, said,
that if the different nations of the world were to be asked
what laws and usages were most reasonable, each would
reply "its own."[a] Still, that there is an Absolute Justice,
whatever mistakes we may make about its application to
human affairs, is, as the old heathen poet knew, a truth
which is not of human origin. It has come to man from
a higher source. It will survive all the revolutions of
human thought. It will last as long as the human mind
itself.

Justice, then, is a primary element of human thought.
But justice takes another idea for granted—the idea of
right. Justice is the virtue which takes care of the rights
of other beings; she not merely avoids interference with
those rights, but she gives them what they claim. And
the right of a being is the claim which it can make in
virtue of the law of its nature. Thus the Rights of God
are the claims which He makes because He is necessarily

<hr>

[a] Hdt. iii. 38.

what He is. And the rights of man or of animals are the claims which they may make in virtue of the law of that nature which the Creator has given them. Rights, in the strict sense, belong to personal beings; inanimate things have no rights whatever. Animals have very limited rights, but certainly such as ought to protect them against wanton cruelty, or being cut up alive in order to promote human knowledge. Men have rights, the full scope of which is traced by the Revelation which God has given to us. And God has rights, which, since He is the Infinite Being, are boundless. Of these various rights justice is the practical recognition; but it also is more. It is not merely a sentiment which recognizes right; it is an operative passion which insists that right should be vindicated. Justice in man is the belief that this vindication is inevitable, and a desire to promote it as far as may be. And justice in man presumes the existence of a Higher Justice; it asks, from generation to generation, "Shall not the Judge of all the earth do right?"

The rights of man! Yes; man, as man, has rights. They are conferred on him by the Being Who has given him existence. They are secured and defined by that moral law which his Creator has discovered to him. The ultimate basis of right is not, as Hobbes of Malmesbury thought, might. It is not true that power is the measure of right. God's right to command is not merely a result of His Omnipotence. Our duty to obey God is not only another name for our inability to resist Him. If this were true, then any man who might be strong enough to subdue the whole human race would have the right to do so, and every human being would be bound to obey him. But it would also follow that any man who could resist him successfully would have the *right* to do so.

Thus the idea of moral obligation would altogether disappear in a conflict of brute force; brute force would reign as right. No! the ultimate basis of right is the Will of the Perfect Moral Being. This Will, being absolutely Holy, is the rule of His Own Rights, and also of the rights of the creatures to whom He has given existence. And therefore, after all, the true Magna Charta of human rights is the Second Table of the Decalogue. The rights of the parent over the child, protecting that authoritative relation in which human life most nearly approaches the Divine, are secured by the Fifth Commandment: "Honour thy father and thy mother." The right of every human being to live; the inherent sanctity of every human life, of the youngest, the weakest, the most useless, is proclaimed by the Sixth Commandment: "Thou shalt do no murder." The right to transmit the gift of life; the mysterious power of invoking the co-operation of the Divine Creator, under the exact conditions prescribed by the Divine Law, is protected against outrage by the Seventh Commandment: "Thou shalt not commit adultery." The rights of property are implied in, as they are guarded by, the Eighth Commandment; the rights of character by the Ninth. Thus far human law may cite, and, after its measure, enforce the Divine; but in the Tenth Commandment the Divine Law ascends into a world of motive where human law cannot follow it, and claims to regulate that unregulated desire which is at the root of all violation of human rights: "Thou shalt not covet." All these six Commandments do recognize and protect human rights; and they form, in their entirety and developments, the law of justice as between man and man.

Human justice is the assertion of the rights of man, and that phrase, or its equivalents, has again and again been a power in human history. Sometimes it has been abused for very selfish purposes; sometimes it has been asserted with a violence which has conspicuously outraged the very rights which were to be vindicated. And yet, so sacred and majestic is the truth which underlies the words that, in some of the darkest periods of history, they have glowed with an almost regenerating power; they have given a new direction to the course of events and to the minds of men.

So it was pre-eminently in the days of our grandfathers, some ninety or a hundred years ago. The right, first of all, to live, and to secure the necessaries of life; the right to protect person and property against violence, conse-crated by long custom, but condemned by the moral law; the right to organize society in such sort that the well-being of the greatest number should be efficiently provided for,—these were ideas which shed upon the first French Revolution, notwithstanding all its hideous excesses and brutalities, a certain lustre which will cling to it. Justice was the idea which broke up the old feudal society of Europe—justice conceived of as the assertion of human rights which, under the old order of things, had been neglected or trampled on. Unless there had been a force like this at work, that old society, so finished and so grace-ful, so associated with a splendid history, so consecrated by the Christian traditions of a thousand years, would have gone on, must have gone on, for centuries. That which broke it up was the fertile and imperious idea of justice, as between class and class, as between man and man. And the cruelties and follies which disfigured the catastrophe must not blind us to the intrinsic nobility and worth of one, at any rate, of the ideas which precipitated it—the idea of social justice.

Yes! justice as between man and man is a power.

What is it which invests the proceedings of our Courts
of Law with such general and popular interest? Certainly not the processes and forms of law itself, which
to ordinary minds are dry, technical, almost repulsive.
Nor is it chiefly a vulgar curiosity about the lives and
fortunes of others, or a criminal satisfaction in their mis-
fortunes or their crimes. These motives do undoubtedly
account, to a certain extent, for the fact before us; but
a truer and more adequate explanation is to be found
in man's deep attachment to the idea of justice. That
justice is to be somehow guarded, asserted, satisfied; that
it has resources for making itself felt as a power in human
life is the fact with which most men concern themselves.
To ascertain this satisfies an appetite, a strong and most
legitimate craving of the human soul. The very eagerness
that justice should be done is sometimes not unlikely to
imperil the character of the justice which is done; while
it witnesses to the hold which justice, as such, has upon
the sympathies of mankind at large.

But the power of the idea of justice between man and
man is seen chiefly in the fact, that the present does not
satisfy it. There is not room for it in the world at any
existing moment; and those who are keen about it, and
anxious that its rights should be respected, are obliged to
look forward. Read Amos from this point of view. He
is so full of the future because the idea of justice which
possesses and inspires him makes him so dissatisfied with
the present. He sees that human justice is refused to
large numbers of people in Samaria; and as he believes
that justice is not a fine sentimental phrase, but a necessary Attribute of the Being Who governs the world, he
is quite sure that there will be a future in which its
claims will be recognized.

Thus, he cries to the governing classes—

" Ye that put far the evil day,
  And cause the scat of violence to come near;
  That lie upon beds of ivory,
  And stretch themselves upon couches,
  And eat the lambs out of the flock,
  And the calves out of the midst of the stall;
  That chant to the sound of the viol,
  And invent to themselves instruments of music, like David;
  That drink wine in bowls,
  And anoint themselves with the chief ointments :
  But they are not grieved for the affliction of Joseph.
  Therefore now shall they go captive with the first that go captive,
  And the banquet of them that stretched themselves shall be removed." [a]

Again, the same sense of a future, in which justice as between man and man will claim her own, appears in the following. He is speaking of some wealthy oppressors—

" They hate him that rebuketh in the gate,
  And they abhor him that speaketh uprightly—
  Forasmuch therefore as your treading is upon the poor,
  And ye take from him burdens of wheat:
  Ye have built houses of hewn stone,
  But ye shall not dwell in them;
  Ye have planted pleasant vineyards,
  But ye shall not drink wine of them." [b]

So again, at a somewhat later time, and with more passion than before—

" Hear this, O ye that swallow up the needy,
  Even to making the poor of the land to fail,
  Saying, When will the new moon be gone, that we may sell corn?
  And the sabbath, that we may set forth wheat,
  Making the ephah small, and the shekel great,
  And falsifying the balances by deceit?
  That we may buy the poor for silver,
  And the needy for a pair of shoes;
  Yea, and sell the refuse of the wheat?
  The Lord hath sworn by the excellency of Jacob,
  Surely I will never forget any of their works.

[a] Amos vi. 3-7.        [b] *Ib.* v. 10, 11.

Shall not the land tremble for this,
And every one mourn that dwelleth therein?
And it shall rise up wholly as a flood;
And it shall be cast out and drowned, as by the flood of Egypt." [a]

The spirit of all these passages is that justice is an imperious force which, though repressed or kept at bay for a time, must sooner or later have its way; that it is like water which will and must find its level; that present appearances to the contrary go for nothing with those who believe in a moral God, and in the ultimate practical supremacy of His Attributes in the world which He has made. These passages in various ways summon Israel to the work of social and moral reformation; they bid it bethink itself of what is coming, of what must come, of that future which is made necessary by the present in which it lives; they bid it arise, in awe and penitence, and prepare to meet its God.

And here is, in fact, an abstract argument for a future life which comes home to the conscience of a good man more powerfully than any other. There are many other considerations which point to a future life, such as those drawn from an examination of the nature of the soul as a simple uncompounded essence, which, therefore, cannot be supposed to dissolve with the material body at death. These arguments have their value; but while they address themselves to minds of a philosophical cast, they do not impress the majority of men, as does the moral argument for a future life which is based on the requirements of justice. That argument is that justice has not room enough in our present existence; that its limbs are visibly cramped and bound; that it cannot breathe freely; that, if all ends with the grave, justice cannot be said to be supreme over the destinies of men; that it must confess

[a] Amos viii. 4-8.

impotence and failure. Yes, most assuredly, either justice
is a dream, or it has not yet said its last word. It demands
a future. And thus belief in a future life varies exactly
with the moral righteousness and vigour of the souls of
men; with their belief in the absolute character of justice.
As a good man looks out on the world, and sees how
many are the failures of human justice here and now; how
domestic justice, social justice, political justice, are alike
maimed or travestied; how hopeless would seem to be
the task of establishing upon the earth, among a generation of clever cynics, a real empire of justice—his
thoughts turn inevitably and with strong confidence
towards the future. And each victory of wrong, each
failure of right, each event, each character, which en-
hances his sense of moral dissatisfaction with that which
he sees around him, sounds in his ears as an echo, more
and more articulate of the summons of Amos, addressed
by justice to a world which might seem to have forgotten
her, "Prepare to meet thy God, O Israel."

## II.

But there are other rights towards which justice has
duties—other rights than the rights of man. What
rights may belong to the blessed intelligences of Heaven
it would be unpractical now and here to discuss; but
there are higher rights still, more imperious and exacting
than can belong to any created being. The most eloquent defenders of human rights have not seldom forgotten that there are any such rights as the Rights of
God. Elaborate treatises on justice, which have traced
the rights and duties of man with the utmost minuteness,
have omitted any notice of these Sovereign Rights, and of
man's duties towards them. Yet it is with these Rights
that the highest department of justice is concerned.

The Rights of God! They are not, like the rights of man, conferred rights; they belong to Him because He is what He cannot but be; they cannot but be His. God, Almighty as He is, cannot place anything beyond the limits of His Own Being. All that exists, exists in God; we live, move, and have our being in Him [a] Who gave it us. We live, minute by minute, because He Who gave us life so many years ago, wills, minute by minute, that we should continue to enjoy it. As our Creator, then, and as our Preserver, God has Rights over us to which there is no parallel in the relations between man and man; we cannot assign limits to them. What is each human life but a drop in the ocean of the Infinite? Each life is free to move within certain limits, but is unable to pass them. It cannot escape for an instant from the encompassing pressure, from the inevitable sovereignty of that Mighty Hand Which has given it being, and has assigned it its place in His Universe, and is really Lord of its every movement, and even now wills that at an appointed moment it shall die.

The Rights of God! Yes, God, too, has His rights; and yet you may hear and read a great deal which implies that He has no rights at all, certainly no such rights as you and I enjoy freely and vehemently assert. For example, you and I have the right of communicating our thoughts to each other; we wrap up our thought in sound which we call language, and pass it from mind to mind, so that it shall exist as perfectly in the mind which receives as in the mind which transmits it. Wonderful, indeed, is the mystery of language, considered as the vehicle and instrument of thought; and yet we are so familiar with this right—for such it also is—of speech, that we exercise it incessantly without thinking of what we do. Yet this

[a] Acts xvii. 28.

very right is constantly denied to God by persons who, singularly enough, do not deny His Existence. He only, it seems, must keep silence amid the millions of voices in His own Universe! He only, Who has given to His creatures alike the gift of thought and the gift of speech, must be deemed unable to unfold His mind in language; and at the bidding of some arbitrary doctrine which would make sure of His impotence while it professes to be guarding His dignity.

No, brethren! God has a right of revealing Himself; and He has the further right of commanding the assent of His creatures to the Revelation which He makes. As the Eternal Truth, He claims the assent of the understandings of men; as the Perfectly Holy One, He demands the obedience of the wills of men; as the Eternal Beauty, He invites the homage of the affections of men. He asks for these things at our hands; He gives us the power, the awful and momentous power, of refusing His request. Yet He thus asks us not to indulge a taste or sentiment, but to acknowledge a right. Yes! we owe to God's Revelation of Himself such tribute as our intellects and hearts can give, as a simple matter of justice. God has a right to be believed by us when He speaks. When He unveils His character and attributes, He has a right to be loved by us; while in loving Him we may, indeed, find that our first strict duty is also the secret of our true happiness. If He were only some one work of His Own Hands—a beautiful scene, or a beautiful form or face, or an exquisite flower-garden, or, perhaps, even a product of human art—we should perchance give what we refuse to the Invisible and Transcendental Beauty, of Whose glory all that most powerfully affects the eye of sense here below is but the faintest ray.

The Rights of God! As the last six Commandments

of the Decalogue affirm, while they guard the rights of man, so do the first four guard and affirm the Rights of God. First comes the Right of God to the highest place in the thought, the affections, the inmost being of His creature; "I am the Lord Thy God:" next, the right to exclude all rival claimants, whether framed by the hands, or by the imaginations of man; then, in the Third Commandment, the right to claim a reverent recognition of His Presence, as hearing every word which touches Himself; and lastly, in the Fourth, the right of occupying a measure of time to be consecrated by His reasonable creatures in acknowledging, by prayer, and thanksgiving, and praise, the real relations which exist between themselves and Him.

Here, then, we may see how the narrow and imperfect conception of justice which confines it to promoting right relations between man and man has to be reconsidered and readjusted, so as to include right relations between man and the Infinite Being Who made him. When we refuse faith and love which God knows that we might give; when we omit prayer, and give neither time nor thought to the claims of God; we do really sin against justice, not less surely than when we take that which is not our own, or bear false witness, or take away a human life. For God has His Rights, too, as well as man. And to be just is to satisfy all rights; the rights of man, assuredly, but also, not less certainly, the Rights of Him from Whom all human rights are gifts; the Rights of the Self-Existent and Perfect Being Who made us.

This, too, was felt by Amos, who is the Prophet of adequate and absolute justice; not merely of justice between man and man, but also of justice as between man and God. And as, in the days of Amos, Samaria was the city in Israel at which justice between man and man was

most conspicuously violated; so Bethel was the sanctuary
in Israel at which most wrong was done to the Rights of
God. There was the centre of the idolatrous worship,
set up and patronized, for reasons of State, by the reigning
dynasty; and there, we may be pretty sure, Amos stood
when, again and again, he proclaimed that this standing
injustice towards God, the King and Friend of Israel,
must entail a judgment. There he uttered the stern
irony, " Come to Bethel, and transgress; . . . and bring
your sacrifices every morning, and your tithes after three
years: and offer a sacrifice of thanksgiving with leaven,
and proclaim and publish the free offerings: for this
liketh you, O ye children of Israel, saith the Lord God."[a]
There, no doubt, he uttered the scathing words, in his
Master's Name, "I hate, I despise your feast days, and
I will not smell in your solemn assemblies. Though ye
offer Me burnt offerings and meat offerings, I will not
accept them : neither will I regard the peace offerings
of your fat beasts. Take thou away from Me the noise
of thy songs; for I will not hear the melody of thy viols.
But let judgment run down as waters, and righteousness
as a mighty stream."[b] Thence it was that "Amaziah
the priest of Bethel sent to King Jeroboam II., saying,
Amos hath conspired against thee in the midst of the
house of Israel," and bade Amos, "O thou seer, go, flee
thee away into the land of Judah, and there eat bread,
and prophesy there: but prophesy not again any more
at Bethel: for it is the King's Chapel, and it is the
King's Court." And there Amos uttered the reply, "I
was no prophet, neither was I a prophet's son; but I was
an herdman, and a gatherer of sycomore fruit: and the
Lord took me as I followed the flock, and the Lord said
unto me, Go, prophesy unto My people Israel. Now

[a] Amos iv. 4, 5.          [b] *Ib.* v. 21-24.

therefore hear thou the Word of the Lord: Thou sayest, Prophesy not against Israel, and drop not thy word against the House of Isaac. Therefore thus saith the Lord; Thy wife shall be as an harlot in the city, and thy sons and thy daughters shall fall by the sword, and thy land shall be divided by line; and thou shalt die in a polluted land: and Israel shall surely go into captivity forth out of his land." [a]

Indeed, in the eyes of Amos, the accumulating injustice of Israel towards God was ever making it more and more inevitable that Israel and God should meet in judgment. Israel, in its blind self-love, might think that a great crisis in its history, which the prophets called "the day of the Lord," could not but be to its advantage; but Amos, who had traced the persistent and deep disloyalty of this people to their true King, knew that it must be otherwise. "Woe unto you that desire the day of the Lord! to what end is it for you? the day of the Lord is darkness, and not light. As if a man did flee from a lion, and a bear met him; or went into the house, and leaned his hand on the wall, and a serpent bit him." [b]

Amos knew—as we Christians should know—that the ever-swelling tide of mental and moral rebellion against the Ruler of the Universe is, by a law which cannot fail to assert itself, bringing judgment nearer and nearer. It is not merely in the obedience of saints, in the conversion of penitents, in the extension of the Divine Kingdom, that we see the tokens of the approaching Advent; it is in the contemptuous rejection of the Rights of God, by populations of Christian stock, and which might be Christian; it is in the resolute exclusion of the King of Heaven from large departments of human thought and life; it is in the coarse blasphemies which meet the

[a] Amos vii. 10-17.          [b] *Ib.* v. 18, 19.

eye and the ear in our streets, but yet more in the
refined ungodliness which underlies the graceful sentences
of well-educated infidelity; it is in the placid indifference
to God, as if He had had His day, and it was high time to
forget Him.

Referring to the dream of Scipio, a thoughtful poet has
sung how

> "Roman conquerors could climb
> Above the things of earth and time,
> Forgetting human hopes and fears
> Amid the music of the spheres;
> Advancing into converse high
> Of goodness, truth, and piety,
> And of a place to spirits given
> In Plato's tranquil seats of heaven."

And then he asks—

> "How is it now the worldly great,
> Men of renown and high estate,
> Turn from the soul-ennobling theme,
> On which e'en heathens loved to dream?
> Is it that truth appears so mean,
> Where Christ the only Door is seen?
> Or that we to the dregs descend
> As the world verges to its end?" [a]

Yes, it is in "the dregs" of descending thought; it is
in the fall of stars from the heaven of faith, in the waxing
cold of the love of many, that Christians may trace the
predestined signs of the last catastrophe; it is nearer
than when they became believers." [b] In these portents
faith sees that which must rouse and consolidate a force
which, in its turn, if we may so speak reverently, must
exert an increasing pressure on the Will of the All-Holy,
tending as the years, and months, and days, and moments
pass, to bring us nearer and nearer to the threshold of the
Judgment. From these, too, one warning, dictated by the

---

[a] Rev. I. Williams, *Christian Scholar*, p. 51.     [b] Rom. xiii. 11.

necessities of the Eternal Justice, is uttered to the world,
"Prepare to meet thy God."


## III.

And yet, brethren, it is not in the outer world only,
or chiefly, that you and I may trace the pressure of the
Law of Justice, as vindicating the Rights of God and the
rights of man, and imperatively demanding some final,
though it be a penal, satisfaction. It is not in the great
events which interest and move mankind, or in the characters which may arrest the gaze of a generation, or in
the public iniquities which may seem to triumph, or in
the conspicuous goodness which may be doomed in appearance to rejection and to shame; it is not on the great
scene of the world's history, but within our own souls
that the tragic requirements of justice, as vindicating the
Rights of God and the rights of man, will and must make
themselves felt. There is a voice within every one of us,
if we will but let it speak, which says solemnly, sternly,
"Prepare to meet thy God." If we hear not this voice
now, we shall hear it hereafter; if not in the day of rude
health, yet, unless the moral nerve has been cauterized,
when we are sick or dying. What a gleam of awful light
was that which fell on the death-bed of Cromwell! His
moral sense had been a while drugged by the then popular
Calvinistic theory of an absolute assurance of salvation.
And as, perchance, he was haunted by some dark spectres,
which the Whitehall banquetting-room, or Drogheda, or
Wexford, might well suggest to a man who felt himself
passing into the Presence of the Everlasting Judge, he
asked his Puritan advisers whether any who had once
been assured of salvation could be finally lost. Then,
assuredly, if not before, if thought and conscience can

still speak, the memory of what has been done, or left
undone, in respect of the Rights of God and the rights
of man, will utter, as never before, the warning, "Prepare,
O soul, to meet thy God."

And this suggests two duties, always incumbent, but
specially at the Advent Season.

The first, the duty of self-examination. We must try,
before we die, to get out of the world of fancy, as far as
our souls are concerned, into the world of fact. We must
endeavour to see for ourselves whether we are on the road
to Heaven; where we are on the road to Heaven; what
we are in the sight of God. We must try, while yet we
may, to strip off the thick coating of illusion with which
the soft words of friends and our own self-love have buried
out of sight our real selves. Every day a little portion of
time—five or ten minutes—should be given to this work.
It will rouse conscience to a new life. It will quicken
prayer. It will enable us, though in tears and sorrow,
to think of what is implied by the Law of Justice in its
bearings on the history of each soul and its future destiny.
If we would thus judge ourselves, we should not be judged.[a]
For thus, as in no other way so efficiently, should we
prepare to meet our God.

And the second is the duty of claiming, as Christians
may and should claim, a part in the perfect Righteousness of Jesus Christ. Alone among the sons of men, He
rendered perfect justice both to the rights of men and
to the Rights of God. There was no claim which He
ever so slightly contravened, no duty which He failed, by

[a] 1 Cor. xi. 31.

ever so little, to satisfy. And thus St. Stephen, in his
dying speech, calls Him " the Just One ; " [a] and St. John,
in his First Epistle, " Jesus Christ the Righteous ; " [b] and
St. Peter says that " He did no sin, neither was guile
found in His mouth ; " [c] and St. Paul, that " He was made
to be sin for us Who knew no sin, that we might be made
the Righteousness of God in Him." [d]

Yes, the satisfaction which He, our Redeemer, offered,
in His Life and Death, to the Law of Justice, is not a
solitary triumph or possession of His Own ; for in His unutterable and condescending love, He allows us, He bids
us share it. Such is His Representative Character, as the
new Head of the race, the Second Adam, that, if we will,
His Justice may be ours. [e] He invites us to hold out the
hand of faith that we may receive that Righteousness of
God which He has thus won for each and for all of us.
Let each here pray : " Eternal Father, I the creature of
Thy Hand, and redeemed by the Blood of Thy Son, offer
Thee His perfect Righteousness, and entreat Thee so to
clothe me in it, that I may be beheld and accepted in the
Beloved." For He both accounts and makes—He accounts
because He makes—us righteous, by virtue of those powers
of the new life which are communicated by His Spirit
acting through His Sacraments on human souls. Thus
may we enter upon the magnificent freedom of the Law of
Justice ; thus may we discover that the " Law of the Spirit
of Life in Christ Jesus has made us free from the law of
sin and death." [f] For what the Mosaic or natural law
could not do, in that it was weak through the conditions
of our fallen nature, " God sending His own Son in the
likeness of sinful flesh, and for sin, condemned sin in the
flesh : that the righteousness of the Law "—the practical

[a] Acts vii. 52.      [b] 1 St. John ii. 1.      [c] 1 St. Pet. ii. 22.
[d] 2 Cor. v. 21.      [e] Rom. v. 15-19.      [f] *Ib.* viii. 2.

recognition of the Rights of God and of the rights of man—"might be fulfilled in us, who walk not after the flesh, but after the Spirit." [a]

Thus may we encounter our remaining years, if any there be, with hope, and peace, and joy. Thus may we hope to meet that hour for which we have been prepared by the voice of Eternal Justice speaking to conscience, and so leading us, like the Law of old, to Jesus Christ. Thus may we prepare to meet our God.

[a] Rom. viii. 3, 4.

# SERMON XXVIII.

## PREPARATION FOR CHRIST'S COMING.

### III. THE SENSE OF REVERENCE.

#### (THIRD SUNDAY IN ADVENT.)

AMOS IV. 12.

*Prepare to meet thy God, O Israel.*

THE words of Amos, as they are understood by Christendom, bidding us prepare for a final and extraordinary meeting with God, appeal, as we have seen, to our sense of prudence and to our sense of justice. The words rouse these original instincts of the human soul to a new activity. Prudence is quickened when we see before us, at an unascertained distance, a vast and certain catastrophe in which we must share. And justice wears a new face for us, when we have come to think it a matter of certainty that we shall be individually judged by an all-surveying, all-powerful, and holy Master. But, behind the sense of justice and the sense of prudence, there is in the soul of man another sense or feeling, more indefinite, yet not less real than these—the sense of awe or reverence. What does this say to us when it hears the words, " Prepare to meet thy God, O Israel " ?

# I.

Reverence,—what is it? It is not exactly fear, nor love, nor admiration. In its earlier stages there is in it more of fear; in its later, more of love. Fear, love, and admiration, all enter into it in different proportions; but it cannot be identified with any one of them. It is the virtuous emotion whereby the soul of man sincerely acknowledges the presence of greatness; and, the human soul being what it is, some acknowledgment of greatness is always natural to it, even in its most undeveloped or most degraded conditions. Thus we may at once brush away one or two misconceptions about it.

First, reverence is not, in any sense, a fictitious sort of virtue. Persons who have little or no eye for real greatness, and see reverent people around them, without seeing the object which provokes their reverence, are led to think, perhaps naturally, that what they witness is a sort of acting. They imagine that no perfectly natural, or, as they would say, no manly person would be reverent; that reverence is the upshot of artificial circumstances, of artificial and stinted convictions; that it is the fruit of forced training and narrow associations, and subjection to teachers or traditions of a peculiar type. In short, they maintain that there is a fictitious element in it, which makes it distasteful to thoroughly honest and strong characters.

No, my brethren, this is an entire misapprehension. The bent head, the bended knee, which mean nothing, which acknowledge no Being or Power That demands this homage, are not reverence at all, but something utterly different. Reverence, like all virtues that merit the name, is based on truth. The truth of some greatness which the soul acknowledges must be sincerely felt if there is to be real reverence.

Secondly, reverence is not an exclusively ecclesiastical or religious excellence, although it is sometimes referred to as if it had been born and bred within the precincts of the Christian Church. Thus it is said to be natural in young children, who do not know the world or the real range of human knowledge; and in women, who are naturally submissive and yielding, if not weak; and in clergymen, to whom it comes as a kind of professional ornament or accomplishment; it is, in short, treated as the virtue of the unreflecting, of the imaginative, of the enthusiastic, of minds in which feeling has free range and empire, but which are possessed of little or no exact knowledge.

Now, of course, the Church is a great school of reverence, because within the Church, as nowhere else, the Highest and most commanding Greatness is continually presented to the soul of man. But reverence, as a human excellence, is older than Christianity; older than Revelation. It is as old as the idea that there is anything in existence greater than man; and though the Christian Church and Religion have heightened reverence almost indefinitely, they did not create it. They found it already in existence, though wandering about the world as if it were sorely at a loss for an adequate object. Nay, more; among men who unhappily reject Christianity at the present day, but who are alive to greatness, whether in nature or in man, no one would deny that there are instances of even conspicuous reverence, of such a kind and within such limits as are possible.

Reverence, then, is the sincere acknowledgment of a greatness higher than ourselves. And, accordingly, the first school of reverence which has been provided for us is the natural world around us.

Think of man, in a primitive and far-distant age, opening his eyes upon that world of nature in which his Maker has placed him, and discovering around him the creatures, forces, processes, catastrophes, which successively arrest his gaze. As yet familiarity has not blunted his sense of wonder; and he feels more than wonder; he feels awe. He is consciously in the presence of a higher greatness, manifold in its forms and activities, but all around him, and more and more impressing him with a sense of his relative insignificance. He beholds a tree, the monarch of some primæval forest, with its head towering heavenwards, and with roots which sink deep into the earth beneath his feet; he marks how it grows, puts out branches, leaves, flowers, fruit; how it is a creature which lives, yet with a life unlike his own; and he feels an awe at it. Or he is the inhabitant of a valley, which is bounded by an impassable mountain : his glance follows the precipices above him up to the point where the mountain-crest buries itself in the clouds; he crouches like a dwarf at the feet of some giant, upon whose head rests the sky above him ; and he trembles at it. Or he lives on the bank of a river, which waters his fields and feeds his flocks, and suddenly swells like an angry enemy to the measure of a destructive torrent, inundating the land on this bank and that, and sweeping all before it ; and he is terrified. Or he lifts up his eyes to the sky above

him, to the sun by day, to the stars and moon by night;
here, too, he feels are objects—vast, distant, mysterious;
they fill him with awe. Or he marks the clouds, changing
their forms from moment to moment as if they were
living things. Or he watches the rain, descending he
knows not whence, sometimes as a gentle friend, sometimes as an implacable scourge. Or he hears the thunder,
uttered above his head as if it were the voice of an awful
being beyond his reach. Or he feels the surface of the
earth rock and quake beneath his feet, and he suspects
the energy of a subterranean power, intent on mischief.
Of the awe excited by the natural world upon primitive
men, we have illustrations in the religious poetry of
India; and although awe is not fully reverence, it is
elementary reverence: man feels behind nature a Higher
Power of some kind which appeals irresistibly to his
sense of greatness.

Undoubtedly, in the absence of revelation, the awe
excited by the resource and mystery of the natural world
has led to abundant error and degradation. Man gazed
at the forest-oak till it took his whole mind and imagination captive; he became a Druid. Or he watched the fire
—so faithful a servant, so terrible a master; his master,
probably, long before he could make it his servant; and
he became the religious ancestor of our Parsees. Or
he dwelt in curious wonder on the productive powers of
Nature; and forthwith throughout Syria, and along the
whole southern coast of the Mediterranean, there arose
those Baal-worships, of which we read so much in the
days of the Jewish kings, and which were so fascinating,
impure, and cruel. Nay, in time, every object around
him became a divinity. If he was an Egyptian, he
worshipped the great river which brought plenty to his
lands, or the monsters which inhabited it; if a Persian,

the sun, the moon, fire, water, the winds; if an Indian, the sky, or the dawn, or the clouds, the earth, the mountains, the streams; if an African savage, representing centuries of progressive degradation, he prayed to a fetish, burying his old awe for an unseen power in his mercantile eagerness to possess a serviceable charm. Idolatry is the grave of reverence; reverence expires when that which meets the eye leads man to forget the Invisible Being beyond. But it was meant to be otherwise as between man and Nature. Nature is God's first revelation to man; His invisible attributes of Wisdom and Power, and, within limits, of Goodness, are clearly seen, being understood by the things that are made;[a] and when we sing the twenty-ninth Psalm, which describes a thunderstorm in the Lebanon, or the *Benedicite*, which calls on all the works of God to praise and magnify Him for ever, we replace Nature on her true throne as the first teacher of elementary reverence.

Ah! the freshness of that early impression of and reverence for the Greatness Which shrouds Itself behind, while It is distinct from, the world of Nature! Do not the jaded and worn-out children of our modern civilization seek to restore vigour of mind and body, at intervals, by the emotions which Nature can inspire; amid the silence of the mountains, broken only by the fall of avalanches, or on the rocky shore which is lashed by the Atlantic waves? Even now Nature speaks to the soul of man; and science does not, as might have been anticipated, break the charm. Science explains just what meets the eye; it carries us one step beyond the touch of sense ; but, then, it only opens out new fields of wonder, whose existence sense does not even suspect. Behind the laws which science discovers, as behind the phenomena which

[a] Rom. i. 20.

are gazed on by primitive men, there is the Higher Greatness of the Legislator, of the Creator. "The more I know," said a man of science, "of the secrets of Nature, the more am I lost in reverence for the Power which I feel to be living and working everywhere around me."

### III.

Nature, then, is our first teacher of that practical sense of a higher greatness which we call reverence; but the lesson is to be learnt secondly, and more efficiently, from man himself. Man becomes an object of reverence whenever a higher greatness rests on him. And this higher greatness may be the greatness of office, or the greatness of character.

High office among men, when legitimately attained, deserves reverence. High office is a shadow of God's Majesty. The commandment to honour our earthly parents includes, in its spirit, the duty of honouring all who have upon them this certificate of greatness. "To love, honour, and succour my father and mother; to honour and obey the Queen, and all that are put in authority under her; to submit myself to all my governors, teachers, spiritual pastors and masters; to order myself lowly and reverently to all my betters;"[a]—this is how every child among us explains the Fifth Commandment. For the Fifth Commandment does not cease to bind when we grow up, or when our earthly parents are removed. When obedience to its letter is no longer possible, obedience to its spirit becomes more than ever a duty, and all upon whom there rests a shadow of the Divine become objects of conscientious reverence. The first magistrate of a state

[a] Church Catechism.

may be an hereditary monarch or an elected president; but the precept which bespeaks for him the reverence of men, as bearing on earth a shadow of the Divine authority, is always obligatory.

My brethren, it is impossible for us to approach so near to the person of the Sovereign without reminding ourselves of the great sorrow which has but yesterday darkened her life.[a] Her people will feel on this occasion, as they felt fourteen years ago, that the Queen's trouble is their own; they will associate themselves with her by their sympathies and in their prayers; they will pray that the evening of a life, in which the highest office has been adorned by such qualities as would bespeak for the humblest of her subjects an involuntary reverence, may be brightened by those consolations which God alone can give.

For, in truth, it is character, rather than, nay, much more than, office which compels reverence. Office is conferred on man; it is in a sense outside him; character is himself. Apart from character, office may only invite that sort of reverence which men pay to the wild powers of Nature; but conspicuous goodness compels a reverence which, with all due allowance for the difference between a created object and the Uncreated, is akin to the love of God. In every generation there are at least a few men who inspire those who approach them with this feeling, which is neither exactly love, nor admiration, nor moral submission, but that compound of all three, which we call reverence. In the old days of paganism there were a few men, who, by some one feature of character, awed their contemporaries; as did Aristides by his justice, and Scipio by his chastity, and Cato by his

---

[a] The Grand Duchess of Hesse Darmstadt, Princess Alice of England, died from diphtheria, caught while nursing her children, on December 14, 1878.

inflexibility. And, as might be expected, the Christian
Church, after receiving the gifts of grace which Christ
has bestowed on her, has, from the Apostolic days until
now, produced an unbroken succession of men and women
who have led lives that are indisputably objects of
reverence. The saints, canonized or uncanonized, conspicuous or hidden, are those Christians on whose characters there has rested the light and beauty of the
Divine Being; and thus they have compelled their contemporaries or their successors to recognize in them a greatness which bespeaks reverence. Nor is reverence less due
from us to these great names because it may have been
exaggerated. Exaggeration becomes impossible when we
remember that the true object to which reverence is due
is no more man himself than it is nature, but only that
Higher Greatness which may be discerned beyond them.

We live in a utilitarian age, and some men, who can
see for themselves the usefulness of prudence and of
justice, ask what are the advantages of being reverent.
Now, the answer to the question is that reverence is a
condition, we may say an indispensable condition, of true
human improvement. Consciously or unconsciously, man
becomes like that which he imitates, and he imitates those
whom he reveres. When you know what are the ideals,
what the heroes, of a boy, of a man, of a nation, you know
a great deal about the character of a nation, the man, the
boy. Reverence, when it is sincere, is no mere sentiment;
it carries with it great practical consequences; and hence
the extreme importance that the objects of reverence
should be, as far as may be, worthy of it; that parents,
teachers, all in authority, all on whom the eye of others
naturally rests, should be entitled to this tribute of respect.
Woe to the man or boy who reveres nothing and nobody!
He is cut off from one necessary condition of improvement;

his own present attainments, his virtues, his failures, his
vices, are the measure of his possible excellence. Woe
to the country or the race which can point to no lofty
characters, whether in the present or the past, on which
it can gaze with thankful reverence! No poverty is so
ruinous as moral poverty like that. It was, indeed, the
need of an object absolutely worthy of human reverence
which formed one of the reasons for the greatest of all
the manifestations of the Love of God. That One Human
Form, One Human Character, might command that
boundless reverence which the absence of any moral flaw
whatever alone can justify; that this supreme condition
of true human improvement might be granted to our
race; the Infinite Being submitted Himself to bonds,
and appeared among us in a Created Form; so that at
His feet all Christian reverence might, without fear
of error or exaggeration, abandon itself to all the impetuosity of its enthusiasm; might pass inevitably but
consciously into the highest expression of reverence—into
adoration.

Below the Throne of Jesus Christ, reverence is paid to
a greatness distinct from and beyond its immediate object.
It is paid to God. Behind Nature, we feel the Omnipotence of God; behind human office, the Authority of God;
behind human character in its higher forms, the Holiness
of God. We do not yet see God; we feel Him. Between
God and ourselves there is a veil; and this veil tempers
the rays of His glory, but at the same time it conceals
something. Thus here on earth the sense of reverence
is only imperfectly satisfied; and yet, if it could now be
confronted with its object, it would be overwhelmed. Just
as the natural eye cannot bear to gaze steadily at the
sun, so in this our earthly state we could not endure the
full effulgence of God; it would be too much for us.

"There shall no man see My Face and live."[a]   This has
been felt by God's truest servants in all ages.   When they
have caught a glimpse of the Divine glory, they have
presently pleaded that it might be hidden from their
eyes, or they have fainted at the sight.   Thus Isaiah,
after the vision in the Temple: "Woe is me! for I am
a man of unclean lips, and I dwell in the midst of a
people of unclean lips: and mine eyes have seen the
King, the Lord of Hosts."[b]   Thus St. John, in his
Apocalypse, after the opening sight of Jesus Christ in
glory: "When I saw Him, I fell at His Feet as dead."[c]

Amos, too, knows the difference between that kind of
apprehension of God which is common among men;
between talking or thinking about Him as men do—while
they think and talk with at least equal eagerness about
a thousand different things besides—and "meeting"
Him.   "Prepare to meet thy God, O Israel."   "Thy
God."   God was Israel's God still; and Israel talked
much of God.   The "manner of Bethel," as it was termed,
was an organized worship of God, though a false one;
the kings of Israel thought much of God, not, indeed,
chiefly as the Lord Almighty, but as, at any rate, quite
necessary to the political well-being of the ten tribes.
Just as Saul had sacrificed without hesitation,[d] because
he thought that, notwithstanding God's command, it did
not much matter; so Jeroboam had set up and his
successors continued a worship which God had disallowed;
no doubt on the principle that, the Divine instructions
notwithstanding, it would all come to the same thing in
the end.   Israel, in short, was irreverent; and Amos bids
Israel prepare to meet God, in quite a different sense
from that in which He had ever been met either at Bethel

---

[a] Exod. xxxiii. 20.        [b] Isa. vi. 5.
[c] Rev. i. 17.        [d] 1 Sam. xv. 9-22.

or in Samaria, in the prosperous days which were now drawing to a close.

Israel was to meet Him in suffering. Suffering does much for man, and among other things, if men will, it does *this ;* it strips off from the eye the conventional films which shut out God. It brings us face to face with Him. Israel would meet God as never before, in sharp and certain suffering. "Therefore the Lord, the God of Hosts, saith thus; Wailing shall be in all streets; and they shall say in all the highways, Alas! alas! and they shall call the husbandman to mourning, and such as are skilful to wailing. . . . For I will pass through thee, saith the Lord." [a]  And therefore Amos says, "Prepare."

And so, too, with us Christians in view of Death and Judgment. Is it not true that, in our ordinary lives, God, if I may say so, takes His chance amidst a thousand objects of interest? We do not, it may be, forget Him. But do we give Him anything like His due? We talk and think of Him, at least, now and then. We talk of the Divine attributes of Power, Wisdom, and Goodness, as to us invisible abstractions. The day is coming when we shall see them. We talk of Him Who was born at Bethlehem, and Who walked by the lake of Galilee, and Who died on Calvary. But He is visible somewhere even now. And "every eye *shall* see Him, and they also which pierced Him." [b]  The veils and films and clouds, material and mental, which intercept Him will pass away. And "we shall see Him as He is." [c]

## IV.

Endeavour to imagine what will meet your gaze within the first minute after death. Many whom we have known,

---

[a] Amos v. 16, 17.  [b] Rev. i. 7.  [c] 1 St. John iii. 2.

who were with us not long ago, have seen already that sight of sights. The Princess whom England mourns to-day has seen it. <u>None ever returns to tell us about it.</u> And we think of the departed too often only as they were while they were with us, and not as they are or may be, after that momentous change, in that new and astonishing world on which they have entered. Yet we, too, have that same experience certainly awaiting us. "We shall see Him as He is," with all His attributes, as living things, inseparable from His Eternal Essence; with the countless ministers of His Will, passing hither and thither on errands of mercy or of punishment beneath His Throne.

What must not that sight mean to those who come upon it suddenly, and without having given it an hour of serious thought in their lives! What may it not mean to those who have been saying every day for years, "Even so, come, Lord Jesus"![a] What should it not exact, in the way of preparation, from that instinct of reverence which neither nature nor man, nor anything short of the Unveiled Face of God, will lastingly satisfy!

Yes, brethren, this is the question. How are we to be educated for the sight of God after death? I answer—and this is a practical consideration with which I conclude—by worship.

"Religion," it once was said to me, "is all very well if by religion you mean morality; if it is something which makes men honest, industrious, useful, benevolent members of society. But," it was added, "if by religion you mean worship, I do not see the good of it; worship is at best the indulgence of sentiment, which loses time, achieves no tangible result, and may promote superstition."

This opinion, I fear, is not altogether singular; and

[a] Rev. xxii. 20.

yet, also, it surely is not altogether reasonable. For
religion is neither morality nor worship; it is the relation which binds a soul to God, of which morality is a
symptom, and worship an exercise. Yet who ever heard
of anything that could be called a religion without a
worship? All false religions which deserve the name
have some kind of worship as their expression; while
worship is of the essence of that one Religion which
claims, as we Christians with reason believe, to have
come from God Himself. A great part of the instructions
of the old Jewish Lawgiver have reference to worship.
And although, under the Gospel, worship has changed
its character because through the Incarnate Son, Christians are brought infinitely nearer to its Object, still in
the New Testament worship is not' represented as less
essential to the very existence of religion than in the
Old. The truth is that, whenever God is thought of as
a living Being, the desire to speak with Him, and that
under the only conditions which befit the approach of
the finite to the Infinite, of the created to the Creator—
that is to say, in worship—becomes irresistible. The idea
of a religion without worship, and, as is implied, without
any clear belief in its Object, is not a religious idea at
all. It is the conception of some shrewd modern minds,
who cannot disguise from themselves the advantages
which religion alone can confer on human society, but
who, being without faith, endeavour to make, for social
purposes, an impossible extract from what religion always
has been and always must be.

What is worship? It is not simply prayer, nor simply
thanksgiving, nor simply confession of sins, nor simply
praise, though praise comes nearest to it. These are acts
of worship; they are not worship itself. Worship is the
conscious self-presentation of a reasonable creature before

the illimitable Greatness of God. Worship is the highest
expression of reverence, which cannot help prostrating itself
in adoration. "O come, let us worship and fall down,
and kneel before the Lord our Maker. For He is the
Lord our God; and we are the people of His pasture,
and the sheep of His Hand. To-day if ye will hear His
Voice, harden not your hearts." [a] This is the invitation
to worship from age to age, whether in the synagogue
or in the Church of Christ.

Observe, then, a main purpose of worship here on earth,
on the part of Christians who believe that they have to
prepare for the sight of God in Judgment. Worship is a
preparation. It is an education for the inevitable future.
It is a training of the soul's eye to bear the brightness
of the Everlasting Sun. If there were no future, no
judgment, nothing but this life and sheer extinction at
the end of it, prayer might still be prompted by faith
in a Ruler of life and a Dispenser of its blessings. And
praise might now and then be suggested by gratitude.
But the greatest of all motives for worship, public and
private, would not exist. As it is, we Christians engage
in it, if intelligently, with a view to that vast Eternity
which is before us, and compared with the claims and
occupations of which all here is infinitely little. We try
to learn in it, as by God's grace we may, the tone, the
manners, the occupation, which will engage us in the
life to come.

Surely, then, as we kneel in the privacy of our chambers,
or as we cross the threshold of a church, each soul
should say to itself, "Prepare to meet thy God." Prepare to meet Him now, and here; for as of old, and in
a more special way, "the Lord is in His Holy Temple;" [b]
He is in the temple of the soul, and the temple of the

---

[a] Ps. xcv. 6-8.　　　　　[b] *Ib.* xi. 4.

Church. But prepare also to meet Him hereafter, in His unveiled Majesty. Prepare, by the very worship which thou art now about to pay Him, in prayer or Sacrament, for that momentous meeting. Surely such a motive as this, if we could do it justice, would transfigure every act of worship; would give it reality, intensity, above all, reverence; would make worship in fact, what in theory it has always been, the best preparation for death, the ante-chamber of Heaven.

# SERMON XXIX.

## PREPARATION FOR CHRIST'S COMING.

### IV. THE YEARNINGS OF AFFECTION.}

### (FOURTH SUNDAY IN ADVENT.)

#### AMOS IV. 12.

*Prepare to meet thy God, O Israel.*

PRUDENCE, justice, reverence,—these virtues have been considered in succession, as they may help us men to prepare for meeting God in death and judgment. True prudence is also justice, both towards God and man ; and true justice towards God is also reverence; it is the acknowledgment that God is What He is. Yet neither prudence, nor justice, nor reverence seems to furnish us with the deepest motive for preparation. Prudence, justice, reverence, are in different ways allied to or based on fear ; fear of consequences, fear of a law of retribution, fear of an awful and as yet unvisited world. My brethren, we could not end here even if there were less than four Sundays in Advent ; and so to-day we pass to an aspect of the subject which you will have already anticipated. What do the words, " Prepare to meet thy God," say to us when they are confronted with that mysterious and pervading element in our nature which in its lower forms we call desire, and in its higher, love?

## I.

We have already satisfied ourselves that the instincts of prudence, justice, and reverence are original elements of the nature which our Maker has given us, and that they are subsequently raised, mainly by God's grace, but also by our faithfulness to His leading, to the rank of commanding excellences, shaping life and controlling the issues of destiny. And thus it is also with that feature of our common human nature which is before us to-day. Every human being is endowed with a certain proportion of desire, that is to say, of impulse, to reach after something beyond himself as necessary to his perfect satisfaction and well-being. Desire is just as much an original endowment of man as is reason; we have no experience of any human being coming into this world without it. Desire, in a moral, self-governing agent like man, corresponds to gravitation in a material body; it is a force which determines a man's relation to beings and objects around him. It is, according to the different objects on which it is fixed, the raw material both of virtue and of vice, and thus it has much more to do with the issues of life and destiny than has reason. Reason may be very active, and yet have no influence upon conduct and character. This was the case with the founder of the inductive philosophy, who was at once the wisest and the meanest of mankind. But desire cannot be active without moulding character profoundly, whether for good or evil; nay, desire determines the direction in which a moral being is moving. And thus, speaking generally, desire may be regarded under two very different aspects; we will look at it

when it is moving towards its one true object, and when
it is not.

If the general truth of what has been said be granted,
the question arises, What *is* the object which desire was
intended to seek?  No believer in God can hesitate about
the answer to this question; and to-day we need not concern ourselves to inquire into that which persons who
unhappily do not believe in God have to say about this
and other features of human nature.  Desire is meant,
first of all, to keep man loyal to the Being Who made him.

Doubtless, according to the constitution of our nature,
desire has a great many immediate and legitimate objects
which fall short of God.  A good appetite, for instance,
and a love of study or inquiry, are both lawful forms of
desire.  But the object of desire in the form of a good
appetite is, or should be, the preservation of health and
strength, with the ultimate aim of employing them to
promote God's glory; and the object of desire in the form
of enthusiasm for study is, or should be, the acquisition
of truth, which must, by whatever paths, lead up to God,
in Whom all the paths of sincere inquiry ultimately meet,
as in the Absolute and Supreme Truth.  In other words,
God Himself is the ultimate Object of desire.  He meant
to be so.  He gave us desire that He might be so.  Desire
is the force intended by the Creator to keep His reasonable creature loyal to Himself, as the Centre or as the
Object and End of their being.  Just as the planets revolve, in obedience to a necessary law, round their central
sun, so souls are designed to revolve in the moral sphere
around the Sun of Righteousness, being held in their
orbits by the force of desire.  Or rather, just as any small
meteoric mass, in the near neighbourhood of this earth,
cannot but draw near to it, in obedience to what we call

the law of gravitation ; so souls, impelled by desire or love of God, ought freely but incessantly to move towards Him, as their Centre of moral gravitation. There is no disputing the old saying, " Amore feror, quocunque feror," " Whithersoever I am borne onward, it is love that bears me." [a] Desire, or love, is always the impelling motive ; it is the weight which determines the gravitation of a soul. It rules both the direction and the rapidity of a soul's movement. When desire achieves its original purpose, it takes the form of the love of God. This, in their days of innocence, was the governing motive in our first parents. This is the governing motive in Christians, who live according to the Law of Christ, in whom He has formed and developed " the new man, which after God is created in righteousness and true holiness." [b] They gravitate, by desire or love, towards God. The motto of their life is, " Whom have I in Heaven but Thee ? and there is none upon earth that I desire in comparison of Thee." [c]

Desire, or love, then, is intended to be directed upon God, to keep the soul true to Him, and to bring it, in the end, into everlasting union with Him. But human nature, as we find it, is like a beautiful instrument in which everything has been dislocated and put out of gear by some terrible shock. And thus desire in fallen man, instead of concentrating itself upon God, lavishes itself like a thoughtless spendthrift upon anything and everything that is not God. No created object is too debased to fail, sooner or later, of attracting it. And as it shatters itself into separated and often conflicting jets of lawless impulse, it becomes the ruling passions, and it results

---

[a] St. Aug., *Conf.*, xiii. 9 : "Pondus meum amor meus : eo feror quocunque feror."

[b] Eph. iv. 24.  [c] Ps. lxxiii. 25.

in the besetting sins of our everyday life. Murder,
adultery, theft, are all products of misdirected desire;
of desire lawlessly concentrating itself on some created
object, and in its impetuous onset breaking down the moral
barriers which forbid indulgence.   Desire, or love, which
has ceased to be loyal to God is like a railway engine
which is off the line, while the steam has not yet been
turned off, and it has not yet encountered any obstacle
capable of bringing it to a standstill.   Its surviving force
is the measure of the danger which it threatens to the
freight behind it.   Desire which is no longer given to
God is even more perilous than moral apathy, in so far
as it may commit the soul more decidedly to evil.   A
soul, the force of whose desire is no longer directed upon
God, is in the moral world what a planet would be in the
material heavens, if it could leave its orbit, and dash
about through space in a course of wild destructive
eccentricity.   St. Jude speaks of a tribe of such souls in
his day, as "wandering stars, to whom is reserved the
blackness of darkness for ever." [a]   And St. James supplies
the reason for this stern language when he describes
the effects of wandering desire which being detached
from God, its true Object, is spending itself on created
things.   "Desire, when it hath conceived, bringeth
forth sin; and sin, when it is finished, bringeth forth
death." [b]   Thus, according to St. James, desire, when no
longer directed upon God, is the active principle which
generates sin.   St. James says that desire is the mother
and sin the child; and assuredly sin, the child, is like its
mother.   For the common word in the New Testament
for "sin" [c] means some act which misses the true mark
or aim of life, that is to say, conformity with His Will,
Who is the Author and the End of our existence.

---

[a] St. Jude 13.      [b] St. James i. 15.      [c] ἁμαρτία.

The object of Religion, then, is, if possible, to restore
desire—this fund of motive force—to its true track, its
true direction, and, having restored, to maintain it there.
To this great object, sermons, prayers, sacraments; all that
illuminates the understanding, all that touches the heart,
all that braces the will, is persistently directed.  For in
this rectification of desire the excellence of man mainly
consists.   There is a famous definition of virtue which
the Christian Church owes to the religious genius of
St. Augustine.  He calls it " order in love," in other words,
" regulated desire." [a]  Augustine clearly saw that if this
formidable ingredient of our nature could only be ordered
well, that is to say, conformably with the laws of God,
all else would settle itself soon and rightly.  Therefore he
called virtue " regulated desire."   Not regulated reason,
which is possible consistently with vice; but regulated
desire.  Not extinguished desire, mark you.  Not even
impoverished desire; because desire is wanted as the
soul's motive force.   But desire, ever moving with all its
strength and impulse; moving according to the original
rule of the Creator; moving among without being
detained by the creatures around it; moving onwards and
upwards towards His Everlasting Throne.

It is not meant that this result can be brought about
only or mainly by human agency.  Experience might
tell us this, if we have ever tried our hands at the work;
and St. Paul says that " the love of God "—in other words,
desire, regulated, reinforced, purified so as to seek its
true Object—" is shed abroad in our hearts by the Holy
Ghost which is given unto us." [b]  St. Paul is just as much
alive as St. James to the havoc which is wrought in fallen

[a] *De Civ. Dei*, xv. 22: " Mihi videtur quod definitio brevis et vera
virtutis ordo est amoris."

[b] Rom. v. 5.

human nature by unregulated and degraded desire; he
says that here is the cause why the Mosaic Law, in itself
" holy, and just, and good," became to man an occasion of
sin : [a] rebellious desire took offence at the Law's restric-
tions upon its wayward licence. Desire is that "other
law in the members," [b] which wars against the law of the
Apostle's mind. And if desire is to be baptized and given
its true direction, a stream of fire from Heaven must be
poured forth into the soul to effect the change; to purify,
to illuminate, to elevate, above all, to direct; to bid the
impulse which has, as concupiscence, long looked downwards and earthwards, raise its gaze to Heaven, and
become the love of God.

## II.

Here, then, let us endeavour to determine the nature
of the appeal which the message of Amos, "Prepare to
meet thy God," makes to this important element of our
nature—desire.

" Prepare to meet thy God ! " When desire is alienated
from God, and is spent on created objects, as if they
were adequate and satisfactory, these words cannot
but carry with them a very solemn meaning. They
mean, evidently, at least this — Prepare, O man, for
a meeting which will show thee that thy life has been
a vast mistake; that thy endowment of desire has been
expended upon what is worthless or worse; that it has
neglected and forgotten the One Being Who is really
worth living for. Prepare for this discovery, when thy
vital force is ebbing or gone; when the shadows are falling

<hr/>

[a] Rom. vii. 8–12.                    [b] *Ib.* 23.

thick around thee; when it is practically too late for recovery and amendment. "Prepare to meet thy God." For if thou art to meet Him in peace, much preparation assuredly is necessary. He does not tolerate the expenditure upon creatures of that mysterious and powerful ingredient in thy nature which He made, that by it He might draw thee upwards to Himself. He has told thee that He is a jealous God;[a] that He will not give His honour to another.[b] He would not be Himself if He could do this. Thou must, therefore, choose. "Love not the world, neither the things that are in the world. If any man love the world, the love of the Father is not in him. For all that is in the world, the lust of the flesh, and the lust of the eyes, and the pride of life, is not of the Father, but is of the world. And the world passeth away, and the lust thereof."[c] Think of that coming moment of disenchantment and of dismay; and, while thou mayest, prepare.

This is the warning; but to obey it is not easy for any of us. Desire, alienated from God, and moving among created objects which attract it, is like Israel among the Canaanities. It obeys forces which it ought to control. "They were mingled among the heathen and learned their works: inasmuch as they worshipped their idols, which turned to their own decay."[d] In order to set desire free to return to its original direction, God has an agent at command in this His human world, which has, indeed, other work to do, and of which much else may be said; but an agent by whose importunity this special work of detaching desire from the unsatisfying objects which woo it is generally effected.

That agent is pain. What a mystery, if we think of

a Exod. xx. 5.  b Isa. xlviii. 11.
c 1 St. John ii. 15–17.  d Ps. cvi. 35, 36.

it, is pain, in a world which a perfectly benevolent Being
has made and governs! How little does pain correspond
to anything that we could have anticipated! How little
do we understand what it is in itself! We know it when
we feel it ourselves; we recognize its presence by its
effects on others; we know and can analyze many of the
causes, physical and mental, which invariably produce it.
But the sensation itself, as distinct from its immediately
antecedent cause, is beyond us; we cannot take it to
pieces, or give any account of it. There it is; we can
but feel it as a simple sensation. No immaterial visitant
from another world, who should make his presence over-
whelmingly plain to us, would more entirely elude our
efforts to understand all about him than does pain. And
yet pain is here—let us be sure of it—with a purpose as
distinct and as beneficent as that of any angel that ever
came from Heaven. Doubtless pain is found far beyond
the frontiers of the human race. What it may or may not
do for the lower creatures, who have a very large share
of it, is an interesting, but not now, and for us, a profitable
speculation. Even within the human family, pain is
sometimes a faithful watchdog, which denotes the near
approach of danger; sometimes it is a penal visitant,
executing a stern sentence which, as conscience whispers,
is deserved. But more frequently pain is or may be a
wise friend, who puts his hand on our shoulders and bids
us think; bids us think about a great many things of
which we think too little, but especially about this grave
matter of misspent desire. Pain is the disappointment
and defeat of desire, arising either from our discovery
that an object is worthless, or that it is vanishing. When
the prodigal son was in the far country, his best friend
was pain. When pain had done its work of disenchantment, desire could turn back towards its true direction.

" I will arise, and go to my father, and will say unto him, Father, I have sinned against Heaven, and before thee." [a]

This was Israel's experience in days long before the birth of Amos. As we may have learnt from the Psalm which occurs in the Church Service of yesterday afternoon,[b] much of the early life of Israel is a long alternation of heart-apostasies from God, and of disciplinary suffering. And in Amos's day the life of the ten tribes was shaped throughout by lawless desire. In Israel, desire had spent itself without reserve on wealth, on luxury, on sensual indulgence, on political ambitions, on everything, in short, but God. The "houses of hewn stone,"[c] the " pleasant vineyards,"[d] the "beds of ivory,"[e] the "melody of viols,"[f] the "bowls of wine,"[g] the "costly ointments,"[h] which Amos mentions, were in themselves or in their associations so many attractions to unregulated desire. When the ten tribes broke away from the religious centre of the nation, the desire of Israel as a people was alienated from God. And God mercifully corrects alienated desire by destroying or removing its objects. Mark the plaintive monotony of the verses which, in another connection, have been already brought to our notice ; verses in which the prophet describes the successive punishments of Israel's godless desire, and their failures to achieve the intended purpose.

Israel's luxury of life was punished by famine :—

"I have given you cleanness of teeth in all your cities,
And want of bread in all your places :
Yet have ye not returned unto Me, saith the Lord."[i]

Israel's avarice in trade was punished by drought :—

| | | |
|---|---|---|
| [a] St. Luke xv. 18. | [b] Ps. cvi. | [c] Amos v. 11. |
| [d] Ib. | [e] Ib. vi. 4. | [f] Ib. v. 23. |
| [g] Ib. vi. 6. | [h] Ib. | [i] Ib. iv. 6. |

> " Also I have withholden the rain from you,
> When there were yet three months to the harvest:
>
> . . . . . . .
>
> So two or three cities wandered to one city, to drink water;
> But they were not satisfied :
> Yet have ye not returned unto Me, saith the Lord." [a]

Israel's unthankful delight in landed property was punished by blight :—

> " I have smitten you with blasting and mildew:
> When your gardens and your vineyards
> And your fig trees and your olive trees increased,
> The palmerworm devoured them :
> Yet have ye not returned unto Me, saith the Lord." [b]

Israel's joyous, bounding confidence in rude health and in military prowess was punished by wasting disease and by defeat in battle :—

> " I have sent among you the pestilence after the manner of Egypt:
> Your young men have I slain with the sword,
> And have taken away your horses ;
> And I have made the stink of your camps to come up unto your nostrils :
> Yet have ye not returned unto Me, saith the Lord." [c]

The confident satisfaction of the separated tribes in their city, their homes, the settled order of things around them, as though these were visible warrants for forgetfulness of God, and worthy objects of the soul's best enthusiasms, was punished by the unwonted terrors of an earthquake, accompanied, it would seem, by a volcanic eruption :—

> " I have destroyed some of you,
> As God overthrew Sodom and Gomorrah,
> And ye were as a firebrand plucked out of the burning:
> Yet have ye not returned unto Me, saith the Lord." [d]

And because all these judgments had failed to restore to God the alienated desire of Israel, another judgment,

---

[a] Amos iv. 7, 8.      [b] *Ib.* 9.      [c] *Ib.* 10.      [d] *Ib.* 11.

more ruinous and comprehensive—it is not said what—
was still impending :—

> "Therefore *thus* will I do unto thee, O Israel:
> And because I will do this unto thee,
> Prepare to meet thy God, O Israel." [a]

As yet, then, pain had not, as Amos complains, done its
destined work for Israel, by turning misspent desire back
upon its true Object—upon God. That, indeed, enhanced
the tragic character of Israel's position. The remedy had
been applied, but as yet the disease had not yielded to
the treatment. Yet all the great penitents of sacred
history, like the prodigal son, have witnessed to the
providential efficacy of pain in detaching desire from
unworthy objects. So it was with David, when his child
was taken ; so with the Magdalen, when she washed the
Feet of Jesus with her tears ; so with the dying thief,
when, exhausted by a lingering agony, he prayed to be
remembered in the Kingdom of his Crucified Lord. So
in later years it was with Augustine. First a philosophical
libertine, then a penitent, then first among all the teachers
of the Church since the age of the Apostles. For many
reasons St. Augustine's *Confessions* will be a classical
work in the Church of Christ to the end of time. But
the special interest of this book is this: it is a history of
the disenchantment, of the rectification of desire, through
the agency of pain. Sometimes it was mental pain ; the
pain which arises from unsatisfied longings after a truth
or a perfection which is never reached. Sometimes it was
weariness of the body, which disgusts men with the present
life, and turns their thoughts upwards and onwards. But
the net result is stated in a saying which puts Augustine's
philosophy of life into a very small compass, and at the
same time has condensed for all Christian time the

[a] Amos iv. 12.

teaching of his wide experience : "Lord, Thou hast made
us for Thyself, and our hearts are restless till they rest in
Thee." [a]

"Prepare to meet thy God!" The action of God
upon a soul in which desire has been spent upon unworthy objects, is not merely a negative one. He does
not merely show it what cannot satisfy. He has positive
attractions in store for it, which will do their work, if
there is not active reluctance or resistance on the soul's
part. Amos is full of reassurance as to the satisfaction
which God has in store for Israel. We do not, indeed, find
in Amos that pathetic tenderness which is characteristic
of the revelations of his contemporary Hosea ; but again
and again with solemn passion Amos recalls the desire of
Israel to its true Object :—

> "Seek ye Me, and ye shall live.
> But seek not Bethel,
> Nor enter into Gilgal." [b]

Again—

> "Seek the Lord, and ye shall live ;
> Lest He break out like fire in the house of Joseph, and devour it." [c]

Again—

> "Seek Him that maketh the seven stars and Orion,
> And turneth the shadow of death into the morning :
>
> .     .     .     .     .     .     .
>
> The Lord is His Name :" [d]

Again—

> "Seek good, and not evil, that ye may live :
> And so the Lord, the God of Hosts, shall be with you." [e]

Certainly God acts upon alienated desire first of all by
the discipline and experience of pain. But He also offers

---

[a] St. Aug., *Conf.*, Bk. i. [i.] § 1.          [b] Amos v. 4, 5.
        [c] *Ib.* 6.          [d] *Ib.* 8.          [e] *Ib.* 14.

it a Love which draws it in its true direction, by drawing it towards Himself.

That which provokes love, is love. The human heart
easily returns an affection of which it feels itself to be the
object; it rouses itself with difficulty to love an invisible
Being, only because He is what He is, the most worthy of
all possible objects of affection. It is not so much because
God is lovable, as because He has loved us from everlasting, that we, in our weakness, are most readily enabled
to return His love. " We love Him," says St. John, " because He first loved us." [a] God so loved this human world
that He gave His only begotten Son for its salvation.[b]
Love is no abstract, unfruitful emotion; it is eminently
energetic. With God, as always and everywhere, love is
the gift of self. " God commendeth His love to us, in that,
while we were yet sinners, Christ died for us;" [c] " Herein
perceive we the love of God, because He laid down His
life for us;" [d] " Herein is love, not that we loved God, but
that He loved us, and sent His Son to be the Propitiation
for our sins;" [e] and therefore, says an Apostle, "the love
of Christ constraineth us; because we thus judge, that if
one died for all, then were all dead: and that He died for
all, that they which live should not henceforth live unto
themselves, but unto Him that died for them, and rose
again." [f] It was the love of God, as shown to man in Jesus
Christ, Incarnate, Teaching, Crucified, Risen, Ascended,
Interceding, but pre-eminently in Jesus Christ Crucified,
which was to win back to God, in the form of a pure, self-
sacrificing love, the truant desire of humanity.

And it has done this in the true representatives of
Christendom, the great servants of God who have appeared
from age to age. The saints are very various in character

[a] 1 St. John iv. 19.     [b] St. John iii. 16.     [c] Rom. v. 8.
[d] 1 St. John iii. 16.     [e] Ib. iv. 10.     [f] 2 Cor. v. 14, 15.

VOL. II.                                                          E

and attainments, but there is one mark which is always upon them; they love God. Christ has perfectly won their hearts by that supreme expression of love, His own self-sacrifice on Calvary. And they, as one after the other they traverse the centuries, whatever be their station, or repute, or attainments, or country, repeat alike in word and by their acts, "We love Him, because He first loved us." [a]  They are men in whom desire has recovered the place which was designed for it; it is the attractive force which binds them to the Centre around which they move; it draws them onwards to the Being Who is the true End of their existence.

"Prepare to meet thy God!" The words bid us detach desire from unworthy and unsatisfying objects while yet we may. They bid us attach desire to the One Object Which can everlastingly satisfy it; to the Being Who made us, revealed in His Adorable Son. They bid us, while we may, wed desire to understanding; to that true understanding of the real meaning and conditions of our existence, which God gives to those who would keep His Law with their whole heart.[b]  Desire and understanding are the parents of will; will is but intelligent desire. And will is, or should be, the monarch among the faculties of the regenerate soul; shaping life in accordance with an apprehension of its true purpose; demolishing or surmounting the obstacles which oppose themselves to the attainment of that purpose; bringing circumstances, habits, passions, even reason, into harmonious co-operation for the attainment of the true end of man. "Prepare to meet thy God!" Yes! where will is supreme in a regenerate soul, soon "the crooked places are made straight, and the rough places plain," as of old across the desert for the passage of God.[c]  Everything is welcome, because everything,

either as an assistance or as a discipline, must further our
purpose, that of reaching the supreme object of desire—
the Vision of God.  Not least welcome is death.  Death
leads the way to Him for whom the soul longs.

> "How pleasant are thy paths, O death !
>   Like the bright slanting west ;
> Thou leadest down into the glow,
> Where all those heaven-bound sunsets go,
>   Ever from toil to rest.
>
> "How pleasant are thy paths, O death !
>   Thither, where sorrows cease,
> To a new life, to an old past,
> Softly and silently we haste,
>   Into a land of peace.
>
> "How pleasant are thy paths, O death !
>   Straight to our Father's home.
> All loss were gain, that gained us this ;
> The sight of God, that single bliss
>   Of the grand world to come."[a]

Yes! this is the true work of Advent as of life ; the training of many other faculties, if you will, but especially of
desire, in order that, transfigured as love—the Love of God
revealed in His Blessed Son—it may be more than a conqueror ; in order that, loving God above all things, we
may obtain His promises, which exceed all that we can
desire, through Jesus Christ our Lord.[b]

[a] Hymns by F. W. Faber, No. 139.
[b] Collect for Sixth Sunday after Trinity.

# SERMON XXX.

## THE FIRST FIVE MINUTES AFTER DEATH.

### (THIRD SUNDAY IN ADVENT.)

1 Cor. xiii. 12.

*Then shall I know, even as also I am known.*

AN Indian officer, who in his time had seen a great deal
of service, and had taken part in more than one of
those decisive struggles by which the British authority
was finally established in the East Indies, had returned
to end his days in this country, and was talking with his
friends about the most striking experiences of his professional career. They led him, by their sympathy and their
questions, to travel in memory through a long series of
years; and as he described skirmishes, battles, sieges,
personal encounters, hair-breadth escapes, the outbreak of
the mutiny and its suppression, reverses, victories—all the
swift alternations of anxiety and hope which a man must
know who is entrusted with command, and is before the
enemy—their interest in his story, as was natural, became
keener and more exacting. At last he paused with the
observation, "I expect to see something much more remarkable than anything I have been describing." As he
was some seventy years of age, and was understood to
have retired from active service, his listeners failed to

catch his meaning. There was a pause; and then he said in an undertone, "I mean in the first five minutes after death."

"The first five minutes after death!" Surely the expression is worth remembering, if only as that of a man to whom the life to come was evidently a great and solemn reality. "The first five minutes." If we may employ for the moment when speaking of eternity standards of measurement which belong to time, it is at least conceivable that, after the lapse of some thousands or tens of thousands of years, we shall have lost all sense of a succession in events; that existence will have come to seem to be only a never-ceasing present; an unbegun and unending *now*. It is, I say, at least conceivable that this will be so; but can we suppose that at the moment of our entrance on that new and wonderful world we shall already think and feel as if we had always been there, or had been there, at least, for ages?

There is, no doubt, an impression sometimes to be met with that death is followed by a state of unconsciousness.

> "If sleep and death be truly one,
>   And every spirit's folded bloom,
>   Through all its intervital gloom,
> In some long trance should slumber on,
>
> "Unconscious of the sliding hour,
>   Bare of the body, might it last,
>   And all the traces of the past
> Be all the colour of the flower."

But that is a supposition which is less due to the exigencies of reason than to the sensitiveness of imagination. The imagination recoils from the task of anticipating a moment so full of awe and wonder as must be that of the introduction of a conscious spirit to the Invisible World. And, accordingly, the reason essays to persuade itself, if it

can, that life after death will not be conscious life, although
it is difficult to recognize a single reason why, if life, properly speaking, survives at all, it should forfeit consciousness.   Certainly the life of the souls under the Heavenly
Altar, who intercede perpetually with God for the approach
of the Last Judgment,[a] is not an unconscious life.   Certainly the Paradise which our Lord promised to the dying
thief[b] cannot be reasonably imagined to have been a moral
and mental slumber, any more than can those unembodied
ministers of God who do His pleasure, who are sent forth
to minister to them that are the heirs of salvation,[c] be
supposed to reach a condition no higher than that which
is produced by chloroform.   No, this supposition of an
unconscious state after death is a discovery, not of Revelation, not of reason, but of desire; of a strong desire on
the one hand to keep a hold on immortality, and on the
other to escape the risks which immortality may involve.
It cannot well be doubted that consciousness,—if not retained to the last in the act of dying, if suspended by sleep,
or by physical disease, or by derangement—must be recovered as soon as the act of death is completed, with the
removal of the cause which suspended it.   Should this be
the case, the soul will enter upon another life with the
habits of thought which belong to time still clinging to it;
they will be unlearnt gradually, if at all, in the after-ages
of existence.   And, assuredly, the first sense of being in
another world must be overwhelming.   Imagination can,
indeed, form no worthy estimate of it; but we may do well
to try to think of it as best we can this afternoon, since it is
at least one of the approaches to the great and awful subject which should be before our thoughts at this time of the
year, namely, the Second Coming of Jesus Christ to Judgment.   And here the Apostle comes to our assistance with

    [a] Rev. vi. 9, 10.    [b] St. Luke xxiii. 43.    [c] Heb. i. 14.

his anticipation of the future life, as a life of enormously enhanced knowledge: "Then shall I know, even as also I am known."[a]   He is thinking, no doubt, of that life as a whole, and not of the first entrance on it, immediately after death.   No doubt, also, he is thinking of the high privileges of the blessed, whose knowledge, we may presume to say, with some great teachers of the Church, will be thus vast and comprehensive because they will see all things in God, as in the Ocean of Truth.   But it cannot be supposed that an increase of knowledge after death will be altogether confined to the blessed.   The change itself must bring with it the experience which is inseparable from a new mode of existence: it must unveil secrets; it must discover vast tracts of fact and thought for every one of the sons of men.   Let us try to keep it before our minds, reverently and earnestly, for a few minutes; and let us ask ourselves, accordingly, what will be the most startling additions to our existing knowledge at our first entrance on the world to come.

## I.

First, then, at our entrance on another state of being, we shall know what it is to exist under entirely new conditions.   Here we are bound up—we hardly suspect, perhaps, how intimately—in thought and affection, with the persons and objects around us.   They influence us subtly and powerfully in a thousand ways; in some cases they altogether shape the course of life.   In every life, it has been truly said, much more is taken for granted than is ever noticed.   The mind is eagerly directed to the few persons and subjects which affection or interest force prominently upon its notice; it gazes inertly at all the rest.

[a] 1 Cor. xiii. 12.

As we say, it does not take them in, until some incident arises which forces them one by one into view. A boy never knows what his home was worth until he has gone for the first time to school; and then he misses, and as he misses he eagerly recollects and realizes, all that he has left behind him. Who of us that has experienced it can ever forget those first hours at school after leaving home; that moment when the partings were over, and the carriage drove away from the door, and we heard the last of the wheels and of the horses as they went round the corner, and then turned to find ourselves in a new world, among strange faces and in strange scenes, and under a new and perhaps sterner government? Then for the first time, and at a distance from it, we found out what our home had been to us. It was more to us in memory than it had ever been while we were in it. All that we saw, and heard, and had to do, and had to give up at school, presented a contrast which stimulated our memories of what had been the rule of home—of its large liberty, of its gentle looks and words, of its scenes and haunts, which had taken such a hold on our hearts without our knowing it. It was too much; we had to shrink away into some place where we could be alone, and recover ourselves as best we could before we were able to fall in with the ways of our new life. No doubt, in time, habit did its work; habit turned school, I will not say into a second home, but into a new and less agreeable kind of home. And as the years passed, we saw repeated again and again in the case of others that which we had experienced at first, and with a vividness that did not admit of repetition in ourselves.

This may enable us, in a certain sense, to understand what is in store for all of us at our entrance, by dying, into the unseen world. I do not, of course, mean that this life is our home, and that the future at all neces-

sarily corresponds to school as being an endless banish-
ment. God forbid! If we only will have it, the exact
reverse of this shall be the case. But the parallel will
so far hold good that at death we must experience a
sense of strangeness to which nothing in this life has
even approached. Not merely will the scene be new—to
us as yet it is unimaginable; not merely will the beings
around us—the shapes, forms, conditions of existence, be
strange—they are as yet inconceivable; but we ourselves
shall have undergone a change; a change so complete that
we cannot here and now anticipate its full meaning. We
shall exist, thinking and feeling, and exercising memory
and will and understanding; but—without bodies. Think
what that means. We are at present at home in the
body; we have not yet learnt, by losing it, what the body
is to us. The various activities of the soul are sorted out
and appropriated by the several senses of the body, so
that the soul's action from moment to moment is made
easy, we may well conceive, by being thus distributed.
What will it be to compress all that the senses now
achieve separately into a single act; to see, but without
these eyes; to hear, but without these ears; to experience
something purely supersensuous that shall answer to the
grosser senses of taste and smell; and to see, hear, smell,
and taste by a single movement of the spirit, combining
all these separate modes of apprehension into one? What
will it be to find ourselves with the old self, divested of
this body which has clothed it since its first moment of
existence; able to achieve, it may be so much, it may be
so little; living on, but under conditions so totally new?
This experience alone will add no little to our existing
knowledge; and the addition will have been made in the
first five minutes after death.

## II.

And the entrance on the next world must bring with it a knowledge of God such as is impossible in this life. In this life many men talk of God, and some men think much and deeply about Him. But here men do not attain to that sort of direct knowledge of God which the Bible calls " sight." We do not see a human soul. The soul makes itself felt in conduct, in conversation, in the lines of the countenance; although these often enough mislead us. The soul speaks through the eye, which misleads us less often. That is to say, we know that the soul is there, and we detect something of its character and power and drift. We do not see it. In the same way we feel God present in Nature, whether in its awe or its beauty; and in human history, whether in its justice or its weird mysteriousness; and in the life of a good man, or the circumstances of a generous or noble act. Most of all we feel Him near when conscience, His inward messenger, speaks plainly and decisively to us. Conscience, that invisible prophet, surely appeals to and implies a law, and a law implies a legislator. But we do not see Him. "No man hath seen God at any time;" even "the only begotten Son, Which is in the Bosom of the Father," is only said to have " declared Him," [a] since in Him the Godhead was veiled from earthly sight by that mantle of Flesh and Blood Which, together with a Human Soul, He assumed in time. Certainly great servants of God have been said to see Him even in this life. Thus Job: "I have heard of Thee with the hearing of the ear, but now mine eye seeth Thee." [b] Thus David: "As for me, I shall behold Thy Presence in righteousness." [c] Thus Isaiah " beheld,"

[a] St. John i. 18.      [b] Job xlii. 5.      [c] Ps. xvii. 16.

while the glory of the Lord filled the Temple.[a] Thus St. John, when he saw the Risen Saviour in His glory, fell at His Feet as dead.[b] These are either preternatural anticipations of the future life vouchsafed to exceptionally good men, or they are, as with Job, cases in which men are said to see God only in a relative sense. Sight does not mean anything spiritual which corresponds fully to the action of the bodily eye, but only a much higher degree of perception than had been possible in a lower spiritual state. Of the children of men in this mortal state, the rule holds good that no one hath seen God at any time.[c]

But after death there will be a change. It is said of our Lord's glorified Manhood, united as It is for ever to the Person of the Eternal Son, that "every eye shall see Him, and they also which pierced Him."[d] Even the lost will then understand much more of what God is to the universe and to themselves, although they are for ever excluded from the direct Vision of God. And they, too, will surely see God, who are waiting for the full glories of the sight to be vouchsafed to them after an intermediate time of discipline and training in the state which Scripture calls Paradise. The spirit of man, we cannot doubt, will be much more conscious of the spirits around it, and of the Father of spirits, than was possible while it was encased in the body. God will no longer be to it a mere abstraction, a First Cause, a First Intelligence, a Supreme Morality, the Absolute, the Self-Existent, the Unconditioned Being. He will no longer reveal Himself to the strained tension of human thought, as one by one His Attributes are weighed, and balanced, and reconciled, and apportioned, after such poor fashion and measure as is

---

[a] Isa. vi. 1.                    [b] Rev. i. 17.
[c] St. John i. 18.               [d] Rev. i. 7.

possible for the finite mind when dealing with the Infinite. None of us will any more play with phrases about Him to which nothing is felt to correspond in thought or fact. He will be there, before us. We shall see Him as He is.[a] His vast illimitable Life will present itself to the apprehension of our spirits as a clearly consistent whole; not as a complex problem to be painfully mastered by the effort of our understandings, but as a present, living, encompassing Being, Who inflicts Himself on the very sight of His adoring creatures. What will that first apprehension of God, under the new conditions of the other life, be? There are trustworthy accounts of men who have been utterly overcome at the first sight of a fellow-creature with whose name and work they had for long years associated great wisdom, or goodness, or ability; the first sight of the earthly Jerusalem has endowed more than one traveller with a perfectly new experience in the life of thought and feeling. What must not be the first direct sight of God, the Source of all beauty, of all wisdom, of all power, when the eye opens upon Him after death! "Thine eyes shall see the King in His beauty,"[b] were words of warning as well as words of promise. What will it not be to see Him in those first few moments—God, the Eternal Love, God, the Consuming Fire[c]—as we shall see Him in the first five minutes after death!

### III.

Once more; at our entrance on another world we shall know our old selves as never before. The past will lie spread out before us, and we shall take a comprehensive survey of it. Each man's life will be displayed to him as a

[a] 1 St. John iii. 2.    [b] Isa. xxxiii. 17.    [c] Heb. xii. 29.

river, which he traces from its source in a distant mountain till it mingles with the distant ocean. The course
of that river lies, sometimes through dark forests which
hide it from view, sometimes through sands or marshes
in which it seems to lose itself. Here it forces a passage
angrily between precipitous rocks, there it glides gently
through meadows which it makes green and fertile. At
one while it might seem to be turning backwards out of
pure caprice; at another to be parting, like a gay spendthrift, with half its volume of waters; while later on it
receives contributory streams that restore its strength;
and so it passes on, till the ebb and flow of the tides upon
its bank tells that the end is near. What will not the
retrospect be when, after death, we survey, for the first
time, as with a bird's-eye view, the whole long range—
the strange vicissitudes, the loss and gain, as we deem it,
the failures and the triumphs of our earthly existence;
when we measure it, as never before, in its completeness,
now that it is at last over!

This, indeed, is the characteristic of the survey after
death, that it will be complete.

> "There no shade can last,
> In that deep dawn behind the tomb,
> But clear from marge to marge shall bloom
> The eternal landscape of the past."

That survey of life which is made by the dying is less
than complete; it cannot include the closing scene of all.
While there is life, there is room for recovery, and the
hours which remain may be very different from those
which have preceded.

It may be thought that to review life will take as long
a time as to live it; but this notion betrays a very imperfect idea of the resource and capacity of the human
soul. Under the pressure of great feeling, the soul lives

with a rapidity and intensity which disturb all its usual
relations to time; witness the reports which those who
have nearly lost their lives by drowning have made of
their mental experiences.  It once happened to me to
assist at the recovery of a man who nearly forfeited life
while bathing.  He had sunk the last time, and there was
difficulty in getting him to land, and when he was landed,
still greater difficulty in restoring him.  Happily there
was skilled assistance at hand.  And so presently my
friend recovered, not without much distress, first one and
then another of the sensations and faculties of his bodily
life.  In describing his experience of what must have
been the whole conscious side of the act of dying by
drowning, he said that the time had seemed to him of
very great duration; he had lost his standard of the worth
of time.  He had lived his whole past life over again; he
had not epitomized it; he had repeated it, as it seemed
to him, in detail and with the greatest deliberation.  He
had great difficulty in understanding that he had only
been in the water for a few minutes.  During these
intenser moments of existence the life of the soul has no
sort of relation to what we call time.

Yes! in entering another world we shall know what we
have been in the past as never before; but we shall know
also what we are.  The soul, divested of the body, will see
itself as never before; and it may be that it will see disfigurements and ulcers which the body, like a beautiful
robe, had hitherto shrouded from the sight, and which are
revealed in this life only by the shock of a great sorrow
or of a great fall.  There is a notion abroad—a notion
which is welcomed because, whether true or not, it is very
comfortable—that the soul will be so changed by death as
to lose the disfigurements which it may have contracted
through life; that the death-agony is a furnace, by being

plunged into which the soul will burn out its stains; or
that death involves such a shock as to break the con-
tinuity of our moral condition, though not of existence
itself; and thus that, in changing worlds, we shall change
our characters, and that moral evil will be buried with
the body in the grave, while the soul escapes, purified
by separation from its grosser companion, to the regions
of holiness and peace.

Surely, brethren, this is an illusion which will not stand
the test—we need not for the moment say of Christian
Truth, but—of reasonable reflection. It is a contradiction
to all that we know about the character and mind of man,
in which nothing is more remarkable than the intimate and
enduring connection which subsists between its successive
states or stages of development. Every one of us here
present is now exactly what his past life has made him.
Our present thoughts, feelings, mental habits, good and
bad, are the effects of what we have done or left undone,
of cherished impressions, of passions indulged or repressed,
of pursuits vigorously embraced or willingly abandoned.
And as our past mental and spiritual history has made us
what we are, so we are at this very moment making ourselves what we shall be. I do not forget that intervention of a higher force which we call "grace," and by which
the direction of a life may be suddenly changed, as in
St. Paul's case at his conversion; although these great
changes are often prepared for by a long preceding
process, and are not so sudden as they seem. But we are
speaking of the rule, and not of the exception. The rule
is that men are in each stage of their existence what with
or without God's supernatural grace they have made themselves in the preceding stages; and there is no reasonable
ground for thinking that at death the influences of a whole
lifetime will cease to operate upon character, and that,

whatever those influences may have been, the soul will be
purified by the shock of death. Why, I ask, should death
have any such result? What is there in death to bring it
about? Death is the dissolution of the bodily frame; of
the limbs and organs through which the soul now acts.
These organs are, no doubt, very closely connected with
the soul, which strikes its roots into them and acts through
them. But, although closely connected with the soul,
they are distinct from it: thought, conscience, affection,
will, are quite independent of the organs which are dissolved by death. And it is impossible to see why the
soul should put on a new character simply because it lays
aside for awhile the instrument which it has employed
during a term of years, any more than why a painter's
right hand should forget its cunning because he has sold
his easel, or why a murderer in fact should cease to be a
murderer at heart because he has lost his dagger and
cannot afford to replace it. True, at death, the ear, the
eye, the hands, perish. But when they are destroyed in
this life by an accident, does character change with them?
The indulgence of the purely animal appetite may depend
on the healthy condition of the organ; but the mental condition which permits, if it does not dictate, the indulgence
remains unaffected. Principles of right action or their
opposites outlive the faculties, as they outlive the opportunities for asserting themselves in act. The habit of
thieving is not renounced because the right hand has
been cut off; nor are sensual dispositions because the body
is prostrate through illness; nor is evil curiosity because
the eye is dim and the ear deaf. And when all the instruments through which in this life the soul has expressed
itself, and which collectively make up the body, are laid
aside by the emphatic act of death, the soul itself, and all
its characteristic thoughts and affections, will remain un-

affected, since its life is independent of its bodily envelope as is the body's life of the clothes which we wear.

One Being there is Who knows us now, Who knows us perfectly, Who has always known us. When we die we shall for the first time know ourselves, even as also we are known. We shall not have to await the Judge's sentence; we shall read it at a glance, whatever it be, in this new apprehension of what we are.

It may help us, then, this Advent to think from time to time of what will be our condition in the first five minutes after death. Like death itself, the solemnities which follow it must come to all of us. We know not when, or where, or how we shall enter on it; this only we know —that come it must. Those first five minutes, that first awakening to a new existence, with its infinite possibilities, will only be tolerable if we have indeed, with the hands of faith and love, laid hold on the Hope set before us,[a] in the Person of Jesus Christ our Lord and Saviour; Who for us men and for our salvation took flesh, and was crucified, and rose from death, and ascended into Heaven, and has pleaded incessantly at the Right Hand of the Father for us, the weak and erring children of the Fall. Without Him, a knowledge of that new world, of its infinite and awful Master, still more of ourselves as we really are, will indeed be terrifying. With Him, we may trust that such knowledge will be more than bearable; we may think calmly even of that tremendous experience, if He, the Eternal God, is indeed our Refuge, and underneath are the Everlasting Arms.[b]

[a] Heb. vi. 18.     [b] Deut. xxxiii. 27.

# SERMON XXXI.

## THE FUTURE CROWN.

### (SECOND SUNDAY IN ADVENT.)

2 TIM. IV. 8.

*Henceforth there is laid up for me a crown of righteousness, which the Lord, the Righteous Judge, shall give me at that day.*

WHEN St. Paul writes thus, he is in full view of the end of his career. He is in prison at Rome, for the second and for the last time. He has already gone through a first trial, in the Forum, or public court of Rome, possibly before the Emperor, certainly with men of all nations and races looking on, assembled as they were in the great capital. On that dread scene, in those anxious moments, St. Paul was alone. No patron, in the legal sense, no man of influence, sat by to show that he was interested in the acquittal of the prisoner, or, at least, in seeing that justice was done to him. No advocate, trained in the technical knowledge or in the great traditions of the Roman law, was there to place his reading and his skill at the disposal of the accused. No humble friend, powerless to sway the will of the judge, or to arrange or to assist the argument for the defence, yet striving by kindly looks to assure the prisoner of the sympathy of at least one human heart among those around him, and to sustain him by doing so,—not even one such friend was near. There were still Christians in Rome whom the forecasts of approaching persecution had not scared away; but they too, it seems, were absent. Demas had fled, "having loved this present world."[a] Titus and Crescens had left for the work of some Christian missions.[b] But where—in these hours of sadness and depression—where was Eubulus; where was Pudens, the rising soldier, as it might seem, and his highly born British wife, Claudia; where was Linus, already Bishop of the infant Church in Rome, and as such working under the Apostles; above all, where was Luke, the beloved physician, who had remained in Rome to care for his great teacher's bodily health in these last days of anxiety and confinement? We know not; this only we know— that they were not at Paul's side in his first public trial. "At my first answer," he sadly writes, "no man stood with me, but all forsook me: I pray God that it be not laid to their charge."[c]

And yet he was not alone. One was there, unseen by the bodily eye, but clearly discerned by the eye of the soul, Who was at once Sympathizer and Advocate and Patron; One from Whose Presence the prisoner drew strength and boldness and inspiration; One Who so stirred him to speak, that the Faith was proclaimed by him again, and for a last time, in such wise that through their representatives all the nations of the world should hear it; and that, for the moment, even the heathen judge was awed before his victim. "The Lord Christ stood by me, and strengthened me; that by me the preaching of the truth might be fully proclaimed, and that all the Gentiles might hear: and I was delivered out of the mouth of the lion."[d] This first trial resulted,

[a] 2 Tim. iv. 10.    [b] *Ib.*    [c] *Ib.* 16.    [d] *Ib.* 17.

in fact, in what the Roman lawyers called a " non liquet ; "
it was not plain to the judges whether the accused was
innocent or guilty.   And, as a consequence, the case was
adjourned; adjourned, perhaps, indefinitely; adjourned,
anyhow, until popular passions or imperial caprice might
determine to bring it on again.

It was during this interval thus obtained that St. Paul
wrote to Timothy about " the crown of righteousness." For
himself, the Apostle was under no illusions whatever as
to what awaited him.   He had seen a great deal of Rome,
with eyes sharpened by anxious waiting some five years
before, and now he had scanned it for a second time from
his Roman prison.   He well knew what social forces were
at work, what was the general drift of affairs, what considerations would come to the front in possible, or probable,
or foreseen contingencies.   He may well, too, have received
some intimation from on high, as a last proof of the high
favour of that Divine Saviour Whom he served, that the
end was now very near, and that he must be ready for it.
Even now he cries, " My blood is being poured out as if
in sacrifice, and the time of my parting from earth is close
before me.   I have fought the good fight ; I have finished
the course ; I have kept the faith : henceforth there is
laid up for me the crown of righteousness, which the Lord,
the Righteous Judge, shall give me at that day." [a]

## I.

"The crown of righteousness ! "   What does he mean
by it ?

In nothing was the whole ancient world more agreed,
than in viewing a crown as the symbol of honour, glory,
or power.   How it came to be so, or when, is a question

[a] 2 Tim. iv. 6–8.

about which much has been said and written, and with
no great prospect of arriving at an answer. Probably the
symbol would have been suggested by the genius of the
human form itself. Very early in our history, human
nature, we may well believe, wreathed rosebuds around
the temples of the maiden, and bound laurels on the
soldier's brow, and set a diadem of gold and gems on the
head of the ruler of men. To the Jews, the crown was
the most familiar of symbols. Their own monarchs long
wore the crown which David took from the King of
Ammon;[a] their women, their bridegrooms, their priests,
wore coronets, or crowns, or tiaras of varied form; and the
great Asiatic conquerors, who trampled their civilization,
and for awhile their religion, in the dust, were crowned
also, as we know from their sculptured forms in our
museums, and from the drawings which travellers have
made of their palaces and tombs. "Thou shalt set a
crown of pure gold upon His Head,"[b] is David's forecast for the great King of the future; nor was the
conception only Jewish or Oriental. In the games of
Greece, crowns of parsley, of pine, of laurel, were awarded
to the conquerors. "Corruptible crowns," as St. Paul
calls them, when, for a great moral object, he refers the
Corinthians to scenes with which they had been familiar
from childhood;[c] "corruptible crowns," but not therefore, at the moment, less precious in the eyes of the men
who won, and of the men who failed to win them. And
thus for St. Paul, with his Jewish birth and education,
and with his long and intimate converse with the Greek
world, a crown was the natural symbol of triumph—
of triumph recognized, approved, rejoiced in; and when
he would think or speak of the state of the blessed, he
weaves, as it were, moral beauty into the ornament which

[a] 2 Sam. xii. 30.    [b] Ps. xxi. 3.    [c] 1 Cor. ix. 24-27.

he associates with the triumphs of Greek or Jewish life, and talks naturally of a "crown of righteousness."

"A crown of righteousness!" Does he mean that it is righteousness which is crowned, or that righteousness is the material of which the crown is made? It is of some importance, if we are to do the Apostle justice, that this question should be answered.

Now, there are two similar expressions in the New Testament to describe the reward of the blessed; they are "the crown of life,"[a] and "the crown of glory."[b] In these it is plain that what is meant is, not that life is crowned, but that the crown of the blessed is life; not that glory is crowned, but that the crown of the blessed is glory. Life, glory, these are—if the word were not too rude—the very material and substance of the heavenly crown. And so it is with righteousness. "The crown of righteousness"—is a crown whereof righteousness is the material; this crown is of the same fabric and texture as that which it should decorate; it is a crown whose beauty is moral beauty; the beauty, not of gold and precious stones, but of those more precious, nay, priceless, things which gold and gems can but suggest to us; the beauty of justice, truthfulness, purity, charity, humility, carried to a point of refinement and high excellence of which here and now we have no experience. Once, and once only, was such a crown as this worn upon earth; and, to the eyes of men, it was a Crown of Thorns.

It may seem to be a difficulty in the way of this statement, that the happiness of the blessed is said elsewhere to consist in the enjoyment of the Beatific Vision, in the unveiled sight of God, Whom they praise and bless to all eternity. We know that, when we shall be like Him, we shall see Him as He is.[c] But what is it that makes

---

[a] St. James i. 12; Rev. ii. 10.   [b] 1 St. Pet. v. 4.   [c] 1 St. John iii. 2.

this vision of God the source of the promised happiness? What is it in God that will chiefly minister to the expected joy? Is it His boundless Power, or His unsearchable Wisdom? Will they cry for ever, "Almighty, Almighty, Almighty!" or "All-knowing, All-knowing, All-knowing"? Will they not, do they not say, without fatigue or desire for change, "Holy, Holy, Holy"? And why is this? Because God is, essentially, a Moral Being; and it is by His moral attributes that He perfectly corresponds to and satisfies the deepest wants in our natures. The "crown of righteousness" means a share, such as it is possible for a creature to have, in His Essential Nature; in His Justice, Purity, and Love. For while we can conceive of Him, had He so willed, as never having created the heavens and the earth; we cannot think of Him, if He has any creatures around Him, as being other than Just, Loving, Merciful, in His dealings with them. This Holiness of God in dealing with His creatures may be, in a sense, shared by His creatures; and thus God is, indeed, Himself "the Crown of Righteousness," with which He rewards the saved. Nor is there any opposition between the idea of such a crown and the Beatific Vision; they are only different accounts of a happiness which is in its essence the same.

Now, this idea of the future life of the blessed, as crowned with righteousness, furnishes us, incidentally, with an answer to two common objections to Christianity in the secularist literature of the day.

We are told sometimes that the Christian Faith is largely responsible for unfitting men to discharge the duties of this life, by fixing their attention too exclusively on a world that is to succeed it. That which happened at Thessalonica between the writing of St. Paul's First and his Second Epistle, the neglect of common obvious daily work in obedience to religious excitement, is alleged to be the rule wherever Christianity is sincerely accepted. Christianity is, accordingly, condemned by those who measure the truth of a religion solely by its effect in this one direction; solely by its capacity or incapacity to enable men to do the best they can with this present visible world.

Here we must admit, in candour, a limited element of truth in the objection. Say what we will, the religion of the New Testament is a renunciation, in whatever degree, of this present world for the sake of the next. It is not really possible to make the best of both worlds; at least, in the sense of making the best of material advantages in this. But if Christianity does thus draw the keenest interests of men away from the seen and the present to the future and the unseen, it also gives more than it withdraws; it endows men during this earthly life with moral excellences, which, by their practical value, more than atone to human society and life for the constant absence of the heart, as our Lord expresses it, with its treasure in Heaven.[a] For the expectation of a crown of righteousness tends to make men resemble that which they expect; just as any object of hope or ideal gradually but surely shapes the thought and character of the man who entertains it. And thus, while for Christians this life is made of less account than the life to come, it is sweetened, raised, ay, invigorated, by virtues which would not be, to say the least, popular or common, if men were to think that all ended with death, and that there was no crown of righteousness hereafter.

We are told, again, by some apostles of virtue which claim to be disinterested, that Christian service, after all, is a poor and mercenary thing. The old question is asked

[a] St. Matt. vi. 19-21.

again, and not without the old bitterness, "Doth Job
fear God for nought?"[a]    It is asked by men who assure
us that they do themselves love virtue because it is virtue;
they love it for the sake of its own loveliness; they find
their happiness and their satisfaction simply in obeying its
dictates; they want no payment, whether in glory or in
gold, for efforts which they would on no account forego;
virtue is at once their inspiration and their prize.    And
then they turn a pitying glance upon Christendom, with
its millions of souls in every generation bent solely upon
escaping the agonies of the pit or upon attaining the joys
of Paradise.  "What a poor conception!" they exclaim,
"of a renewed world is this, whereby virtue is only the
price that is paid for glory; what a travesty within the
sanctuary of the serious transactions of that world of
commerce, which pretends to no disinterestedness, and
which is honestly brutal in its avowal of selfish motives!
How far higher and nobler is a virtuous life, which
knows of nothing and expects nothing after death, but
which is virtuous because virtue is the law of its being,
the joy of its existence!"

This is at first sight a telling objection; it seems to
turn the flank of Christianity with an argument profoundly Christian, and to defeat our Lord Jesus Christ
on His own chosen ground.  But this is the appearance;
it is not the fact.  The fact is, as we have just now seen,
that virtue is its own reward in Christendom not less
truly—to use guarded terms—than among the thinkers in
question.  The Christian life is not a life of virtue undertaken in order to win a life of a different kind—a life of
glory or a life of pleasure—in a future state of existence.
It is a life of righteousness, and only counts on such glory
and pleasure as righteousness brings with it.  It is a life

[a] Job i. 9.

of righteousness, which, most assuredly, in its origin, is not our own,[a] but the gift of the Perfect Moral Being, our Lord Jesus Christ. It is a life of righteousness begun on earth, but continued into a higher sphere, where righteousness takes new and transcendental proportions, and becomes its own crown and recompense. The real difference between us Christians and these thinkers does not turn upon the question whether virtue is its own reward, but upon the question whether this reward can be sufficiently secured within the narrow limits of an earthly existence. The real question is whether at death men cease to be. If they do not, the Christian Heaven, with its crown of righteousness, is but the prolongation on a splendid scale of the ever-progressing strength and beauty of a life of virtue; the crown of righteousness is given, not to fade away on the sod that covers an earthly grave, but to beautify an undying being through the ages of Eternity.

## II.

"The crown of righteousness!" Some crown or other, I apprehend, most men are looking for; if not always, yet at some time in their lives; if not very confidently, yet with those modified hopes which regard it as possibly attainable. Human nature views itself almost habitually as the heir-apparent of some circumstances implying improvement. An expectation of this kind is the very condition of effort in whatever direction, and no amount or grossness of proved illusions can permanently extinguish it. But the crowns which, as many of us hope, may be laid up for us, somewhere and by some one—what are they?

There is the crown of a good income. In a great mercantile community like our own, this is the supreme dis-

[a] Phil. iii. 9.

tinction for which many a man labours, without thought
of anything beyond. He begins as a salaried clerk in a
great firm; he sees rising above his head, in a hierarchy
of ever-ascending splendours, the upper clerks, the junior
partners, the retired partners, the millionaires; the men
who count their incomes by hundreds, by thousands, by
tens of thousands. And this is his world, his firmament;
this is the sphere in which he hopes to rise. He hopes for
the day in which he shall say, "I have struggled hard
by day and by night; I have lived the life of a thorough
man of business; I have kept the rule of honesty and the
rule of hard work: henceforth there is laid up for me the
distinction of an income which will enable me to spend
my remaining years in easy affluence; and, after all,
money means comfort and money means power, and the
toil that I have undergone is not ill rewarded by this
golden crown."

And closely akin to this is the crown of a good social
position. In a country like our own, this is a crown for
the winning of which many a life is spent from first to
last. We English as a people reach forward into the
future not less eagerly than do other European nations;
but, more resolutely than they, or at least than most of
them, we also cling to the bequests of a distant past. Our
social system strikes its roots far back into the Middle
Ages. We often combine the ideals of the subjects of the
Plantagenets with the practical aptitudes of the subjects
of Victoria; and the enterprise of a society profoundly
modern in its tendencies and temper is directed to the
attainment of positions which derive their splendour from
ages which have passed away. And thus, in England, if
class-envy is reduced to moderate proportions, it is mainly
because, in his secret heart, each ambitious member of all
classes but the highest hopes to rise. And if, as we survey

the ceaseless activity of every section and department of
the social world, we could seize the undertone of desire
which is the soul of so much incessant effort, we should
find, probably, that it is directed to a time when each
struggling aspirant might say, " I have made great efforts,
tempered with due discretion; I have finished a course
which has appeared to bring unbounded pleasure, and
which has really meant incessant weariness; I have observed those laws of social propriety which are never dis-
regarded with impunity: and so henceforth there awaits
me an assured position, in which I may, indeed, be rivalled,
but from which I cannot be dislodged; a position which
society cannot but award, sooner or later, to those who
struggle upward faithfully in obedience to its rules."

Then there is the crown of political power.   In our
day and country that crown can be said to be beyond the
reach of no man.   In the days of our forefathers there
was what is called a governing class; in our days, as we
know, any man with sufficient ability and fair opportunities
may become a member of the Government.   And thus we
see also, naturally enough, all over the country, the budding ambitions which would fain some day control the
affairs of England.   To become a member of a municipal
corporation; to represent a popular constituency, or even
to stand for it with some distinction; to raise a voice
which shall command attention, even for twenty-four
hours, at a crisis in the national fortunes;—these are the
first steps in the ascent.   But how many are the steps,
the flights of steps above; the steps which must be
scaled and traversed ere the summit is reached!   How
many the failures, the rebuffs, the disappointments; how
transient the successes; how keen the humiliations which
must be encountered, ere the prize is won!   And yet in
every young man who ventures on that often thankless

career there is a hope in his heart of hearts that a day
may come when it may be his to say, "I have fought a
good fight against the foes of my country or my party; I
have finished a course of public activity with credit or
distinction; I have kept to my principles, or have shown
that I had reason to modify or abandon them: henceforth there is laid up for me, if not a peer's coronet,
yet certainly a crown of political influence so sure, as to
be independent of office; a crown which a great country
will never refuse to those who have served it long and
served it well."

And there is the crown of a literary reputation. There
is many a man who cares little for society and less for
wealth, who has neither spirits nor skill for the active
struggles of political life, but in whom intellect is active
and creative, and imagination is enterprising and taste
refined, and to whom, therefore, the pursuits of literature
are less of an employment than a recreation. In our own
day, when education has become so general, the literary
class—to use that word in a wide sense—is much more
numerous than are the opportunities of literary occupation,
or than the chances of even moderate distinction. And yet
we may be pretty sure that each young writer, as he tries
his hand at his first article or his first review, hopes devoutly
that a day may come when, at the conclusion of some
work which shall have caught the fancy of the world, and
shall have made criticism respectful, or perhaps enthusiastic, he may be able to say, "I have had a hard time
of it; I have finished what I proposed to do; I have been
true to the requirements of a great and exacting subject:
henceforth there is reserved for me the rare pleasure of a
reputation which wealth and station cannot command, and
which envy cannot take away; henceforth I have a place
in the great communion of the learned, a name among

those elect minds in whom genius is wedded to industry, and whose works are among the treasures of the human race."

These are the crowns, or some of them, for which men toil, and with which not seldom they are rewarded. But do they last? Of the wearer of one it is written, " He shall carry nothing away with him when he dieth;"[a] of another, " Man being in honour hath no understanding, but is compared unto the beasts that perish;"[b] of a third, " How art thou fallen from Heaven, O Lucifer, son of the morning!"[c] of a fourth, "Of making of books there is no end, and much study is a weariness to the flesh."[d] They pass away, these crowns, even the brightest of them: they are put off in the dying hour; they cannot be preserved in our coffins, much less worn into the Eternal Presence-chamber. They pass, with all their tinsel, and all their adornments of such real beauty as belongs to time; they pass, and are forgotten. Do I say that it is always wrong to look for crowns like these? That, surely, would be an exaggeration; because it often happens in life that the expectation of some earthly crown is closely intertwined with something nobler beyond it. The income may be valued chiefly as a means of charitable effort; the social position, as an opportunity for helping and guiding others; the political triumph, in order to carry out some great moral or religious principle, or social improvement; the literary success, as a means of disseminating truth or of improving conduct. God only knows how it is with each expectant of an earthly crown. But, at least, to rest in the expectation of any earthly crown, as if it were a sufficient and satisfactory end of thought and action, cannot be right in a Christian, to whom the Kingdom of Heaven

[a] Ps. xlix. 17.   [b] *Ib.* 12.
[c] Isa. xiv. 12.   [d] Eccles. xii. 12.

has been laid open by his faith. He knows that he has an imperishable soul, made that it may commune with and enjoy an unchangeable Object; and a decoration which, however fascinating for the moment, does not pretend to last, only trifles with the deepest needs of his being.

Let us place ourselves for a few moments, by way of conclusion, in St. Paul's position, and we shall understand the character of his expectations, and perhaps, too, his confidence in entertaining it.

St. Paul writes with death in full view. Long before this he could write sincerely, " I count all things but dung, that I may win Christ, and be found in Him."[a] Now this view of life is even clearer, and more decided. " Henceforth there is laid up for me a crown of righteousness."

When a thoughtful man knows that he has not long to live, he does not take much account of that which he knows must end with life. He may be wealthy, but at his death his wealth will be as much beyond his control as if he had never earned a penny. He may have achieved a great social position ; how will it profit him when he is once in his coffin ? His name may have become a household word in all the courts, in all the newspapers, of Europe ; will their estimate of its importance be ratified in the world unseen ? His books may be classics, translated into all the languages of the civilized world ; yet it may matter as little to him as if their first copies had been sold for waste paper. As we approach death, the exaggerations of self-love cease to assert themselves ; we see things more nearly as they are ; we distinguish that which lasts from that which passes ; we understand the difference between perishable crowns and "a crown of righteousness." That one crown does not pass ; it is laid up, or set

[a] Phil. iii. 8.

aside, for its destined wearer by that Merciful Redeemer, Who is also the Eternal Judge, Who watches with tender interest each conqueror as he draws nearer to the end of his earthly course, and as, in the name of the Great Redemption, he dares to claim it.

Yes! place yourselves side by side with St. Paul, and you will understand why he cares only for " a crown of righteousness," and why he is so confident that it is laid up for him. " Henceforth there is laid up for me a crown of righteousness." St. Paul did not always write thus. In earlier years he felt and expressed his anxiety lest that by any means, when he had preached unto others, he himself should be a castaway.[a] And long after he "counted not himself to have apprehended;"[b] he could only forget those things that were behind, and reach forward unto those things that were before; he was still pressing forward to the mark of the prize of his high calling in Christ Jesus.[c] But now he has no misgivings; now all is clear; "henceforth there is laid up for me a crown of righteousness." And why? Is it not because, in the solitariness of his last trial, he has had an assurance from on high which was withheld before; which was only vouchsafed when all human aid and human sympathy had failed him, and when he was thrown, without any reserve whatever, upon his hope in the Unseen and the Future? And even now, not seldom, they who fashion their lives as did St. Paul, by faith in an Unseen Saviour, do learn to know that there is for them a morally assured future of happiness in the World of Light. It is not an arrogant confidence, it is a humble yet well-grounded hope; it is a hope which grows in strength as the solitudes of the advancing years press with more and more gloom upon the natural spirits, and when, in the absence of departed

[a] 1 Cor. ix. 27.    [b] Phil. iii. 13.    [c] Ib. 13, 14.

or of alienated friends, the majesty and consolation of One
sacred, overpowering Presence makes itself increasingly
felt.   " The Lord stood by me, and strengthened me ; " [a]
" Henceforth there is laid up for me a crown of righteousness."

"In *that* day."   There is no need to say more ; every
Christian knows what day he means.   It is the day
described in to-day's Gospel; the day on which "the
Son of Man will come in a cloud with power and great
glory." [b]   " Wherefore," being such as we are, " let us
beseech Him to grant us true repentance and His Holy
Spirit, that those things may please Him which we do at
this present, and that the rest of our life hereafter may
be pure and holy, so that at the last we may come to His
eternal joy." [c]

[a] 2 Tim. iv. 17.                    [b] St. Luke xxi. 27.
      [c] The Absolution in the Order for Morning Prayer.

# SERMON XXXII.

## SOCIAL POWER OF THE GOSPEL.

### (THIRD SUNDAY IN ADVENT.)

#### PHILEM. 15.

*For perhaps he therefore was parted from thee for a season, that thou shouldest receive him for ever.*

A GREAT many Christians, who are not careless readers of the New Testament, know, it may be presumed, very little indeed about the value of St. Paul's Epistle to Philemon. Its destination, its shortness, and, at the first sight, its subject-matter, alike combine to divert attention from it. It is not written to a great Church, like those to the Romans or the Corinthians; it is not written to rulers of Churches, like the Epistles to Timothy and Titus; it is written to a private member of a Church, which, in its collective capacity, is addressed elsewhere—to Philemon of Colossæ. It is shorter by far than any other of St. Paul's letters. At first sight it seems to be concerned, not with any great and vital truth of revealed religion, but only with a detail of domestic life in a private family. And thus it comes to be read hurriedly and with scant attention; we trip lightly over it, thinking that we can soon know all about it; we trip, I say, lightly over it, perhaps not without a passing thought of wonder that a man who could write a treatise so perfect in its structure, and covering so vast an area of thought, as the Epistle to the Romans, should have spent any time at all upon such by-play as the Epistle to Philemon. It will not be without practical advantage, I hope, to inquire whether this estimate is altogether accurate; and in order to do this let us begin by reminding ourselves who St. Paul's correspondent was, and what induces St. Paul to write to him.

Philemon, it has been said, was a private member of the Church of Christ in Colossæ. He was, plainly, a man of some substance; he was married to a Christian wife, Appia; and he was on intimate terms with Archippus, an influential clergyman, as we should now say, in the place, who was honoured with the Apostle's affectionate confidence. Philemon, Christian though he was, still had slaves in his household; they belonged to him before his conversion, and in this respect matters still went on as before. One of these slaves, named Onesimus, or "Useful," had robbed his master, fled from Colossæ, and found his way along one of the main lines of communication to Rome. Perhaps he drifted there, as many a countryman comes up to London, from a vague notion that something was to be done or got in Rome which could not be done or got elsewhere. Perhaps he was afraid of being taken up, and hoped to lose himself in the dense population, in the courts and alleys of the great capital. But at Rome he found his way into the presence of St. Paul, who was at that time undergoing the first of his two Roman imprisonments. How this intercourse came about must be a matter for conjecture. It may well be that in a Christian household like Philemon's St. Paul's imprisonment would have been a natural subject of frequent and anxious conversation. And Onesimus may have resolved

to discover St. Paul, from recollecting what he had observed
of the tenderness, the sympathy, the attractiveness of
the preacher, who in years gone by had converted his
master Philemon to the Faith of Christ, and who might
now speak to him, too, a word of comfort in a time of
trouble. It is less probable that, after his arrival in
Rome, Onesimus was arrested, and thrown for a time
into the same prison with St. Paul; because this supposition fails to explain how, soon after his conversion,
Onesimus was free to go back to Colossæ with a commission from the Apostle. But, however it happened, St.
Paul and Onesimus did at this time come into close
relations of intimacy with each other; and the result was
the conversion of Onesimus to the true Faith. We see
from this Epistle, and from the Letter to the Colossians,
how tenderly St. Paul loved and how entirely he trusted
his humble convert.[a] St. Paul was, indeed, at first disposed to keep Onesimus in Rome that he might be of
service to himself.[b] But, on reflection, he felt that Onesimus ought to go back to his master, come what might
of it;[c] and this letter is an intercession with Philemon
that Onesimus, still a slave in the legal sense, but also a
baptized and believing member of Christ, might be received as a Christian brother by his Christian owner.
The whole letter is a model of that true delicacy and
tact which Christian convictions can alone inspire; but
it seems to reach its climax in the verse which is before
us in the text, where St. Paul suggests that the misconduct of the slave had been permitted in order that
he and his master should be friends to all eternity.
"Perhaps he therefore was parted from thee for a season,
that thou shouldest receive him for ever."

There is no room for doubt of the success of St. Paul's

---

[a] Col. iv. 9.      [b] Philem. 13.      [c] *Ib.* 14.

appeal; but from this time Philemon and Onesimus
disappear from the New Testament. Their names occur
in Church traditions of a later time, as bishops of sub-
Apostolic Churches; but here we are on less solid ground,
or at any rate on ground which is foreign to our immediate subject.

There are three lessons among, and perhaps above,
others, which present themselves to us as we think over
this touching history.

### I.

We see here, first of all, what sort of results St. Paul
expected to flow from the reconciling and combining force
of the Christian Faith. "Perhaps he therefore was
parted from thee for a season, that thou mightest receive
him for ever." In nothing does Christianity differ more
profoundly from some philosophies which seem to have a
superficial resemblance to it, than in this: it does not
allow a man to think of himself as an isolated unit, while
forgetful of other men; it does not allow a class to entrench
itself in its privileges or excellences, and to ignore the
claims of other classes; it does not allow a race to stiffen
itself in its prejudices, and to forget that other races are
also members of the human family, and have gifts and
endowments that are all their own.

What was Onesimus? He was two things which
seemed to put him beyond the range of respectable sympathies : he was a felon, and he was a slave.

Onesimus was a felon. And St. Paul, by birth, was a
Pharisee ; the son of a Pharisee. He belonged to a class
which would not willingly soil its robes by the lightest
contact with a sinner. Recollect that scene in the house
of Simon, when the Magdalen washed the feet of our Lord

Jesus Christ.[a]   Often must St. Paul have found it hard to
repress with a strong hand the rising prejudices of his
early years, especially when face to face with a runaway
thief like Onesimus.   But in St. Paul the spirit of the
Pharisee had been expelled, or killed, by the Spirit of
Jesus Christ.   He knew that he too was a sinner, who
could not hope to meet the Judgment of God unless he had
been robed in the righteousness of our Lord Jesus Christ.
He knew that he himself owed everything to the Love
Which had come down from Heaven, and Which had died
on Calvary.   What, then, was the real difference between
himself and Onesimus?   It was merely that the one had
found the pardoning love of the Redeemer, and the other
has not yet found it.   In the light of this truth there
was no room for what he himself so often denounced as
" boasting ; "[b] it was as impossible to his reason as it was
impossible for his heart.   Onesimus the felon had as good
a claim on the All-merciful as had Paul the Pharisee ;
each could but say, " When we were yet sinners, Christ
died for us."[c]

This would have been, but for the grace of Christ which
had remade and which ruled him, St. Paul's great difficulty in having dealings with Onesimus.   Onesimus was
a thief who had escaped from justice.   But this was not
all.   Onesimus was not only a felon ; he was a slave.   We
need not go very far to observe that human nature is
often more tolerant of crime than of anything which
violates a social prejudice.

Certainly St. Paul, though in civil rank a Roman,
would not have shared the feeling about slaves which
was current in the best pagan society.   But how about
Philemon?   He had only recently been converted; he
was a master of slaves; he was hardly likely, as yet, to —

<hr>

[a] St. Luke vii. 37-50.        [b] Rom. iii. 27.        [c] *Ib.* v. 8.

have expelled from his mind the settled prejudices of his
class. In the eyes of a Roman proprietor of the imperial
period, a slave differed much less from the horses and
cows around him than from the members of the master's
family. Varro, a Roman writer of authority and learning,
gravely divides agricultural implements into three kinds:
mute implements, like the plough; implements which
make inarticulate noises, like the horse and the ox; and
implements which talk, like the slave.[a] A slave had no
rights; he was insulted, flogged, crucified, at the master's
pleasure. Often he was a man of much greater education
and refinement than his owner; he had been bought,
perhaps, because he was known to possess some accomplishment in which his owner was deficient. It made no
sort of difference; he was just as much a chattel as the
chairs and tables around him, in the eye of the Roman
law. If, while hunting, he should accidentally kill a wild
boar before his master had time to do so, we know, from
what actually happened in a famous case, that he was
liable to crucifixion; and if he lived long enough to
become entirely useless, he might be left to starve to
death on an island in the Tiber.[b]

In Christian households like Philemon's, we may be
sure that the purely brutal feeling of good pagan society
about slaves would have been greatly softened; that the
conventional barbarities would have been impossible.
But it is probable that, in a man of Philemon's position,
a good deal of the old prejudice would survive. This
pagan slave who had robbed him, and had run away,
would have deserved, in his master's judgment, hard

[a] Varro, *De re Rusticâ*, i. 17.
[b] The best account of slavery as it existed in the ancient Roman world
is given by Allard, *Les Esclaves Chrétiens.* Paris, 1876. 2me ed. Cf.
especially pp. 112–184.

measure. We see St. Paul's consciousness of this in
the extreme delicacy with which he urges his request.
Certainly Philemon had law on his side; on the side of
St. Paul and of Onesimus there was only a reasonable
and equitable charity. So St. Paul feels that he is on
tender ground. He might, indeed, issue a command, as
an Apostle ruling in the Church of God; but he will
not insist on his Apostolic position. He approaches
Philemon as an equal; he pleads with him as a friend.
He pleads the memories which cluster around his own
name—Paul;[a] he glances at his own advancing years;[b]
he permits himself to mention the imprisonment which
he was undergoing for the cause of Christ;[c] and then
he introduces Onesimus as his own spiritual child, as
the object of his warmest affections: "My son Onesimus,
whom I have begotten in my bonds;"[d] "mine own
bowels,"[e] or, as we should say "heart;" "a brother
beloved, specially to me."[f] He pleads his own wish
to have retained Onesimus about his person; a wish
which was set aside from his sense of what was due to
Philemon himself.[g] And then he presses his request upon
Philemon, who is reminded that he owes him nothing less
than his own salvation.[h] He protests that he is willing to
pay anything that Onesimus may have taken from his
master, if Philemon will have it so;[i] he professes his
confidence in Philemon's willingness to meet his wishes;
and then he begs that Onesimus may be received again as
something more than a slave; as "a brother beloved," in
the common bonds of the Redemption. It is very difficult
for us, in a social atmosphere which has been largely
formed by the Christian teaching of fourteen centuries,
to understand what all this meant at first for the man

---

a Philem. 9.　　b *Ib.*　　c *Ib.*　　d *Ib.* 10.　　e *Ib.* 12.
f *Ib.* 16.　　g *Ib.* 13, 14.　　h *Ib.* 19.　　i *Ib.* 18.

who wrote, and for the man who received it. It meant at
least this; that Christianity was bridging over a vast
social chasm. Onesimus was the predecessor of millions
of slaves, Philemon of millions of proprietors, in the
centuries to come.

It may be asked, Did not St. Paul beg Philemon to
give Onesimus his freedom? It must be answered, No;
he did not. He hinted at this, perhaps, when he expressed his confidence that Philemon would do more than
he was asked to do.[a] But he did not prefer a formal
request to this effect, much less did he insist on it; and
he has sometimes been reproached with this by critics
who cannot understand what is possible or equitable in
a position of which they have never had personal experience. Certainly slavery was repugnant to the spirit
of Christianity; to the spirit of Him Who had vindicated
the true rights of man, and had indefinitely enhanced
the dignity of our nature by taking it upon Him at
His Incarnation. But the business of the Apostles was
of a higher and Diviner kind than that of inaugurating
a violent social revolution. The revolt of Spartacus and
all that had followed was still fresh in the memory of the
world. And the Apostles addressed themselves to the
strictly practical task of lodging the Christian faith and
life in the minds and hearts of masters and slaves alike;
confident that, in time, the Faith would act as a powerful
solvent upon such an institution, by creating a new
estimate of life. The Christian master would remember
that the slave was certainly his equal as a man; possibly,
in the Kingdom of the Redeemer, his superior. He
would bear in mind that he, too, had a Master in heaven.
The Christian slave would feel that the circumstances
of this life mattered little if he were really secure of the

[a] Philem. 21.

next; and he would see in his master's will, wherever he could, the Will of God. The Apostles would not anticipate the slow but certain action of Christian principles upon society; the infiltration of the Christian spirit into the Imperial Codes; the gradual legislation of the great Catholic Councils; the noble work which, too long delayed, is associated in later days with the great names of Wilberforce and Clarkson. When Philemon received Onesimus, the great Christian enterprise of reconciling classes had indeed begun. What are we doing to further it?

## II.

Secondly, we may note here how entirely, for the time being, St. Paul's interest is concentrated on a single soul. He writes as though there was no person in the world to think about except Onesimus, and, relatively to Onesimus, his master Philemon. "Perhaps he therefore was parted from thee for a season, that thou mightest receive him for ever."

Remember that, as an Apostle, St. Paul had world-wide jurisdiction, and therefore world-wide responsibilities. As he puts it, "That which cometh upon me daily is the care of all the Churches." [a] He had to watch over populations, to defend truths, to protect and extend religious interests throughout the civilized world. Upon his heart and head there rested the burden of all the questions, great and small, which local animosities or local ignorance could not or would not settle for the early Churches. In the First Epistle to the Corinthians he discusses and decides on a catalogue of such questions; from the head-dress of Christian women during worship,[b] up to the necessity of faith in the resurrection of the body.[c] As an Apostle,

---

[a] 2 Cor. xi. 28.        [b] 1 Cor. xi. 5-13.        [c] *Ib.* xv.

like the prophetic watchmen of an earlier century,[a] he was
set upon a tower to survey all the horizons of the time;
to note the approach or the menace of danger; to welcome
all that was hopeful and opportune in the circumstances
of the Church; to keep his eye clearly and constantly
fixed on those general and governing considerations which
bear upon the prospects and work of that kingdom of
souls in which he was, by Divine commission, a ruler
and leader. In this great world of thought and administration, in and around which he had for so many years
been moving, he might have been pardoned, we may
think, if he had found no time to soothe the anxieties of
individual lives. With so many large subjects on his
mind, of vital and far-reaching import, as we see in his
Epistles; with so many errors arising in succession one
after another, as if only to wreck his work—the Judaizers
of Galatia and Corinth, the Theosophists of Colossæ, the
budding Gnosticism at Ephesus and in Crete; with so many
young and growing Churches depending almost entirely
on his advice and sympathy—at Antioch in Pisidia, at
Lystra, at Ancyra, at Hierapolis, at Troas, at Colossæ, at
Miletus, at Ephesus, at Cesaræa, at Philippi, at Thessalonica, at Berœa, at Athens, at Corinth, at Rome itself
—to name only a few; he might well have said to himself
that he must leave the care of single souls to others.
This is the usual course of things, whether in the Church
or in other spheres of administration. Men commonly
begin to work at details, then they ascend to general
principles; they begin with individuals, and they go on to
influence classes and bodies of men; and, in this sphere
of abstract thought and comprehensive efforts, they not
merely lack leisure for the detailed work with which they
began life, they not seldom lose the secret of doing it.

[a] Isa. xxi. 6, 8; Hab. ii. 1.

This, then, is so admirable in St. Paul, that, with a
burden of speculative thought and of practical anxiety
upon him, on the very largest scale, he yet found time,
in his Roman prison, to devote himself to the instruction
and conversion of this poor slave; to enlightening his
understanding and touching his heart by the history of
the Divine Redemption; just as if he had had nothing
else in the world to do.  We know that he had dealt thus
with others; with Aquila and Priscilla,[a] with Timothy,[b]
with Lydia,[c] with each one of those whom he met on the
strand at Miletus,[d] and whom he had warned, as he says,
one by one, by night and day, with tears.  So here we
see how he has given his whole heart to the work of
winning Onesimus for Jesus Christ.  Consider the depth,
the tenderness, of his language : " My child Onesimus,
whom I have begotten spiritually in my bonds." [e]  During
that travail, we may be sure, St. Paul felt as though
there were only two souls in the world—his own and that
of the poor slave.  And the great questions of the time,
and the Churches with all their anxieties, and the budding
heresies, and the threatening ferocities of the pagan world
around, were all in the far background of his thought,
or rather altogether outside it.  This is a lesson which is
much needed, as it seems, in our day.  The fashion is to
think and speak of religion as an abstract influence; and
to forget that, to be worth anything, it must be a power
reigning in individual lives.  We talk grandly and
vaguely of the tendencies of the age, of the dangers of
the age, of the characteristics of the age, of the modern
spirit, of a number of fine abstract conceptions, which just
slightly stimulate the imagination, and exact no sacrifice
whatever from the will.  We utter, or we listen to, these

a Acts xviii. 1–4.      b *Ib.* xvi. 1–3.      c *Ib.* 14, 15.
d *Ib.* xx. 31.                        e Philem. 10.

imposing abstractions at a public meeting, and we forget that they mean nothing, nothing whatever, apart from the life and experience of separate souls. They are creations of our own thought; but souls are independent realities. Souls are there, whether we think about them or not; and all the real good that is ever to be done in the Church or in the world must begin with individual characters, with single souls. Phrases die away upon the breeze, but souls remain; they remain in their ignorance, in their perplexities, in their sorrows; awaiting death, awaiting eternity.

The teacher of two or three young children, the tutor with a few pupils, who seem dull and irresponsive and little likely to do their instructor credit, is often tempted to wish that he had what is called a larger sphere of action, where he might control great issues, and become a leader or a fashioner of the thought of the time. If any such be present, let him think of St. Paul, the aged Apostle of the nations, spending his labour, as the dreary hours passed, on the dull brain and the sluggish affections of the slave Onesimus. The world, depend upon it, is not saved by abstract ideas, however brilliant; it is saved by the courageous individualizing efforts of Christian love.

### III.

Thirdly, let us note here how a Christian should look at the events of life; at the commonplace and trivial events, as well as at those which appear striking and important. Every such event has a purpose, whether we can trace it or no; a purpose to be made plain in the eternal world, in that mysterious state of existence which awaits every one of us, when we have passed the gate of death. Onesimus did not rob Philemon, take flight from Colossæ, and find out St. Paul at Rome, all for nothing.

No. "Perhaps he was therefore parted from thee for a season, that thou mightest enjoy him for ever."

This is not, let us be sure, a common way of looking at life among those who have lost faith in Christ, or who catch sight of Him only occasionally as a very dim and indistinct Figure, Whose outline can hardly be made out, as they gaze at Him through the thick vapours which constantly ascend from their mental laboratories. For them there exists no working theory of human life, or of the events which make it up. They tell us that we may study the causes, or, as they would say, the immediate antecedents of what we are and of what happens to us; but that of any purpose beyond we are ignorant. We must, it seems, take facts as they come to hand; we may, if we can, account for their shaping themselves as they do; but we must give up the unscientific attempt to connect them with a purpose. To do so is to forget that teleology is generally discredited; that it has been placed under the ban of science.

Here the real difference is not as to whether a given purpose for each event of life can be satisfactorily made out, but whether or not there is any future existence towards which this life is properly directed as its completion and development. That larger question must be settled before the narrower one can be at all profitably entertained. For us Christians it is settled. For us Christians it is certain that this life, and every incident in it, has a purpose, which the future will interpret. If life and immortality had not been brought to light,[a] it might be reasonable to suppose that the events of our existence here could only be referred to the causes which immediately produced them, and that they had no relation to anything beyond themselves. But if we have learnt that this world is but the ante-chamber of the next, and a

[a] 2 Tim. i. 10.

very insignificant ante-chamber too, by comparison with that to which it introduces us, then it is, at least, no more irrational to think that particular parts of this earthly life have their explanation and counterparts hereafter, than to think that the whole of it has no other purpose than that of preparing us for it. To St. Paul the future life was as clear as the shining of the sun in the heavens; and, therefore, he naturally wrote to Philemon, "Perhaps Onesimus was therefore parted from thee for a season, that thou mightest enjoy him for ever."

And yet remark that "perhaps." St. Paul will not encourage us in a rash and presumptuous confidence, when we endeavour to interpret in detail God's providences in this life by the light of the next. We may conjecture that such and such an event is permitted for such and such an end, which would be agreeable to the known Will and attributes of God. We cannot know that it is so. Some well-meaning but unthinking people undertake to interpret a human life as they undertake to interpret the Revelation of St. John, with an easy reliance on their own insight, which nothing but ignorance of the real difficulties of the subject can possibly explain.

St. Paul saw as far as most men into the purposes of God; yet, when he would interpret God's design in respect of a given human life, he reverently adds, "perhaps." "Perhaps he was therefore parted from thee for a time, that thou mightest receive him for ever." St. Paul describes what took place in his own religious language. Onesimus had robbed Philemon, and had fled: St. Paul says, "was parted from thee" for a time. St. Paul sees a higher agency in what seemed to be only the act of Onesimus. If Onesimus robbed and fled from his master, God permitted him to do so; and this permission, we are told, was probably given in order to bring about

the conversion of Onesimus to the Faith, and his reunion
with his master Philemon, first in this life at Colossæ, and
then for ever in the life everlasting. What is remarkable
here is, that even the misconduct of Onesimus seems to
have been, according to St. Paul, permitted with a purpose, which would be made plain in the future life.

A large number of the difficulties which are felt in our
day on the subject of religion run up into that one great
difficulty of all, the existence of evil. How many a man
says to himself, " If I were God, All-good, All-wise, All-
powerful, I should not wish evil to exist; I should know
how to prevent its existing ; and I should use my power,
either to strangle it in its birth, or to crush it out of
being "! God, of course, is not the author of evil; it
cannot be fastened on Him without blasphemy ; but He
does permit it to exist, and, so far as we can see, because
its existence is involved in the gift of free-will to such a
creature as man. God willed to be served by a race of
beings who should have it in their power freely to choose
His service ; differing in this from planets and suns and
from vegetable and animal creatures, which cannot but
serve Him, whether they will or not. But this freedom to
choose carried with it the freedom to refuse His service ;
and the freedom to refuse involved the possibility, to say
the least, that His service would be refused. And this
refusal is moral evil, which emerges when a created will
freely decides not to serve the Perfect Moral Being,
Almighty God. This is moral evil, bringing in its train
physical and all other sorts of evil ; and thus we see that
moral evil arises incidentally from man's abuse of the
consummate goodness and generosity of God, Who does
not withhold His own highest gift, although it may be
made to produce that which is so hateful to Him.

You rejoin, In giving man free-will, God must have fore-

seen what would happen ; and how, then, could He give
it ?   The answer is that He doubtless foresaw what would
presently happen, and saw a great deal further too.   He
foresaw, not merely the birth of moral evil from the abuse
of free-will, but the overruling of moral evil, through the
Divine Redemption, to purposes of a higher good beyond.
This is what St. Paul teaches in the fifth chapter of the
Epistle to the Romans, when he explains how, though sin
had abounded, grace had much more abounded.[a]   We
cannot believe sincerely in God's attributes of perfect
Goodness and Wisdom and Power without being certain
that in the end, and in ways entirely beyond our present
faculties of comprehension, the permitted existence of evil
will be somehow justified by a magnificent victory of good.
Meanwhile, we are able to see that this is the case, over
and over again, on a small scale and in detail.   Onesimus'
theft and flight was a fragment of moral evil ; but it was
overruled, first to his conversion, and next to his reconciliation with his master, whose friend he thus became for
time and eternity.   St. Paul will not now dwell on the
evil, but only on the good to which it may lead.   God knew
what He was doing, in permitting the misconduct of
Onesimus.   It was for Philemon to forget the petty and
personal aspects of the case ; to recognize God's Hand
and Mind in it ; to throw his thought forward and upward ;
forward from the present to the future, upward from the
little world of sense and time to the mighty world, with
its immense perspectives, of Eternity.

This, you will observe, is a rule of thought ; but for us
men it is not a rule of action.   Never are we authorized to
do evil that good may come ; although we are bound to
extract all the good we can out of the evil that may be
done by others, and to trace God's Hand in bringing

[a] Rom. v. 20.

good out of the evil which He permits His creatures to do. Onesimus did not rob and desert his master with a view to his own conversion and reconciliation. He " was parted " by God's providence from Philemon for a season, that Philemon should receive him for ever.

Eighteen hundred years and more have passed since Philemon and Onesimus entered into the World Unseen. But they are there now, in some seat, we may believe, of glory, near the great Apostle who brought first the master and then the slave to the feet of the Crucified. They are there now, bound to each other by the bonds of a charity that will never cease to bind, as they gaze incessantly upon the Immaculate Lamb slain and glorified in the midst of the Throne. There they are now; and when they think of us who are, in our poor, feeble way, sharers in the Faith which has made them what they are, they surely must desire and pray that we, in this day and country, might know more than we do of the reconciling and combining power of the Faith of Christ, more of the worth and dignity of each individual human existence, more of the majestic strength by which God overrules to His own high purposes of good the evil which disheartens us. Nay, rather, under slightly altered conditions, One-simus and Philemon live on in their successors; they are still here, as servants and masters, with the Church of Christ; and she has no less work to do in the way of conversion on the one side, and of persuasion and entreaty on the other, than she had eighteen centuries ago. Here, surely, we have materials in abundance for Advent lessons and for Advent resolves; since it is certain that, when placed in the light of the Second Coming of our Lord, neither the passing incidents of the humblest life are really insignificant, nor yet the proudest deeds of the most renowned among men really great.

# SERMON XXXIII.

## THE INSCRIPTION ON "GREAT PAUL."

### (FOURTH SUNDAY IN ADVENT.)

#### 1 COR. IX. 16.

*Woe is unto me, if I preach not the Gospel!*

DURING the course of the last week or ten days, many of you will have gathered from the public prints that a new bell, of great weight and size, is to be shortly placed in the north-western tower of St. Paul's Cathedral. It will be of heavier metal than any other in London, or in this country;[a] it will take its rank among the six or eight largest bells in Europe; and there is good reason to hope that its rich and melodious tone will not be unworthy of its weight and bulk. Like most other works of public interest and usefulness in the metropolis, the bell is largely indebted for its existence to the munificence and public spirit of the Corporation and Companies of the City of London; while for the excellence of its tone we must trace its obligations to the genius and perseverance which within the last ten years has already done so much for the music of this Cathedral Church.[b] Londoners, per-

[a] The bell weighs 16¾ tons.

[b] It is unnecessary to say that the reference is to Dr. (now Sir John) Stainer, of whose great services St. Paul's has recently (1888) been deprived.

haps, will feel that it will add a new circumstance of interest even to this great city; and we may hope that, however indirectly, it will also benefit that which we, the clergy of this Church, must have most at heart—the cause of religion.

It is as easy, my brethren, to underrate as to overrate the real, that is the religious, importance of a matter of this kind. Certainly, a church bell is not a vital or saving truth; it is not a purified and consecrated heart. It belongs to the world of matter, and not to the world of spirit. It lies on the extreme circumference of that complex mass of interests which go to make up or to assist the practical manifestations of religious life; it cannot for a moment enter into comparison with anything that lies near or about the centre. But it is not, therefore, without its due measure of importance. Anything external and artistic that asserts for the immaterial world its due claims upon the thoughts and hearts of men; anything that resists the encompassing pressure and importunity of matter; anything that, though itself matter, proclaims and advertises the reality of a higher and spiritual existence, has a certain value which cannot be overlooked. It acts insensibly upon the public imagination; it moulds and sways the less conscious processes of popular thought. No religious man will assign too much importance to this; no prudent man will altogether neglect it.

It has been observed that here, in London, the place which is assigned to religion in public thought owes something to the fact that the most striking building in the metropolis, taken altogether, is its Cathedral; and it may be that hereafter something less, yet something worth having, may be traced to its great bell. For a church bell, in virtue of the associations of centuries,

reminds us of two things, at least, which concern religion
most nearly ; it reminds us of prayer, and it reminds us
of death. And this new bell has upon it an inscription
which will account for my having said so much about it
now and here: " Væ mihi si non evangelisavero ! "—" Woe
is unto me, if I preach not the Gospel ! "

## I.

What were the circumstances which drew from St. Paul
this exclamation, " Woe is me, if I preach not the
Gospel " ?

Some events had occurred at Corinth which led St. Paul
to assert his claim to be maintained, if he chose, at the
cost of the Church. He pleads that he only claims what
was already granted to other apostles. He points to the
analogy of other occupations: no soldier lives at his own
expense ; the vinedresser and the shepherd are alike
supported by the produce of their labour.[a] The Levitical
Law, when ruling that the " ox which trode out the corn
was not to be muzzled," had a broader and deeper object
in view than the " care of oxen." [b] The spiritual workman
was not to be hampered with the duty of providing for
the necessaries of physical life. It surely was not much
to ask that the sowers of spiritual blessings should reap
the " carnal things "—the temporal aid—of their people ?[c]
Under the old Law, the ministrants at the altar live of the
sacrifices ;[d] and it was by the ordinance of Christ our Lord
Himself that the Gospel labourer was to live of the
Gospel.[e]

We might suppose that the Apostle is on the point of
pressing his own claim at the conclusion of this chain
of arguments. But no. There is no doubt about his

---

[a] 1 Cor. ix. 7.    [b] *Ib.* 9, 10.    [c] *Ib.* 11.    [d] *Ib.* 13.    [e] *Ib.* 14.

right; but, in view of higher considerations, he never did, and never will, exact what it should secure to him. He refuses to do this, not because he admits that his opponents are justified in saying that he is no true Apostle at all; but because, in waiving it, he finds that he gains immensely in moral power; that he has enlarged opportunities of access to all sorts and conditions of men. This, then, is his "glory," or ground of thankful exultation, that he works for the Gospel of Christ and for souls while supporting himself by his own labour, although he has, by the Law of Christ, by the old Jewish Law, and as a matter of natural justice, a full right to be supported by the Church. But his work in preaching the Gospel is not itself a subject of glory. He has no discretion about it. To others it may seem that his life and work are what they are, because such incessant movement, struggles, persecutions, proclamation of unwelcome truth, is agreeable to an eccentric taste or to an energetic and restless character. He himself knows that it is otherwise; he is driven forward in his great life-work by one particular instinct of commanding power; the instinct of moral self-preservation. "Though I preach the Gospel, I have nothing to glory of: for necessity is laid upon me; yea, woe is unto me, if I preach not the Gospel!"

"Woe is unto me!" We can remember, perhaps, some modern writer with whom an exclamation of this kind is almost conventional; with whom it implies nothing more than a passing sensation of modified annoyance at something which haunts the memory or which traverses the will. But this is not the case with the deeply serious and impassioned Apostle. "Woe is me!" is an exclamation which occurs nowhere else in the writings of St. Paul. But it has a history in the prophetic literature of the Hebrews, and St. Paul uses it with a full knowledge of its meaning. Under the cover of this indefinite but weird word "Woe!" the Prophets called down penal suffering upon persons, countries, causes, enterprises, which were opposed to the Will of God; and our Lord employed the same word in the same sense as the Prophets, though with higher authority. He invoked woe upon the Scribes and Pharisees; woe upon the lawyers; woe upon the selfish rich; woe upon the unthinking and light-hearted; woe upon the universally popular; woe upon those by whom offences come. Some of His sentences run thus: "Woe unto you that are rich! for ye have received your consolation. Woe unto you that laugh now! for ye shall mourn and weep. Woe unto you, when all men shall speak well of you! for so did their fathers to the false prophets."[a] "Woe to that man by whom the Son of Man is betrayed! it had been good for that man if he had never been born."[b] Thus the word is a prophecy and an imprecation; it anticipates and invites most real although indefinite evil; and it does not change its character when it is invoked by a speaker upon himself. "Woe is me," cries a captive Psalmist, "that I am constrained to dwell with Mesech, and to have my habitation among the tents of Kedar!"[c] "Woe is me!" exclaims Isaiah, deeply conscious of his own sinfulness, at the vision in the Temple; "for mine eyes have seen the King, the Lord of Hosts."[d] "Woe is me, my mother," cries Jeremiah, in the despair of his protracted and seemingly fruitless struggles, "that thou hast borne me a man of strife!"[e] "If I be wicked," says Job to his friends, with reference to their cruel and false explanation of the calamities which had come on him—"If I be wicked, woe unto me!"[f]

St. Paul, then, is employing an expression of acknow-

[a] St. Luke vi. 24-26.     [b] St. Matt. xxvi. 24.     [c] Ps. cxx. 5.
[d] Isa. vi. 5.     [e] Jer. xv. 10.     [f] Job x. 15.

ledged solemnity which for him, we may be very sure,
had not lost its freshness. He predicts and invokes evil
upon himself if it should ever happen that he ceased,
while in this life, to preach the good news of God to men.
" Woe is unto me, if I preach not the Gospel ! "

## II.

As we think over the words, we are perhaps at first
disposed to credit the Apostle with a touch of exaggeration. It was, we grant, a very good, even an heroic, thing
to preach the Gospel. If the Roman society thought
him mad, the Christian Church was sure that he was
inspired; and, at any rate, as a free man he was within
his rights, and as a good man he was doing what he
believed to be the best that could be done with his life.
But supposing he had settled down quietly, as a private
Christian, in Tarsus or elsewhere, putting what truth he
knew into practice as best he could, and saying little or
nothing about it, why should he think that any harm
would happen to him ? There are many men who have
in them the tastes, the habits, the capacities of mind and
temper which go to form a great statesman—men, too,
who are conscious of their power—but whose voices are
never even heard on a platform or in Parliament. Would
they be using sober and serious language if they were on
this account to imprecate woe upon themselves ? There
are born artists who never paint, born architects who
never build, born authors who never write, born military
leaders who never wear an epaulette; men with natural
capacity for this or that kind of work, but who somehow
never undertake it. It is a misfortune, no doubt, in a
certain sense, for themselves and for the world. it is
better for all of us, and indisputably better for each man

himself, when he finds himself doing that work for which
God has fitted him by nature and circumstances. But if
we were to hear such a man say, " Woe is me, if I do not
practise medicine, or plead at the bar, or keep the accounts
of a great firm, or command a merchant-ship," we should
think him exaggerating. We should say to him, " My
good man ! it is a pity that you are not making the best
you can of yourself. But, after all, there are other things
in the world to be done besides that on which you have
set your heart; and it is better to take a quieter and more
moderate view of your case." Why may not something
of this kind be said of St. Paul, exclaiming, with such
vehemence, to the Corinthians, " Woe is me, if I preach
not the Gospel " ?

Ah! why? It is, first of all, because St. Paul felt
that if he were not to preach the Gospel he would be
doing violence to his sense of justice. The Gospel was
not his in such a sense that he had any right to keep it
to himself. What was the Gospel? It was the good
news of God. It was the Divine message, warranted to
be Divine by certificates whose worth could not be mistaken. It was the message which announced that, if men
would believe, earth and Heaven, God and man, might
be reconciled. " Preaching the Gospel " is one of those
phrases of the Bible which, like coin that has been long in
circulation, have been degraded and vulgarized by constant
use. It may mean here or there only a distorted view of
some seven chapters of the New Testament, to the practical
neglect of all the rest; only the recurrence of a few stock
phrases addressed to some very narrow mood of feeling.
We know some of the meagre associations which have
clustered, to its detriment, around this inspired expression. By the Gospel is sometimes meant only a thin

extract from the religion of the New Testament, according to which we are justified by emotions divorced from morality, and may measure our Christian freedom by our indifference to the means of grace, and our spirituality by the licence of general irreverence. The Gospel which St. Paul preached was larger, nobler, more generous, more true. The very word "Gospel" implied that mankind was in a bad case, and needed something to reassure and to help them. It implied that men were conscious of being ill at ease, and were looking out, at any rate at intervals, for a deliverer. We find traces of this in the whole Jewish and pagan world ; and we know, as St. Paul knew, that these misgivings and yearnings were well grounded. A dark shadow had passed between God and man since the first age of man's life on earth ; it was the shadow of sin. Sin had veiled from man the face of God ; it had opened a gulf between earth and Heaven. It had given a perverse bent and twist to all in human nature that was meant to lead to God ; it had robbed man of his original robe of righteousness, and thereby had darkened his understanding ; it had blunted his affections ; it had weakened and warped his will. We often know that we are ill without knowing precisely what is the matter with us ; and this was the case with the large mass of human beings in the ancient pre-Christian world. Therefore, first of all, God opened the eyes of men to see what their case really was. Nature and conscience did something in this way for the heathen nations ;[a] the Law of Moses did a great deal more for the Jews. By the Law was the knowledge of sin ;[b] the Law was a lantern, burning with a bright moral light, and revealing the dark and unlovely forms which human life had assumed under the impetus and operation of sin. But the Law only discovered to the

---

[a] Rom. i. 20 ; ii. 15.          [b] *Ib.* iii. 20.

patient his real condition; it did not and could not cure him. It only made his misery more intense, because more intelligent; it made the moral demand for a real remedy greater than ever, but it did not supply that for which it made men crave.

Then came the real cure, not from earth, but from Heaven; not from man's strength, or virtue, or intelligence, but from God. God so loved the human world, that He gave His Son to save it.[a] When no other or lesser being could bring help, the Infinite and the Eternal appeared among us, under the conditions which we call space and time. He came clothed in a Human Body and in a Human Soul, and in this created form He laid Himself in a manger; He died upon a Cross. He offered a life of perfect symmetry, faultlessness, obedience, culminating in a death of entire self-sacrifice, to the Father in Heaven; and henceforth all who are truly united to Him, by faith on their part, by gifts of grace, given through appointed channels, on His, are, as His Apostle says, " accepted in the Beloved." [b]

This is the core or essence of the Gospel, although it has collateral and dependent truths which cannot really be separated from it, ranging forth in this direction and in that, and worthy of all men to be believed. But clearly such a Gospel as this was not meant only for one or two men, for a company of men, for a single nation, for a single race. " Is He the God of the Jews only ? " [c] was St. Paul's indignant question addressed to those who would have limited His favours to the Jewish people. Like the sun in the heavens, the Incarnate Sun of Righteousness is the property—we may dare to use that word—of all the members of the human family; all have a right to the light and warmth which radiate from His Sacred Person,

---

[a] St. John iii. 16.     [b] Eph. i. 6.     [c] Rom. iii. 29.

from His Redeeming Cross. And this explains St. Paul's
sense of the justice of proclaiming the good news of the
reconciliation in Christ of earth and Heaven to all members of the human family. Every man, as such, had a
natural right to his share in the Gospel; just as every
man has a right to air, and water, and freedom, and, at
least, sufficient food to preserve bodily life. Not to preach
the Gospel; to hoard it as if it were the luxury of a small
clique, like some of the old philosophies, or a rare book in
a library, or a family portrait—was to offend against the
sense of natural justice, and to increase the woe which,
as Nature whispers, is sooner or later inseparable from
doing this. "Woe is me, if I preach not the Gospel!"

But, in St. Paul's mind, not to preach the Gospel was
yet more emphatically to sin against the instinct of
generosity. The feature in the Redemption, which strikes
St. Paul, which takes possession of him, which awes his
reason while it takes his heart captive, is the extraordinary
generosity of the Redeemer. What was there in the
human race, what was there in the individual sinner,
I do not say to compel, but to invite, such an effusion of
Divine Love? For, if any one point is clear in the New
Testament, it is that not merely the collective Church, but
each single member of it, has a distinct place and recognition in the Eternal Counsels, and in the All-embracing
Heart of God. Each may say, as though each was alone
the object of the Redemption, "He loved me, and gave
Himself for me."[a] St. Paul felt this to be especially true
in his own case. He was a Jew, a Pharisee, an active
persecutor, an enemy of the Crucified, a ravager and
destroyer of His Church. He was sincere in that old life
of fanatical error and violence, and God would not leave

[a] Gal. ii. 20.

him to himself. On the road to Damascus, he was brought, by a flash of light from Heaven, into real spiritual contact with the Divine Lord, risen and glorified, Whom he had so bitterly opposed ; and the result was a change in his whole view of himself and of God, of life and duty ; a change, profound, vital, ineffaceable. And then followed the visions in which the Lord Jesus Himself sketched out the great work which he was to do.[a] And then, later on, the Ordination ; at which older ministers of Christ formally transmitted to him the powers which they had already received from Heaven.[b] All this left upon St. Paul's mind an indelible impression. He felt that, whatever he might once have seemed to be, he was no longer his own master ; that the Eternal Love had swept down upon his life in its misery and shame ; had transformed it ; had translated him to a new sphere of glory and of labour. " This is a faithful saying, and worthy of all acceptation, that Christ Jesus came into the world to save sinners ; of whom I am chief. However for this cause I obtained mercy, that in me first Jesus Christ might show forth all long-suffering, for a pattern to them which should hereafter believe on Him to life everlasting." [c]

This, then, was the second reason which prompted St. Paul's exclamation. As he dared not offend against the law of justice, which bade him give to the world the truth which belonged to it ; so, even more, he could not outrage the law of gratitude which bound him to the Redeemer, Who had bought him with His Blood. Even with heathen moralists the obligations of gratitude are reckoned imperative. Even the lower animals show their share in some departments of our moral nature, by their practical acknowledgment of kindnesses received at the hand of man. We all remember the story of the lion in the

[a] Acts ix. 11–16.     [b] *Ib.* xiii. 2, 3.     [c] 1 Tim. i. 15, 16.

amphitheatre, who recognized the Christian by whom he had been tended in former years in the desert. Such a sentence as " While we were yet sinners, Christ died for us," [a] measures St. Paul's sense of obligation to his Lord and Saviour; and if this sense was to take a practical form, it could only be by his doing his best to spread abroad among men a knowledge and love of the Redemption. " Woe is me, if I preach not the Gospel!"

But, once more, not to preach the Gospel would have been, in St. Paul's case, to be false to the imperious commands of truth. Truth is a stern mistress, and, if we serve her at all, we serve her, not on our own terms, but on hers. We cannot really make selections, and choose so much service and leave the rest undone; we must do her bidding, or be dismissed. The Gospel came to St. Paul as it comes to all of us, as a body of truth which could only be really held on condition of its being propagated by the holder. Not to do something towards propagating the Gospel is not to believe it; it is to treat the Gospel as though it were at best only partially or relatively true. The Gospel is nothing if it be not absolutely true; true for all men and for all times. It is nothing if it is not the Universal Religion; " the power of God unto salvation to *every* man that believeth." [b] Hence, that the Gospel should be propagated according to the opportunities of the believer, is not merely a legitimate inference which may or may not be drawn from it; it is as much an integral part of the Gospel as anything else in it. The case is very different with false religions, with private speculations, with human philosophies; to hold them is one thing, to make efforts to disseminate them is another. To believe the Gospel, and to do nothing for its accept-

[a] Rom. v. 8.          [b] *Ib.* i. 16.

ance among men, is a contradiction in terms. Unless you can separate in fact, as well as in idea, the convex and concave sides of a circular vase, you must, when you believe a Religion which, as being absolutely true, is also the Universal Religion, do what you may to induce others to believe it also.

Enough has, perhaps, been said—though it is little enough in view of what might be said—to explain St. Paul's conditional imprecation of woe upon himself. He could not trifle with the great laws which lie at the basis of the moral life of every human soul; with the law of justice, the law of gratitude, the law of truth. These laws bade him preach Christ's Gospel. And to turn a deaf ear to them, to resist them, was to break up his moral nature from within; it was to tear it up by the roots; it was to incur, first, in the solemn depths of his own conscience, and then at a higher tribunal, a sentence of penal woe, the dark misery of which it was impossible to exaggerate.

## III.

"Woe is me, if I preach not the Gospel!" This is a motto for every portion and member of the Church of Christ. Particular Churches have their periods of energetic life, and their intervals of inertness and decay. There are epochs when the great truths of the Christian Creed are prominently and livingly present to the conscience of a particular Church. There are intervals when truth is obscured, or kept in the background, or mutilated, or overlaid by matter of comparatively slight importance. At such times a Church is in danger. A Church's strength ever lies, not in her external supports, but in her inward vitality; in her faithfulness to that whole body of truth,

which alone accounts for her existence. When she forgets
this, she is in a fair way to forfeit her candlestick.[a]

Not seldom in her history has the Church of Christ
been tempted to proclaim something other or less than
the Gospel. So it was in the Apostolic age, and in the
presence of St. Paul himself. There were clever and
accomplished Greeks at Corinth and elsewhere, hovering
around the doors of the Church, feeling and expressing
much sympathy with many sides of Christianity, but
withheld from conversion, at least so they said, by what
seemed to them the strange and repulsive doctrine of the
salvation of the world by Jesus Christ crucified. They
wanted a Gospel without the Cross. And what was St.
Paul's reply? "God forbid that I should glory, save in
the Cross of our Lord Jesus Christ;"[b] "We preach Christ
crucified . . . to the Greeks foolishness; but to them that
are called . . . the power of God and the wisdom of God."[c]
He could say no otherwise. Woe to him, had he not thus
preached the Gospel!

So it was in the fourth century. Arianism, that shrewd
endeavour of human ingenuity to keep some terms with
the language of the New Testament, while denying the
real Divinity of our Lord Jesus Christ—that celebrated
effort to project into the Christian imagination the idea
of a Christ who should be more than human, yet less
than absolutely Divine,—Arianism, in alliance with the
Byzantine Court, and with a large section of the literary
class, tempted the Church again to say something less
on the subject of our Lord's Adorable Person than she
had said and believed since Pentecost. And what was
the Church's reply? It was the famous sentence which
we repeat to-day in the Nicene Creed: "I believe in One
Lord Jesus Christ, the only begotten Son of God . . . of

---

[a] Rev. ii. 5.          [b] Gal. vi. 14.          [c] 1 Cor. i. 23, 24.

One Substance with the Father, by Whom all things were made." She could say nothing else or less. Woe to her, if she had not then preached the Gospel!

So it was in the fifteenth century, the age of the Renaissance. The old literature of pagan Greece and Rome had been just rediscovered; and for a time the learned fairly lost their heads at the discovery. Such was the attraction of this long-buried world of classical thoughts and writings, that Christians actually professed themselves ashamed of "the jargon of St. Paul," and unable to express even religious ideas except in the phrases of Plato or of Cicero. The Church was bidden refashion herself upon the model of the very paganism which she had conquered by suffering a thousand years before. And what was her answer? The Renaissance might be very well; but for Christians, the first consideration was the Law and honour of Christ. The reply of Christendom took widely different forms in Northern and in Southern Europe; but, in either case, its spirit was substantially this, " Woe is me, if I preach not the Gospel!"

And in our own day the old temptation presents itself, but in an altered mien. To-day the Church is face to face with a world of thought, which is in a hundred ways hostile to her, but which is often willing to be friendly, if friendship can be secured on its own terms. "There is much good still in Christianity," so we are told; "its moral precepts, or some of them; the example of its Founder, or parts of it; the literature which was created at its birth, and which, with few intervals, marks its passage across the centuries;—these will always be among the treasures of the world. But, then," it is added, "the day has arrived for something more than a change of front. If Christianity is to keep on good terms with the modern world, Christians must give up the supernatural.

They must be content with a Christ who is perfect, but
simply human; with a Calvary that is the scene of a
self-sacrifice, but not of an atonement; with prayer that
refreshes the suppliant, but does not move the Will of
God; with Sacraments that are poetical signs of absent
blessings, not means whereby we are actually united to
the Divine Redeemer."

And what are we to say to all this, as we look at our
title-deeds in the New Testament, as we review the history
of Christendom all down the centuries, as we ask ourselves what is wanted to meet the real needs of the human
soul, as we reflect that, within a few years, the generation
which confronts us will be lying with ourselves beneath
the sod, and some new mood will have passed over the
ever-changing mind of man? Ah! what can the Christian Church say but that which her great Apostle said
eighteen hundred years ago?—" Your demands can never
be conceded; unless we are to be traitors to the Truth
which we have received, and to your own dearest interests.
'Woe is unto me, if I preach not the Gospel!'"

These, too, are words which no ordained man can afford
to forget. You, my brethren of the laity, expect much,
and you rightly expect much, of us the clergy. You
are quick to note our failures, and our inconsistencies;
and we certainly have no right or wish to complain of
you, if you judge us by the Divine standard which it is
our business to enforce. But, perhaps, if you knew more
of the temptations of a clerical life, you would not, as I
hope, judge us less sternly, but you would help us better
by your prayers. To preach the Gospel, the whole Gospel
and nothing but the Gospel, out of the pulpit as well as
in it, in general intercourse as well as at home, before its
opponents as well as before believers, is not easy. Many

are the temptations to mutilate known truth, to twist it,
to exaggerate it, to mistake the inspirations of passion for
the inspirations of faithfulness, to mistake the promptings
of cowardice for lofty spiritual prudence. Many are the
temptations to substitute doing good in a general way,
which is, indeed, often one of our accompanying privileges, for that which is our proper work as Christ's
ambassadors; to substitute a Gospel of benevolence, of
philanthropy, of literary refinement, for that real message
from Heaven which was ever on the lips of Christ's first
Apostles, and without which all else is but a poor and
heartless trifling with the most solemn interests of dying
men. And on this day in the year especially,[a] if on any,
this should be borne in mind, when, in almost every
diocese, young clergymen are being sent forth, furnished
with a heavenly commission, on their difficult task, and
when they need the prayer and sympathy of all good
Christians to enable them to be true, even in a moderate
degree, to their Ordination vows. May it not be that
if no prayers, no living interest, follow on their steps,
and they fail grievously to do justice to the truth and
grace entrusted to them, the resulting woe will not be
altogether theirs; that it will be shared, according to
a law of inexorable justice, with those who might have
helped them, and who left them to themselves?

"Woe is me, if I preach not the Gospel!" Every
Christian man and woman may, in a true sense, make these
words his own. For most assuredly every life preaches
something, not necessarily in set discourses, not perhaps
by anything that passes the lips, but by its whole drift and
character. Not Apostles only, but the humblest Christians, may be a savour of life unto life, or of death unto

[a] Fourth Sunday in Advent, 1881.

death;[a] every soul has its special Apostolate of this kind
or of that. The days and hours pass, and we are all of us
leaving around us moral effects, impressions, convictions of
truth or the reverse, which will not cease when we ourselves
pass away from this earthly scene, or when those who
receive them follow or precede us. In view of this vast
vista of responsibilities, surely every Christian soul may
well exclaim, " Woe is me, if I preach not the Gospel ! "

Well, then, it is that this inscription is to be written
on the great bell of St. Paul's. The sentence comes
straight from the heart of the great Apostle whose Church
this is; and it summarizes, in a brief and vigorous form,
all that was characteristic of the thought and temper of
his noble and saintly soul. When, as we hope, this bell
sounds forth over London next Easter Day, when it sounds
on in the years that will follow, after we of this generation shall have gone to our account, let us trust that it
will suggest other and higher thoughts than any which
belong only to this passing scene; that its deep and
solemn tones will bear in on the soul of many a listener
the thought of the Second Coming, the thought of
Eternity, the thought of the many and intricate issues
which depend on each man's making the best efforts
that he may to know and to spread abroad Christ's everlasting Gospel during the fleeting days and hours of
time.

[a] 2 Cor. ii. 16.

# SERMON XXXIV.

## THE GREAT ANTICIPATION.

### (ADVENT SUNDAY.)

**2 St. Pet. iii. 12.**

*Looking for and hasting unto the coming of the day of God.*

AS we move on in life, Advent, so it seems, becomes more and more welcome. It is in keeping with those deeper thoughts which, if we think at all, present themselves more frequently with advancing years. As the space within which any future is possible on this earthly scene steadily contracts, Advent reminds us of the illimitable life which lies beyond. And the natural year, in these first winter months, seems to lend its aid to the truths and reflections which are brought before us by the Church of Christ. These short, damp, cold, dark days, when the sun generally hides his face during the few hours of his hurried visit to us; these nights, always long, often wild and tempestuous, when the savage forces of nature seem to have broken loose and to be for the time in the ascendant; and then the sense that we are still, for some while yet, sinking lower and lower into the realm of winter gloom;—all this tends to create and to maintain the subdued state of feeling in which man best thinks of the last things—Death and Judgment, Heaven and Hell.

The natural features of the season become, in the course of years, associated with the sacred and familiar words. To-day's Gospel,[a] which records the entry into Jerusalem, when, on the eve of His condemnation, our Lord really judged the Jewish people; and that more solemn Gospel of next Sunday,[b] which describes Him as He has yet to come in the clouds of Heaven; and then those well-known lessons from the Prophet Isaiah,[c] so stern and so pathetic; —all seem to gather force year by year, as the other world throws its shadows more and more distinctly across the path of life.

And to-day there is another consideration which will be present to the minds of many of you. This morning the shadow of death has fallen on the highest See in the English Church.[d] It is the close of a career which already, in a very ample and distinguished sense, belongs to history; it is the end of a life which for twelve years was devoted to the pastoral care of this vast Diocese; while it also, as we cannot here and now forget, means the full measure of sorrow which death inflicts on the hearts of an affectionate family. At such times it is of great importance if we can to be definite and practical; and here St. Peter comes to our assistance in the text. He gives us a motto for the Christian life which it will be well to keep in memory, at least during Advent: "Looking for and hasting unto the coming of the day of God."

St. Peter's language takes it for granted that man, as man, looks forward to something. Absolute satisfaction with the passing moment has been the dream of poets and philosophers. It has not often been embodied in general experience. Certainly the light-hearted poet of antiquity

[d] St. Matt. xxi. 1-13.    [b] St. Luke xxi. 25-33.
[c] Isa. i., ii., v., xi., xxv., xxvi., xxx., xxxii.
[d] Archibald Campbell Tait, Archbishop of Canterbury, died December 3, 1882.

advised his friend to snatch joyfully the gifts of the passing hour, and leave the anxieties of life to themselves.[a]
And a very recent moralist tells us, as the last word of
modern wisdom, that our life is best spent in extracting
the largest amount of possible satisfaction out of each
successive sensation as we experience it.  It is in a very
different sense that our Lord bids us take no thought for
the morrow;[b] He deprecates anxiety about the things of
this world, because He would have the soul constantly
given to anticipation of the next; constantly engaged, as
His Apostle bids it, in "making its calling and election
sure."[c]  And, as a matter of fact, anticipation of some
future is a part of human nature.  The child looks forward
to what he will do when he is grown up.  The young man
or young woman thinks constantly of being married, and
of the shape and hue that married life will take.  The
man who is married looks for professional success or for
promotion.  The loyal wife desires her husband's wealth
or reputation as, in a true sense, her own.  And then,
when success or advancement has been attained, the
interest of life, ever future, is transferred to a younger
generation; and the aged parent, himself on the brink
of a new and illimitable existence, lives over again in his
children the hopes and enthusiasms and ambitions that
were once his own.  There are, of course, men and women
who, even in early life, have put aside all lesser and poorer
ends, and have resolved to set before their eyes only that
vast eternity which lies beyond all earthly horizons; but
we are looking for the moment at human nature of the
average type, and as we see it around us and in ourselves.
Average human nature is ever stretching forth towards a
future; ever building castles in the air, mean or splendid
as the case may be; ever showing, all unconsciously, that

[a] Hor.          [b] St. Matt. vi. 34.          [c] 2 St. Pet. i. 10.

the present does not satisfy it perfectly; that no passing sensation, however exquisite, can quite prevent it from looking onwards to the unexplored and the unknown. And what is the event that lies beyond all else; what is the occurrence upon which, according to St. Peter, the eye of the soul must rest, whether in buoyant hope, or in wistful apprehension, or in terror-stricken despair? The answer is, "The coming of the day of God."

## I.

"The day of God!" What is meant by this striking expression?

Can it be intended that God has left the present time to itself; that He has retreated into a distant future, where He will claim rights and exert a jurisdiction that do not now belong to Him? Certainly this notion cannot be entertained together with any worthy idea of the Almighty and the Ever-living. All days most assuredly are His, Who, being Eternal, is the Lord of time; all days most assuredly, and in particular this very day which is now drawing to its close, not less than any which have preceded or which will follow it. Each hour, each minute, as it passes by, is passed beneath His Eye; it is passed in His encompassing Presence, for Whom time, with its sequence of artificial or natural measurements, cannot exist. The idea of His not being Lord of any one day is not to be reconciled with belief that, being what He is, He exists at all.

No; such a phrase must describe, not God's absolute relation to any one moment of time, but our human way of looking at it. By the "day of God" is meant a day which will not merely be His, as all days are, but which will be felt to be so; a day in which His true relation to time and life, which, in the case of the majority of men, only is dimly perceived, or almost obscured during the great part of their earthly existence, will be unreservedly acknowledged ; a day which will belong to Him, because, in the thoughts of every reasonable creature of His Hand, whether for weal or woe, He will have no rival.

That the "day of God" means, first of all, a day in which God will take the first place in the thoughts of men, seems to result from an examination of the language of the Bible.

In the Old Testament, this word "day," meaning not seldom a season or epoch, is constantly joined to some word: denoting an event, or idea, or characteristic with which the particular time referred to was associated in the minds, whether of men in general, or of the sacred writer. Thus the Psalmist speaks of "the day of temptation," [a] "the day of his trouble," [b] "the day of God's power," [c] "the day of God's wrath ; " [d] and Isaiah, of "the day of visitation," [e] "the day of God's fierce anger," [f] "the day of grief and desperate sorrow ; " [g] and Jeremiah, of "the day of evil," [h] "the day of affliction," [i] "the day of calamity." [j] These several periods, thus described, are sometimes present, sometimes not distantly future ; while sometimes they point on to a very remote time, of which the present or the near future is a pledge or an anticipation. Or, again, some city or nation is named, which has had a tragic history, and its day means the epoch of its suffering or ruin ; and thus Isaiah speaks of "the day of Midian," [k] and Ezekiel of "the day of Egypt," [l] and Hosea of "the day of Jezreel," [m] and one of the later Psalmists of "the

<hr/>

| | | |
|---|---|---|
| [a] Ps. xcv. 8. | [b] *Ib.* cii. 2. | [c] *Ib.* cx. 3. |
| [d] *Ib.* 5. | [e] Isa. x. 3. | [f] *Ib.* xiii. 13. |
| [g] *Ib.* xvii. 11. | [h] Jer. xvii. 17. | [i] *Ib.* xvi. 19. |
| [j] *Ib.* xviii. 17. | [k] Isa. ix. 4. | [l] Ezek. xxx. 9. | [m] Hos. i. 11. |

day of Jerusalem." [a]  That which is common to all these
phrases is the prominence in men's thoughts of the subject, whether it be a race, or a city, or a vicissitude, or a
mode of feeling, or a particular experience at some given
epoch ; and thus we see how words which are at first sight
so strange and embarrassing, as "the day of the Lord,"
might come to be used.  It means a time when the
Lord is to take precedence of all else in the thoughts of
men.

"The day of the Lord !"  The phrase occurs again and
again in the Hebrew Prophets, and, as far as the Old
Testament is concerned, it is peculiar to them.  Sometimes, indeed, they speak of "the day of the Lord's anger," [b]
"the day of the Lord's sacrifice," [c] "the day of the Lord's
vengeance," [d] but more frequently, as do Isaiah, [e] Joel, [f]
Amos, [g] Obadiah, [h] Zephaniah, [i] Jeremiah, [j] Ezekiel, [k] Zechariah, [l] Malachi, [m] of "the day of the Lord," or more
fully, "the day of the Lord God of Hosts." [n]  By this
expression, too, they often refer to very various events.
Sometimes to some near exhibition of God's power in the
history of Israel, or of the adjacent peoples ; sometimes
to a far-off occurrence, general and comprehensive in its
scope, of which the nearer events are premonitory shadows
on the dial of time.  And thus the phrase passes into the
hands of, and is, so to say, baptized by, the Apostles, who fix
its meaning, in view of that fuller revelation of the world
beyond the grave which was laid open to them by the
Holy Spirit.  St. Paul prays that the Corinthians may
be "blameless in the day of the Lord :" [o] he trusts that

[a] Ps. cxxxvii. 7.　　[b] Lam. ii. 22.　　[c] Zeph. i. 8.
[d] Isa. xxxiv. 8.　　[e] *Ib.* ii. 12.　　[f] Joel i. 15.
[g] Amos v. 18.　　[h] Obad. 15.　　[i] Zeph. i. 18.
[j] Jer. xlvi. 10.　　[k] Ezek. xiii. 5.　　[l] Zech. xiv. 1.
[m] Mal. iv. 5.　　[n] Jer. xlvi. 10.　　[o] 1 Cor. i. 8.

God, Who has begun a good work in his spiritual children
at Philippi, will perform it until the day of Jesus
Christ;"[a] he hopes that, through the discipline of the
Church exercised on the incestuous Corinthian, his "spirit
may be saved in the day of the Lord;"[b] warns the Thessalonians that "the day of the Lord cometh as a thief in
the night."[c] The expression is made at home in the
New Testament, and it now has a clearly defined meaning; it points to a day beyond the limits of what we
call time, when God will be first in the thoughts of all
men.

There are two modifications of the expression which
lay stress upon this side of its meaning.

Of these, one is the "great day." Thus Jeremiah had
exclaimed, "Alas! that day is great: none is like it;[d]
and Joel, "The day of the Lord is great and very terrible,"[e] and that "the sun shall be turned to darkness, and
the moon into blood, before the great and terrible day
of the Lord come;"[f] and Malachi had told of the turning
of the hearts of the fathers to the children, and of the
children to the fathers, before the coming of the great
day of the Lord.[g] And thus St. Jude speaks of the fallen
angels, who are reserved unto the judgment of the great
day;[h] and St. John of the battle of the great day,[i] and of
the great day of the wrath of God.[j]

The other expression, which is even more suggestive,
is "*that* day;" as if, when the soul's eye had once caught
the true outline of the future, one day only could be
in question. Sometimes, in the Prophets of Israel, "that
day" means, indeed, the day of the promised Christ,
the day of the Church of Christ in which we are living

[a] Phil. i. 6.        [b] 1 Cor. v. 5.        [c] 1 Thess. v. 2.
[d] Jer. xxx. 7.      [e] Joel ii. 11.        [f] *Ib.* 31.
[g] Mal. iv. 5, 6.    [h] St. Jude 6.    [i] Rev. xvi. 14.    [j] *Ib.* vi. 17.

—as when Isaiah speaks of the new song that shall in *that day* be sung in Judah;[a] or Hosea, that in *that day* God will make a covenant with His people;[b] or Joel, that in *that day* the mountains shall drop new wine[c]—meaning the spiritual blessings of the Gospel; or Zechariah, that the nations shall be joined to the Lord in *that day*;[d] or that in *that day* there shall be a Fountain opened for sin and for uncleanness[e]—meaning the Precious Blood; or that in *that day* there shall be One Lord, and His Name One.[f] But, in our Lord's mouth, *that day* commonly means the great day of the Lord hereafter. "Many will say unto Me in that day, Lord, Lord;"[g] "Of that day knoweth no man;"[h] "It shall be more tolerable in that day for Sodom than for you."[i] And thus St. Paul is anxious lest *that day* should overtake the Thessalonians as a thief;[j] and he assures them that *that day* shall not come except there come a falling away first, and the revelation of the Antichrist who is to precede it;[k] and he tells Timothy that he has committed the treasure of his hopes and fears to our Lord against *that day*;[l] and he prays that the deceased and faithful Onesiphorus may find mercy of the Lord in *that day*.[m]

## II.

"The day of God!" It means, secondly, a time when all human things will be rated at their true value; when man's life, and all that belongs to it, will be seen in the light of the Infinite and the Eternal, and therefore in its relative insignificance. "The day of God" thus implies

---

a Isa. xxvi. 1.　　b Hos. ii. 18.　　c Joel iii. 18.
d Zech. ii. 11.　　e *Ib.* xiii. 1.　　f *Ib.* xiv. 9.
g St. Matt. vii. 22.　　h *Ib.* xxiv. 36.　　i St. Luke x. 12.
j 1 Thess. v. 4.　　k 2 Thess. ii. 3.　　l 2 Tim. i. 12.　　m *Ib.* 18.

a contrast and a catastrophe.  It means that the days of man's earthly life, and all that concerns it, will have passed away.

This is the idea of "the day of the Lord" which Isaiah describes in the First Lesson for this afternoon.[a]  Isaiah was living in a generation for which this present life was well-nigh its all.  Each feature of its civilization, each personal decoration, each possession, each dignity, each exercise of power, was inexpressibly dear to the men of that time.  The trees and hills of Lebanon and Bashan furnish the imagery which clothes the burning words that predict the coming revelation of human insignificance.  "The day of the Lord shall be upon every one that is proud and lofty, and upon every one that is lifted up; and he shall be brought low: and upon all the cedars of Lebanon, that are high and lifted up, and upon all the oaks of Bashan, and upon all the high mountains, and upon all the hills that are lifted up, and upon every high tower, and upon every fenced wall, and upon all the ships of Tarshish, and upon all pleasant pictures.  And the loftiness of man shall be bowed down, and the haughtiness of men shall be made low: and the Lord alone shall be exalted in that day."[b]

Most men who have lived until middle life have experienced something that will enable them to understand this.  You have gone on for years, without any shock to the even tenor of existence; and insensibly, this visible world has become your all, or nearly so.  Its striking scenes, its great personages, its objects of ambition, may easily so occupy the mind as to shut the unseen out from view.  A spirit of slumber or stupefaction,[c] such as St. Paul, appealing to prophecy, says took possession of the Jews, may have taken possession of you.  You have

[a] Isa. ii.  [b] Ib. 12-17.  [c] Rom. xi. 8.

fallen under the empire of nature and of the bodily senses; and everything belonging to this world is seen in exaggerated proportions, because you have lost sight of a higher.

Now, a state of mind like this is abruptly broken in upon by a great trouble; by a loss of income, or a loss of reputation, or the death of a loved relative, or the ruin of health. Each of these may be a staggering blow to a man in certain circumstances; and one effect of such a shock may be to convince him that his former way of looking at life was a mistaken one. He has made too much of it, in detail and as a whole. He has attributed to it an importance and stability which is not borne out by experience; and he wakes up to see that there is another world beyond it, compared with which it is poor and worthless indeed. This is for him a "day of the Lord;" and, in the light of it, he learns that "all flesh is grass, and all the goodliness of man as the flower of the field; that the grass withereth and the flower fadeth, but the Word of our God shall stand for ever." [a]

And every such experience is a preparation for the awful day, when we shall learn, as never before, the insignificance of all that only belongs to time. This lesson, indeed, is surely learnt at the moment of death. The Psalmist says of the great and powerful, that "he shall carry nothing away with him when he dieth, neither shall his pomp follow him." [b]

When Tertullian thinks of the poor oppressed Church of the second century face to face with the powerful and splendid society of the Empire, which scorned when it did not persecute, he carries his thoughts forward to a time when all the prominent figures in Romish society will have heard the sentence of the Universal Judge, and will

[a] Isa. xl. 6–8.　　　[b] Ps. xlix. 17.

learn how little the lasting reality corresponds to the transient appearance.[a] And if any of us are ever tempted to dwell on outward advantages, on the means at our disposal, on the reputation we may bear among our friends, on the deference that is paid us, on any of those circumstances of life which mean social or public consideration without meaning inward penitence and peace, let us think steadily of the coming day, when we shall stand before the Eternal Throne, unclothed spirits unless we be clothed with the Righteousness of Christ, while all that we have cared for here will then be worthless, or worse than worthless.

### III.

"The day of God!" It means, once more, the day of an Universal Judgment. Such a day would be the day of God, if only because His moral attributes would be conspicuously displayed and satisfied.

Thus our Lord says, "For every idle word that men shall speak, they shall give an account thereof in the Day of Judgment."[b] Thus St. Peter says that "unjust men are reserved unto the Day of Judgment to be punished."[c] Thus St. John is anxious that good Christians should have boldness in the Day of Judgment.[d] And this character of the day is more fully explained when St. Paul tells the Romans that it is "a day of wrath and revelation of the righteous judgment of God; Who will render to every man according to his deeds: to those who by patient continuance in well-doing seek for glory, honour, and immortality, eternal life: but unto them that are contentious, and do not obey the truth, but obey unrighteous-

---

[a] Tertull., *Des Spectacul.*, vi. 30.     [b] St. Matt. xii. 36.
[c] 2 St. Pet. ii. 9.     [d] 1 St. John iv. 17.

ness, indignation and wrath, tribulation and anguish, upon
every soul of man that doeth evil." [a]

Certainly, God is always judging us. Moment by
moment we live beneath His all-seeing Eye; and He
registers each act and word and thought, each movement
of passion, each truancy of will, each struggle, by His
grace, to live for Him, each victory "over the craft and
subtlety of the devil or man." Moment by moment He is
"a discerner of the thoughts and intents of the heart;
neither is there any creature which is not manifest in His
sight: for all things are naked and open to the eyes of
Him with Whom we have to do." [b] He discerns; and as
He discerns, He judges; He judges as we think, and feel,
and speak, and act. And this life, too, is largely made
up of the rewards which He bestows and of the penalties
which He inflicts. His "judgments are already in all the
world," [c] although it may be hard to say which sufferings
in our own lives or in the lives of others have been certainly penal, and which of them remedial or intended to
educate for a higher life. But it is to Him, as our present
Judge, that we pray with the Psalmist, "Judge me, O
Lord, according to Thy righteousness;" [d] or, "Judge me,
O Lord, and seek the ground of my heart; prove me, and
examine my thoughts;" [e] or, "Enter not into judgment
with Thy servant, O Lord; for in Thy sight shall no man
living be justified." [f]

Yes! God is always on the Throne of Judgment; but
this does not prove that no time is coming when He will
judge as never before. The predicted Day of Judgment
will differ from the continuous judgment of the Divine
Mind in two respects; in its method, and in its finality.
It will be carried out, that Last Judgment, by the Man

[a] Rom. ii. 5–9.    [b] Heb. iv. 12, 13.    [c] Ps. cv. 7.
[d] Ib. xxxv. 24.    [e] Ib. cxxxix. 23.    [f] Ib. cxliii. 2.

Christ Jesus in Person. "For," as the Judge Himself has told us, "the Father judgeth no man, but hath committed all judgment unto the Son."[a] And so, as St. Paul taught the Athenians, "God hath appointed a day, in which He will judge the world in righteousness by that Man Whom He hath ordained; whereof He hath given assurance unto all men, in that He hath raised Him from the dead."[b] And, accordingly, "we must all appear before the judgment-seat of Christ, that every one may receive the things done in his body, according to that he hath done, whether it be good or bad."[c] And then "every eye shall see Him, and they also which pierced Him; and all the kindreds of the earth shall wail because of Him."[d] Yes, Lord Jesus, "we believe that Thou shalt come to be our Judge."

And as the Last Judgment will be administered by a visible Judge—by our dear Lord, Who was crucified for us, and rose from the grave and ascended into Heaven—so it will be final. There will be no appeal, no rehearing, no reversal possible. Every grace corresponded to or neglected will be taken into account. Every thought, word, act, habit, that has gone to make us what we shall have become; and every thought, word, act, from childhood to the dying hour, contributes something;—all will be taken fully, unerringly, into the reckoning. If there could be error, there would be room for reconsideration; but where all is weighed by Absolute Love and Justice; where each award is seen to be, not the dictate of supreme caprice, but the necessary resultant effect of those moral laws which could not be other than they are; then we shall understand that such a judgment must be final. And thus, in the Epistle to the Hebrews, it is called an

[a] St. John v. 22.      [b] Acts xvii. 31.
[c] 2 Cor. v. 10.      [d] Rev. i. 7.

"eternal judgment,"[a] meaning a judgment from which there is no appeal in the new and everlasting ages; and the dream of a lapse of the blessed, or of the restoration of the lost, must be dismissed as finding no warrant whatever in the words of Christ.

We cannot easily picture to ourselves this judgment; but that does not prove that it will not take place. When men had not yet crossed the equator, the old Greeks could not believe the report of some travellers who said that at noon their shadows had fallen towards the south. Our little world of experience is no measure of the eternal realities; our limited idea of time does not enable us to argue that, because as yet *the* day has not come, it will never come. The French saying, that "nothing is probable, except the unforeseen," has a great element of truth in it; and the day of the Lord will come, when it comes, as a thief in the night.

To-day we are on the eve of an event which will be in a sense historical; to-morrow Her Majesty the Queen is to open the New Law Courts. For some years past the splendid pile has been rising, and it is now in a large measure completed; but the great artist who designed it[b] has not been spared to witness the fruit of his genius and his toil. For many days or weeks past, the inaugural ceremony has been in preparation; and to-morrow will open a new chapter in the history of the great profession of the law.

We do not see them, but most assuredly preparations have been and are going on for another occasion, infinitely more momentous. Human justice is a shadow of the Justice of God, and the palace in which it is administered may suggest that more awful audience-chamber,

---

[a] Heb. vi. 2.

[b] George Edmund Street, Esq., R.A. He died December 10, 1881.

whose Judgment-seat is the Great White Throne, and whose officers are the high intelligences of Heaven, and at whose bar we shall all of us, small and great, stand one day, to be acquitted or condemned. Even now the angels are moving to and fro throughout the realms of the living and of the dead, to prepare for that supreme moment, when, in the counsels of God, all will at last be ready, and the Judge will be seen on the clouds of Heaven.

"Looking for and hasting unto the coming of the day of God." That is St. Peter's account of the way in which a Christian should live. Does this description apply to us? Is our present relation of faith and love to our Lord Jesus Christ of such a character that we can look forward with humble confidence to being accepted in Him? Or are we whirling on through the advancing years of this brief life; whirling on towards that tremendous future, and closing our eyes as the flash of premonitory lightning breaks ever and anon from the Heavens, stopping our ears to the roll of the distant thunders of the eternal storm? This is indeed a vital question; and its bearing upon human life, in the departments of the understanding, the affections, and the will, will, please God, be the subject of our consideration during the remaining Sundays of Advent.

# SERMON XXXV.

## THE DAY OF JUDGMENT AND THE UNDERSTANDING.

(SECOND SUNDAY IN ADVENT.)

2 ST. PET. III. 12.

*Looking for and hasting unto the coming of the day of God.*

THE solemn truth that a day is coming, at a date known only to the Eternal Mind, when God will judge the secrets of men by Jesus Christ His Son, was said last Sunday to have important bearings on the understanding, the heart, and the will of man. And obviously this truth, like any other truth, must address itself in the first place to the understanding. If a man is to take St. Peter's advice, and be "looking for and hasting unto the coming of the day of God," his understanding must hold out some kind of welcome to it. The mind has its eyes, its range of vision, its horizons, no less than the body ; and the use of the mental eyesight is just as much under our control as the use of the bodily eyesight. And just as astronomers predict the arrival of a comet, or the transit of Venus, or an eclipse of the sun or moon, and we, who cannot follow their calculations, get ready our glasses, and hope, if the weather permits, to make the most of the sights for which they prepare us, so it is with the spiritual realities which are foretold by Christ and His Apostles. Only in this last case no dates are given; "of that day and that hour knoweth no man." [a] No dates are given, in order that we may be constantly watching. "Watch, therefore, for ye know neither the day nor the hour when the Son of Man cometh." [b] But the eye of the mind has its duty assigned to it; it is to be constantly "looking for the coming of the day of God."

Here it is well to consider how great may be the influence of an idea or truth kept steadily in view during a long term of years. History is full of illustrations of this. Almost all men who have achieved anything considerable, whether in active life or in literature, whether in the world or in the Church, have done so under the influence of an overmastering idea. Doubtless there are ideas and ideas; ideas which, like fleeting clouds, only please or entertain us for a passing moment; and ideas which, having been received into the mind as convictions, give a direction to the whole course of life, and permanently mould the thoughts and the character. If an idea is to be fruitful, it must be believed to be true; nobody is really influenced by that which he holds to be the work of fancy. If an idea is to be fruitful, it must be made a great deal of; it must be dwelt on often and perseveringly by the mind which perceives it; it must remain, as it were, in attendance, always ready to claim an audience when thought is not otherwise engaged; it must make itself welcome during the intervals of work, during the stated hours of recreation, during the spare minutes in which we pass from one duty to another. It is these recurring importunate ideas which really mould and govern us. It is during these spare moments of life when, letting our thoughts take their own course, we instinctively

<hr>

[a] St. Mark xiii. 32.  [b] St. Matt. xxv. 13.

fall back on that which lies nearest to our hearts, that
we can often best discover the direction in which we are
moving, and the kind of convictions which have a real hold
upon, and are shaping our characters. In this way an
idea will in time saturate the whole texture of the mind
and temper ; it will be so appropriated as to become part
of a man's very self; it will reappear unbidden in his
language and conduct, and without any new sense of
intellectual effort ; it will in the end control him, so that
he will become not so much its possessor as its servant ;
not so much the conscious owner and producer of a mental
treasure as the almost unconscious instrument of a domi-
nant force.

Take as an illustration the life of Von Stein, the North
German patriot who witnessed the humiliation and ruin
of his country in the days of the First Napoleon. Stein
was a man of one idea ; how to enable his country first to
throw off the yoke of France, and next to defend herself
in the future against French aggression. How this idea
haunted, possessed, controlled him ; how it enabled him
to work and struggle, when all around him had well-nigh
lost hope ; how it upheld him against powerful opposition
and great discouragement in unexpected quarters ; how,
under its light and impulse, he wrote, and entreated, and
protested, and organized ; how, at last, others awoke from
their stupor and were fired by his patriotism ; and then
how the effort became more and more general, until at
last it became completely national ;—all this has been
lately told us again by an accomplished writer. And we
of this generation have seen the full result. Not only
did Stein contribute largely to the German resistance to
the First Napoleon, but the impulse which he gave has
lasted on to our time ; and the Prussia which conquered
at Sadowa, and at Gravelotte, and at Sedan, and which

made Berlin the capital of the most powerful of European States, was very largely the work of Stein; the result of his devoted obedience to the idea which possessed him in early life. And if this is the power of an idea, when concerned with the things of sense and time, what may we not expect when man's endless destiny is in question, and all that it implies now and here!

In religious history, the power of a single truth, constantly dwelt upon, has been again and again shown by the lives of the great servants of God. St. Paul, after his conversion, surrendered himself to one ruling and practical idea; the conversion of the heathen to the faith of Christ, and their incorporation, together with the Jews, into one Catholic or world-embracing Church. "Unto me, who am less than the least of all saints, was this grace given, that I should preach among the Gentiles the unsearchable riches of Christ; and to make all men see what is the fellowship of the mystery, which from the beginning of the world hath been hid in God;"[a] that is, what it is to be one with our Lord Jesus Christ, Whose Incarnation and Death for the salvation of man, ever present to the Eternal counsels, have been at last revealed in time. To this idea, as we know, St. Paul devoted his life. And what the conversion of the heathen was for St. Paul, that the translation and explanation of the Holy Scriptures was for St. Jerome; and the vindication of the necessity and operations of God's grace in the salvation of man for St. Augustine; and the introduction of Christian principles into civil and social life for Savonarola; and the exposure of the intellectual difficulties of Deism, considered as an assailant of Christianity, for Bishop Butler; and the evangelization of Central Africa for the late Bishop Steere. And to most of us will occur the names of some men or women,

[a] Eph. iii. 8, 9.

moving in less public spheres, who have, early in life,
given themselves up to be controlled by one ruling conviction, and have carried out its behests through a long
succession of years. The enunciation of one forgotten
truth, the reform of one conspicuous abuse, the resistance
to one form of besetting evil, the practice of some one
much-needed virtue; these have inspired, do inspire lives,
and everything, or almost everything, about them can be
seen in the retrospect to be governed by it. It may be
said that such men are sometimes narrow; but human
nature is what it is, and if you would make a small
stream of water turn a large wheel, you must confine it in
a narrow channel. In the case of the majority of men, to
be interested in a great many ideas is to be feeble and
unfruitful in action; the dissipation of interest means a
corresponding loss of force. But a single truth really
accepted and acted on means great moral power and fruit-
fulness, and it means this because it moulds, first, thought,
and then character, in the way which has been described.

Let us apply this to the matter before us. If a man
really does look for and haste towards the coming of the
day of God, his life cannot but be profoundly influenced
in a great many ways; but it will be influenced first of all
in the department of his understanding. This, we must
here remember, is the point now more immediately before
us; we have to answer the question, How is human
thought affected by belief in a coming day of God?

## I.

The expectation of a coming day of God affects Christian thought, in the first place, by reminding us of what
human life really is and means.

There are a great many side views, so to call them,

which we men are in the habit of taking of our human nature. Some of us are physiologists, and we are entirely absorbed in considering the structural peculiarities of man's animal frame. Some of us are psychologists, and we are no less interested in observing, cataloguing, analyzing, the various powers of the human mind. Some in our day seem curiously bent upon degrading the idea of man to a point at which it is impossible to make out, from the accounts they give of him, that he differs in any serious respect from the higher apes. Others are no less determined to exalt him to the first place—I do not say in creation, for creation implies a Creator, Whose existence they deny, but—in the whole existing universe. Man, whatever be the history of his bodily frame, is said to be the highest being known to himself, since the invisible is only another word for the imaginary. Man is the being, so we are told, in whom the Divine soul of nature attains to consciousness of its own existence ; as a French Pantheist, in reply to a question " what he was doing on that sofa," answered, " I am adoring my own divinity." Now the expectation of a Day of Judgment breaks in upon these sickly delusions with a trenchant emphasis. Springing as it does out of the very idea of duty, being as it is the inseparable concomitant of a reasoned conception of right and wrong —as the Law planted within us by a Moral Being Who must have the will and the power to enforce it — the expectation of a coming judgment at once raises man into his true place, as the first of created beings here below, while it also keeps him there. Whatever may be said about the resemblance of our animal frames to that of the higher apes, we know that, unlike the apes, we have a law of duty in our heart, a conscience by which we shall be judged, and that in this we differ from all creatures below us. Whatever may be said about man,

as the highest existing being of which Science can take
account, and therefore, as is often but unwisely assumed,
the highest actually in existence, we know that we have
an account to give for our faithfulness to the law of
Right and Wrong within us, and that this of itself implies the existence of a Being Who differs from us as does
the Creator from the creature. In short, the knowledge
that we have to be judged at once guarantees our dignity
and defines our subordination. It is only as moral beings,
having free-will, that we are capable of undergoing judgment at all; and, as having to undergo it, we cannot
but be infinitely below Him Whose right and duty it is
to judge us.

## II.

A second way in which the expectation of the day
of God powerfully affects Christian thought is that it
illuminates the sense of responsibility.

The sense of responsibility is as wide as the moral
sense of man; it is co-extensive with the human race.
Ask any man whom you meet in the street whether he
is a responsible agent; and what will he reply? If he
is not offended at the question he will say, "Of course
I am; I am in possession of my senses." He can draw
no distinction between having his faculties at command
and being responsible. "Responsibility" is, with ninety-
nine men out of a hundred, another word for being of
sound mind. To know that right differs from wrong,
to know that certain things are right and that certain
things are wrong, is practically to know that we are
responsible for what we do or leave undone, for what we
say or leave unsaid, for the thoughts which we encourage
or dismiss, as the case may be.

"Responsible!" Yes; but to whom? What does

responsibility mean? It means having to give an account of what we are, do, and say; but an account points to some one who will receive and has a right to exact it. We cannot be responsible to an idea, to a sentiment, to an abstraction, to the blue heavens or to the vasty deep. This primal idea, rooted in our first instinctive perceptions of moral truth, that we are responsible beings, necessarily implies that some one exists to whom this responsibility is due. Who is it? We look around us, and we see—most of us—some fellow-creature to whom we have to answer for our good conduct. The child knows that he must answer for it to his parents; to his mother in early, and to his father in later, years. The schoolboy thinks of his master; the clerk of his employer; the curate of his vicar or his bishop; the soldier of his commanding officer. As we mount higher in the scale of society, it may seem at first that there are personages so exalted as to be subject to no human masters to whom responsibility is due. But in reality it is otherwise. Those who govern us are answerable to what is called public opinion for their conduct of public affairs; that is to say, they have to give an account, not to one, but to many millions of their countrymen; and it would be difficult to name any situation in life in which there is not somebody entitled at some time or other to exact an account of the proceedings of its occupant.

But if conscience speaks to us at all with clearness and honesty, it tells us one thing about the responsibility which we owe to our fellow-creatures; and this is that such responsibility covers only a small part of our actual conduct. A great deal goes on in every life which is either right or wrong, yet for which a man feels in no way accountable to any human critic or authority whatever. Is he, therefore, really not accountable for acts and words which do not fall under any human jurisdiction? Does conscience, when fairly cross-questioned, limit responsibility strictly to that part of our life of which our fellow-creatures can or ought to take account?

We know that it is not so. And this knowledge obliges us to look above and beyond this human world for One to Whom our responsibility is really due. As He only can take account of much which is withdrawn from the eyes of our fellow-men, so He assuredly does take account of all in which others may have a right to judge us. We are responsible at times to our fellow-men; we are always responsible to our God.

"We are responsible to God." Yes, all who seriously believe that He exists, as the Moral Governor of this world which He has made, must admit this responsibility. But then the question arises, When is the account to be rendered? That God keeps His Eye on it day by day, in the case of every one of us, is as certain as that He exists. But suppose this account to be perpetually made up, yet without any prospect of a settlement; like the books of an estate, which are regularly kept, while the rents are never asked for during half a century. Would not the sense of responsibility towards a Ruler, believed to be so little careful to vindicate His rights, die gradually away into a mere phrase, meaning at first very little, and then meaning nothing?

So it is, depend upon it, with men who, professing to hold themselves answerable to God for their lives, do not believe in a judgment after death. It is faith in a future judgment which makes the sense of responsibility living and operative, by making the prospect of a reckoning definite and concrete. If we mean the Creed when we say that the Crucified and Risen Christ has "ascended into Heaven, and sitteth at the Right Hand of God the

Father Almighty, from whence He shall come to judge the quick and the dead," we mean by our being responsible creatures something unspeakably solemn, which cannot but colour our whole thought and deeply influence our conduct.

## III.

Once more, belief in a coming day of God affects our whole view of human history and of human life.

When we take up a volume of ancient history, or of the history of our own country, of what does the narrative mainly consist? It describes royal and noble personages succeeding one another; their birth and training, their coronations, their weddings, their successes, their failures, their deaths, sometimes tragical enough, their reputations in their own and succeeding times. It describes the varying fortunes of multitudes of human beings, associated together as a nation; their privations, their conquests, their gradual improvement, their progressive degeneracy, the hopes which animate them, the passions which agitate them, the benefits which they are able to confer on the world, the crimes for which they are collectively responsible. We read page after page, chapter after chapter, volume after volume; we read of centuries, epochs, dynasties, modes of thought and feeling, succeeding each other; and the long procession passes before us until the mind grows wearied, and takes refuge in general impressions, and above all in the idea of the perpetuity of change. And thus we speak of this or that personage as going off the scene, as though no more were to be said about human life than that

" All the world's a stage,
And all the men and women merely players."

And we find ourselves talking of masses of human beings

as of counters who are from time to time cleared off the board. In short, we read history too often as though it told us all that was to be said about man; as though when he had done with life there was really an end of him.

Ah! we forget the truth which makes history so inexpressibly pathetic, that all is not really over with those whom it describes; they have only ceased to be visible; and the most important part of their career yet awaits them, namely, the account they have to give of it.[a]

All those kings and queens, those generals, those rebels, those favourites of fortune, as we call them, those children of sorrow, all those multitudes of people of whose general circumstances history talks with such an airy off-handedness, while every unit that composed them had a heart and mind that was and is as dear to the God Who made it as that of any monarch or ruler of men—they all live on now, though we do not see them. Our Saxon forefathers and the Britons whom they so ruthlessly exterminated; our Alfred, and William the Conqueror, and Rufus, and Cœur de Lion, and John; the great Plantagenets; the Edwards, and the Henries; Elizabeth, and Mary Stuart; Charles, and Cromwell; the Georges, and the Pretenders; the great English statesmen of the beginning of this century, and the men of the French Revolution; and, no less they who left us but yesterday. All these are no mere names, they are still living beings. And one pathetic fact is common to all of them; they are waiting for the Final Judgment, and each of them already knows enough to know what it will mean for him.

And this view of history, considered in the light of a coming Day of Judgment, extends itself at once and inevitably to human life in our own day and around us. Our first and, so to call it, natural view of human beings

[a] Cf. Newman, *Par. Serm.*, iv. 6.

around us takes note simply of their positions in this
world, and of the points wherein they differ from or
resemble ourselves. We think of them as better or
worse off; as more or less educated; as friendly, or as
distant acquaintances; as belonging to a past or to a
younger generation, or to our own; as standing in this
or that relation to the public life of the country; as
belonging to this or that profession; as occupying this,
or that, or a third position in the social scale. But once
let us have steadily thought upon the truth that, like ourselves, every human being that lives is certainly on trial,
and has judgment before him; and how insignificant do
all other considerations about our fellow-creatures appear
in the light of this solemn fact! Yes! those possessors
of vast influence, which they use, if at all, for selfish ends;
those owners of accumulated wealth, which they spend so
largely, if not altogether, upon themselves; those men of
cultivated minds, who regard cultivation as an end in itself,
and without a thought of what it may be made to do for
others or for the glory of God; those tens of thousands
who have had no opportunities, no education worth speaking of, nothing but a long struggle with discouragement
and misery, with or without light enough to make them
fully answerable for what they have become to the Author
of their life;—yes, the consideration that all will be judged,
and that every hour that passes brings all nearer to the
judgment, makes us think of human life around us in
quite a new light. All whom we have ever known in
past years, and who now are gone; all of whom we have
caught glimpses; all whom we have seen on one occasion only, without really knowing them; all those whose
careers, viewed from afar, have interested or have shocked
us; all the most winning and lovable characters we have
met with, and all the most selfish and repulsive;—there

they are, hurrying onwards, as if in a confused and tangled
multitude, towards the tremendous scene of the Universal
Judgment. And as with them, so with ourselves. Be our
outward circumstances what they may; whatever our
age, our health, our prospects, the consideration we enjoy,
the anxieties we feel, the hopes we cherish; one thing is
certain, we have to be judged. Well were it if, when we
rise in the morning, we would say, each one to himself,
"The Judgment is before me." Well were it for us if,
ere we lie down to rest at night, we would each one say,
"The Judgment is awaiting me." Well were it for us if,
before each duty we undertake, each recreation we allow
ourselves, each conversation, each act of worship, each
exertion, in whatever way, of our responsibility as men
and as Christians, we could remind ourselves of the real
state of the case, by saying, " I shall one day give account
of this; I have to meet the Day of Judgment."

Surely this must, if anything can, make us tender in
our thoughts of others, and severe in our decisions
respecting ourselves! Surely in this new outlook upon
life we have a warning against the insolence which is
but a concentrated assertion of self, and the scorn which
is impossible when we have sounded the pathos of every
human existence, and the light-hearted indifference which
means an absence of all serious thought whatever respecting the deepest things in human destiny!

Ah! we could not bear to think steadily of human
history, or of human life around us, or of our own unfathomable hopes and fears, in the light of the coming
day of God, if it were not for the Eternal Mercy manifest
in our Lord Jesus Christ, incarnate, crucified, risen, and
ascended for us men and for our salvation. We know
that His mercy is over all His works,[a] though we cannot

a Ps. cxlv. 9.

trace its operation among the intricacies of stubborn or reluctant wills.    We know that He hateth nothing that He has made,[a] and that He forgives the sins of all them that are penitent, though we do not know in whom, by His grace, there have been created new and contrite hearts.    But in His light we may see light;[b] and the thought of judgment is not only tolerable, but welcome, when we reflect that our Judge is also our Saviour, and that He is ever ready to help His servants whom He has redeemed with His precious Blood.

[a] Wisd. xi. 24.                [b] Ps. xxxvi. 9.

# SERMON XXXVI.

## THE DAY OF JUDGMENT AND THE AFFECTIONS.

(THIRD SUNDAY IN ADVENT.)

2 St. Pet. iii. 12.

*Looking for and hasting unto the coming of the day of God.*

LAST Sunday we were engaged in considering some of the effects upon a Christian's habits of thought which are produced by serious expectation of a Day of Judgment. To look for a coming account which has to be given of life, of its secret as well as its public side, of thoughts as well as of words and actions, is to have accepted and to be under the influence of a great principle. This principle makes itself felt in several respects, as colouring and shaping a Christian's mind. It enables us to take and to maintain an accurate measure of our manhood; neither degrading it to the condition of animals, who have no free wills, nor raising it to the rank of the One Being Who has no judgment to undergo from a superior. It makes the sense of responsibility definite and strong, by keeping before the mind's eye the Person to Whom, and the occasion on which, an account of it must be rendered. And it invests human history and human lives around us with a pathetic interest that cannot otherwise be realized; while it lights up within each living man a keen sense of the awfulness of the gift of life, which is, indeed, only tolerable in view of the mercy of God manifested in Jesus Christ our Lord. In these and other ways the expectation of the Day of God shapes and colours Christian thought; imprinting on it a distinct character, which is at once and universally recognized. Certainly, to look and hasten for the coming of the day of God is to live by the light of a great principle; the principle of our accountability, reduced to a definite, concrete, and working form.

And principles give strength and purpose to the understanding. They are the soil into which the tree of the mental life must strike its roots deep and wide; or, rather, they are the rocks around which its roots must entwine themselves, if it is to rear its trunk and branches high into the air without risk of overthrow.

To have learnt in boyhood a number of subjects, which constitute mere separate additions to knowledge, but which do not belong to those guiding and governing facts which we term principles, is to have made no real provision for the stability of the mental life, when it is assailed by the fierce tempests of passion or by the secret corroding action of doubt. And if we are to select a principle which, almost beyond any other, will keep the mind true to its bearings in times of trial, it is the anticipation of the coming day of account.

But this anticipation does not merely affect a Christian's understanding; it provides a satisfaction for his heart.

## I.

What, let us ask, is the most necessary condition of human happiness in this life?

Is it the having something to think about? No, most assuredly. We must all know many men, who have full occupation for their thoughts from morning until night, and yet who are far from happy. Is it regular occupation? No doubt regular occupation keeps us out of harm's way, since

> "Satan finds some mischief still
> For idle hands to do."

But no persons are more occupied than the inmates of a convict prison, yet, unless when they are led by God's grace to true repentance, and can accept their lot as coming from Him, and as sent to them in mercy here, that they may be spared hereafter, they cannot be said to be happy. Still less is happiness secured by any outward advantages, such as wealth or station. These are at their best related to the true seat and secret of happiness much as a great-coat is to the action of the heart; they imply the absence of certain external sources of discomfort. But all that is permanently worth having is independent of them; they cannot, at any rate, guarantee its continuance.

Man's most immediate need is something to satisfy his affections. In this particular satisfaction, supposing it to be pure and durable, lies the secret of his happiness. When the Persians conquered Lydia, it was hard, no doubt, for King Croesus to lose both his wealth and his throne; but he learnt to bear the loss resignedly, when his dumb son Gyges, in the agony of defending his father, had gained or had recovered the power of speech.

Here we touch upon one of the secrets of life, which we cannot think over too often or too anxiously. We each of us come into this world furnished with an active pre-disposition towards objects of various kinds without us. This predisposition is "desire." Desire should be in

moral beings what the force of attraction is in material
bodies; it should keep them in their true relations towards other moral beings; it should, above all, keep them
revolving round the Central Sun of the moral world, Whose
light and warmth are essential to their prosperity. When
desire fulfils this its true function, we name it "love;"
it is the love of God keeping the soul of man true
to the law of loyalty to its Almighty and Benevolent
Creator. But desire differs from material attraction in
that it is not a force which operates necessarily; it is
more or less under the control of the being which experiences it. And accordingly, since the Fall, we see in
the moral and human world every variety of perverted
desire; we look out upon a scene of confusion parallel
to that which the heavens would present if it were possible for the planets to detach themselves from the law
which binds them to their revolutions round the sun,
and to dash about wildly through space in search of some
new suns around which to circle. In the moral world,
desire, which is the raw material of supernatural love, is
also the raw material of the grossest forms of earthly
passion; it may develop into one or the other in different circumstances; and the most vital question, perhaps, in every human destiny, is which of the two it
will become; whether it will be purified into the love of
God, carrying the soul continuously upwards towards Him;
or whether it will be degraded into some lower kind of
attachment to matter, burying the soul in its folds, and
imbruting it progressively with each successive indulgence.

In any case, the presence and operation of desire is one
of the most important, if not the most important fact in
human nature; it is the material out of which, on this
side saints, and on that sinners, are being fashioned every
hour that passes.

# II.

Man's first need, then, in order to his true happiness, is the right satisfaction of desire. How has this been provided for?

No doubt a great provision for our happiness has been made in the love of our fellow-creatures, and especially of those who are related to us by the ties of blood. On this account a man feels in his home a tranquil happiness which he misses elsewhere; his affections are drawn out and satisfied by the presence of his nearest relatives. And another and entirely adequate provision for our happiness has been made in the love of God, Whose Eternal and Unfading Beauty alone can lastingly satisfy the affections of the soul which He has made. He is Himself the true Provision for the happiness of His reasonable creatures. He has made them for Himself, and their hearts are restless till they rest in Him.[a] But the objects of our home affections fail us; they are withdrawn from our sight, and leave our hearts sore and blank; or they disappoint us by some conduct which is destructive of that likeness of the Eternal Beauty which is what we really loved in them. And as for the love of the Invisible, Immaterial, Infinite, Incomprehensible Being, do we not often find that even good men speak of it as if it were rather something which they ought to know by experience than something which they do know; as if God were too remote, and His attributes too abstract, and the air of Heaven too refined and rare, for the constant vivid exercise on the part of the human soul of anything that could be properly called love? I am not saying that this is right—God forbid; I am de-

[a] St. Augustine, *Confessions*, Bk. i. [i.] § 1.

scribing a matter-of-fact weakness of human nature. And the question is whether any provision has been made for our truest happiness, by rendering it easier to love with that kind of love that we give to our fellow-creatures, yet without risk of disappointment in its object; to love as we should love the Infinitely Perfect and Beautiful Life of God, yet without the accompanying sense of making a wasteful expenditure of desire upon the abstract and the inaccessible.

Now, this want has been supplied by our Lord Jesus Christ, very God and very Man. He presents Himself to us in many characters; as the Author of our salvation,[a] as the Revealer of the Father,[b] as the Judge of the quick and dead.[c] But especially does He come to us as the rightful Object of our love. He dares, He alone dares, to undertake to satisfy this fathomless desire of the human soul; and to claim its affections as due to Himself, that He may thus satisfy them. "Love Me," He says in effect, 'and in loving Me you combine the love of God with the love of man; love Me, and you love One Who will never fail or disappoint you; love Me, and you love the Immaterial and Self-existent, but presented to you under the veil of sense, coming to you in your own human nature, and so able to claim the warmest homage of your hearts." And this love, He urges, must take precedence of all other love. "Whosoever loveth father or mother more than Me is not worthy of Me;"[d] "If a man love Me, he will keep My words."[e] And His Apostles, in like manner: "Grace be with all them that love our Lord Jesus Christ in incorruptedness;"[f] "If any man love not the Lord Jesus Christ, let him be Anathema Maran-atha."[g]

<hr />

[a] Heb. v. 9.   [b] St. Matt. xi. 27.   [c] Acts x. 42.
[d] St. Matt. x. 37.   [e] St. John xiv. 23.
[f] Eph. vi. 24.   [g] 1 Cor. xvi. 22.

In short, love of Jesus Christ is to be the central feature
of the life of Christians; since love implies faith in its
Object; and love prompts obedience to the Will of its
Object; and love is quick and sensitive to all that
implies inward disloyalty and decay of that which its
Object loves; and so love is the very soul of growth in
holiness, at once supplying its impulse and determining
its form.   Yes; the love which our Lord claims, and
which, by His grace, true Christians give Him, is the
central feature of the Christian life.

What are the grounds of the love of our Lord?

What is it, let us ask ourselves, that provokes love?
Surely, always and everywhere, beauty.   The lower forms
of love are provoked by physical beauty, the higher by
moral and spiritual beauty; but it is beauty, both at this
and that end of the scale, that challenges man's love.
And our Lord presents Himself as the Eternal Beauty,
rendered intelligible by being translated into the language
and actions of a human life; veiled beneath the outward
accidents and incidents of our common lot in this world;
but not hidden from those who have eyes to trace and
ears to hear the everlasting harmonies.   "Never man
spake like this Man;"ᵃ "I find no fault in Him;"ᵇ
"Truly this was the Son of God;"ᶜ "The world is gone
after Him."ᵈ   This was not the language of disciples, but
it seems to account for the impression which was made on
disciples.   "Lord, to whom shall we go? Thou hast the
words of eternal life;"ᵉ "Depart from me; I am a sinful
man, O Lord;"ᶠ "We believe and are sure that Thou art
the Christ, the Son of the Living God."ᵍ

Not that a man need always be a believer to recognize

---

ᵃ St. John vii. 46.        ᵇ *Ib.* xviii. 38.        ᶜ St. Matt. xxvii. 54.
          ᵈ St. John xii. 19.                ᵉ *Ib.* vi. 68.
          ᶠ St. Luke v. 8.                    ᵍ St. John vi. 69.

the beauty of the Life recorded in the Gospels; to enter
into such scenes as that of our Lord and the adulteress;[a]
or into such addresses as the Sermon on the Mount.[b] Unbelievers have acknowledged the classic perfection of many
parts of the Gospel narrative; and we, who know our Lord
as a living Being, owe them more than the cold, although
sincere, admiration which we might yield to lines of beauty
traced on canvas or chiselled in marble; we know that a
Human Heart still owns what It thus inspired, whether
in word or act, eighteen centuries ago; and we love our
living Lord by reason of the incomparable moral beauty
of this His manifestation of Himself in time.

But, secondly, love is provoked by sacrifice; the sacrifice of self. Such sacrifice is the essence of love itself,
since love is the gift of self, and love rouses love by the
very energy of its own existence. And our Lord appeals to
this motive for loving Him: "Greater love hath no man
than this, that a man lay down his life for his friends."[c]
Jesus "having loved His own that were in the world, He
loved them unto the end;"[d] He expressed His love in the
last humiliations and agonies of death. He died for us
that we, whether we wake or sleep, should by the tie of
love live together with Him.[e] Nothing has won the love
of heathen savages like the story of the Passion; and for
this reason, that that story is throughout the language
which every human heart can understand; it is the
language of love. "God so loved the world, that He gave
His only begotten Son;"[f] He gave "Him that loved us,
and hath washed us from our sins in His own Blood, and
hath made us kings and priests unto God and the
Father."[g]

---

[a] St. John viii. 1-11.   [b] St. Matt. v.–vii.   [c] St. John xv. 13.
[d] *Ib.* xiii. 1.   [e] 1 Thess. v. 10.   [f] St. John iii. 16.   [g] Rev. i. 5, 6.

And here we see how the love of our Lord combines, and while it combines, purifies and spiritualizes the two strongest forms of affection which a man can feel in this life; love for his mother and love for his wife. What is it that provokes love for a mother ? It is first the experience, and then the recollection of her incessant sacrifice of self; it is her anxious, watchful, importunate care ; it is that language which has no meaning, those glances which are even unintelligible, that devotion which is so exaggerated, except in the judgment of love, to which, indeed, it has all the meaning and sense and ingenuity of nature. And what is it in a bride that provokes love ? It is beauty, whether the lower beauty of physical form, or the higher beauty of mind and character ; beauty, it may be, idealized and over-estimated ; beauty which, on nearer acquaintance, may conceivably prove to be other than strictly beautiful; but still it is beauty, whether imagined or real, which thus invites and secures the homage of love. And these two separate streams of a man's experience—his love for his mother and his love for his bride—meet and roll into one mighty tide of passionate affection at the Feet of the Divine Redeemer, Who bids us love Him as Moral Beauty and as self-sacrificing Love ; and thus from the heart of Christendom there goes up incessantly, from age to age, and from generation to generation, the cry, "Thou art the King of Glory, O Christ. . . . When Thou tookest upon Thee to deliver man, Thou didst not abhor the Virgin's womb. When Thou hadst overcome the sharpness of death, Thou didst open the Kingdom of Heaven to all believers." And urged by this double motive, love protests, "Whom have I in Heaven but Thee? and there is none upon earth that I desire in comparison of Thee."[a]

[a] Ps. lxxiii. 24.

This may lead us to note the proper use of one of the books of the Old Testament, the place of which in the Canon of Scripture is not easily to be accounted for, on grounds of internal evidence, if it be read only in its first or literal sense. The Song of Solomon is the account of a Shunamite maiden of singular grace and beauty, who is taken by the great king of Israel from her quiet northern home, and raised by him to the height of earthly happiness and honour as his bride and queen. How he won her love on a spring morning; how she dreamed of him at night; how he persuaded her to forsake the village of her birth; how, amid the splendours of his palace, she retained the simplicity and sweetness of her earlier years; how her thoughts turned again to the scenes of her youth; to the walnut-garden where she first had met the king, to the sacred dances of the northern country-folk; and how their vows were finally sealed when they revisited the bride's birthplace;—all this may be an idealized picture of the married state, while there are passages up and down the book which make any interpretation of this kind, to say the least, difficult. But suppose that we interpret this book as really intended by the Holy Spirit to form a manual for Christian times; and that it is an ideal representation of the communion of love between Christ and His believing Church, based on the earlier election of Israel; suppose that we see thus under the letter a second and deeper meaning, as in the Epistle to the Galatians we are taught to see one in the history of Isaac and Ishmael,[a] and in the Epistle to the Hebrews in the history of Melchizedek,[b] and in the early Fathers of the Church in large portions of the Old Testament; suppose that we recall St. Paul's comparison, when writing to the Ephesians, of the relation between Christ and His Church with that between a

[a] Gal. iv. 21-31.  [b] Heb. v.-vii.

bridegroom and a bride,[a] and that with this key in our hands
we read through this singular and interesting book, we shall
find, at any rate, in it, a striking and consistent meaning
which will more than explain its place in the Sacred Canon.
And thus we shall understand how the greatest and wisest
Christians have repeated the language of the bride, as not
more than an adequate expression of their devotion to the
Divine Redeemer.

> " O set me as a signet on Thine heart,
> A signet on Thine arm :
> For love is strong as death ;
> Inflexible is jealousy as Hell :
> Her flames are flames of fire,
> A lightning-flash from the Eternal.
> Many waters cannot quench this love,
> Nor water-streams overwhelm it :
> Though one should give his all to buy it,
> With scorn should he be scorned." [b]

## III.

Our Lord Jesus Christ, then, is the Supreme Object of
Christian affection ; He perfectly satisfies the desire of
the heart of man, and, in satisfying it, He purifies and
raises it to the highest form of love.   He it is " Whom,
not having seen, we love ; in Whom, though now we see
Him not, yet believing, we rejoice with joy unspeakable
and full of glory." [c]   But love is exacting ; and it is not
satisfied unless its object is constantly before its eyes.
And our Lord Jesus Christ, as we know, has not been
visibly present among us since His Ascension into
Heaven.   He knew full well what His departure would
mean for His affectionate disciples.   He softened the
blow by promises which we actually enjoy, of His Invisible Presence among us, by the agency of His Spirit,

[a] Eph. v. 23-32.      [b] Song of Sol. viii. 6, 7.      [c] 1 St. Pet. i. 8.

under the veils of His Sacraments, in the hearts and lives
of His true servants. "It is expedient for you that I go
away: for if I go not away, the Comforter will not come
unto you;"[a] "I will not leave you comfortless: I will
come unto you;"[b] "Lo, I am with you alway, even unto
the end of the world."[c] And thus "the tabernacle of God
is" still "with men,"[d] in His Church; and every Christian
may say, "I have found Him Whom my soul loveth."[e]

And yet something must be wanting, or Heaven would
be so fully upon earth in the Christian's soul as to have
lost the attractiveness which belongs to a still future
good; something must be wanting, or there would be no
room in the Christian soul for hope. What is that something but the *visible* Presence of Christ? Faith is, in
one sense, sight; but it is a second sight rather than a
direct sight; it is the evidence of things *not* seen.[f] The
promise which is still unfulfilled is that "we shall see
Him as He is;"[g] that, in the deeper sense of Isaiah's
saying, "thine eyes shall see the King in His Beauty."[h]

This promise appeals to elements of love which have
their counterpart in our natural experience in this life.
Some of you can remember—it may be across an interval
of a quarter or half a century—what it was to leave home
and go to school for the first time. In many a life, the
keen distress of those hours is never forgotten, as it
never repeats itself. You remember how the day of
departure at last arrived; how everything was done that
affection could suggest to disguise its character; how—
just as if you were capable of taking an abstract view of
your case from outside—you were told to be thankful
that your parents had the means of sending you to school

---

[a] St. John xvi. 7.  [b] *Ib.* xiv. 18.  [c] St. Matt. xxviii. 20.
[d] Ezek. xxxvii. 27.  [e] Song of Sol. iii. 1.  [f] Heb. xi. 1.
[g] 1 St. John iii. 2.  [h] Isa. xxxiii. 17.

at all; and then how at last the thing was done, and the
last trace of home had vanished, and you were left face
to face with the not unkindly yet strange and grim
countenance of the master, and with the boys who were
to be your companions, but who as yet eyed you as if
you were a wild creature, whose nature had yet to be
investigated. You remember, perhaps, how, when the
first anguish was over, and things were getting better, and
indeed, in a way, enjoyable, you yet made a calendar,
perhaps on a stick or on a desk, and counted day by day
the time that must pass before the holidays should arrive,
when home, now precious to you as it had never been
before, would be revisited.

Or, in later life, some near relation has left you for a
distant colony, and is expected to return. What will he be
like? Will you know him? Will he know you? What
will he say when he first sees you? What will you say
or do in the transport of that anticipated meeting?

Or, as actually happened to Israel, a people is exiled
from their fatherland; among "a nation of fierce countenance," whose words they cannot understand;[a] "where
they sit in darkness and the shadow of death, being fast
bound in misery and iron;"[b] where oppression, imprisonment, torture, death, are their daily portion. Then their
ancient home, with its sanctuary and its worship, acquires
in their eyes a value which they never felt so consciously
before. "If I forget thee, O Jerusalem, let my right hand
forget her cunning: if I do not remember thee, let my
tongue cleave to the roof of my mouth."[c] How they pray
for the day when they will be again restored to their
country! "Wilt Thou not turn again, and quicken us
that Thy people may rejoice in Thee?"[d] "For why? Thy

---

[a] Deut. xxviii. 49, 50.        [b] Ps. cvii. 10.
[c] *Ib.* cxxxvii. 5, 6.        [d] *Ib.* lxxxv. 6.

servants think upon her stones, and it pitieth them to see her in the dust. The heathen shall fear Thy Name, O Lord, and all the kings of the earth Thy Majesty; when the Lord shall build up Zion, and when His glory shall appear." [a] "Turn Thee again, O Lord God of Hosts, look down from Heaven: behold, and visit this vine." [b]

Thus the human heart plays around the Object of affection—for awhile separated from sight, but to be here-after restored to it—with a persistent and delicate inten-sity which shows what depths of affection there are in the nature which we wear.

And yet, as I have said, these are but shadows; shadows of that great return home, of that meeting of all meetings, of that restoration to the Object of the heart's best affec-tions which awaits us all. What will it be for those who have indeed loved Him, to see Him coming on the clouds of Heaven, with ten thousand of His saints, to be admired of all them that believe? [c] What will it be to behold that Crucified Form, still bearing the Wounds with which for love of us He was pierced on earth, but radiant and glorious beyond all that imagination can conceive, at the moment of the final award? What will it be to see in His train or in His keeping those whom, in Him and for His sake, we have loved best on earth, and who now in their measure are the associates of His glory? Ah! there are many anticipations in life; but none that can compare with this, the greatest and the last, to which true love looks forward across all that intervenes. It is because the deepest desire of the Christian soul will be finally and for ever satisfied that, notwithstanding its awfulness, notwithstanding our clinging sense of personal sinfulness, a true Christian is so carried forward by the love of Christ as to be constantly "looking for and hasting

[a] Ps. cii. 14-16.    [b] *Ib.* lxxx. 14.    [c] 2 Thess. i. 10.

unto the coming of that day of God" which will make
Jesus Christ visibly present to him for all eternity. Are
we conscious, brethren, of anything like this expectation
in ourselves? If not, why not? If, by God's grace, we
are, what is the practical form in which such an expectation must express itself? That is a question which we
shall do well to think about, and some answer to which
will be attempted, please God, when we next meet here
in His Presence, a week hence.

# SERMON XXXVII.

## THE DAY OF JUDGMENT AND THE WILL.

(FOURTH SUNDAY IN ADVENT.)

2 St. Pet. iii. 12.

*Looking for and hasting unto the coming of the day of God.*

THE impulsive force of love for our Lord Jesus Christ, directed towards His visible appearance on the clouds of Heaven at the Day of Account, was the subject before us last Sunday afternoon. Love is, in truth, a mighty agent; it surmounts or it pierces obstacles which, to a purely intellectual perception of what is right and true, appear to be, and practically are, insuperable. But love does and is much more than this; it is patient and submissive, as well as enterprising and progressive. And so on this occasion we have to consider how the force, thus set in motion by love for Jesus Christ, will operate; how love will express itself in conduct; or, as the Apostle puts it, "what manner of persons we ought to be in all holy conversation and godliness." [a]

## I.

One effect, then, of a true love of our Lord, in view of His coming to judgment, will be to keep the mind and heart free from distracting forms of excitement.

[a] 2 St. Pet. iii. 11.

Suppose that the day of the Lord is sincerely believed in, while there is no love of our Lord in the soul. The result may be general unsettlement, neglect of plain duty, indeed of all regular occupation. So it was at Thessalonica, in the early part of the Apostolic age. At Thessalonica, as at Athens, St. Paul began his work by laying stress upon Christ's coming to judgment.[a] The fear of the Lord, he knew well, is the beginning of that wisdom[b] which welcomes a revelation of love. His First Epistle to the Thessalonians is full of the subject. He describes the Christian life as " a waiting for the Son of God from Heaven."[c] He tells his Thessalonian converts that he looks upon them as his own hope and crown of rejoicing at Christ's coming.[d] He prays that their hearts may be established unblamable before God, at the coming of our Lord Jesus Christ with all His Saints.[e] He guards them against hopeless sorrowing for the dead, by assuring them that at that day the dead will rise before the living are caught up to meet the Lord in the air.[f] He reminds them that they know perfectly that the day of the Lord cometh as a thief in the night.[g] The prayer of his parting blessing is that their whole spirit and soul and body might be preserved blameless unto the coming of our Lord Jesus Christ.[h]

This constant reference to the Second Coming in one short Epistle led the Thessalonians to think that it was very near at hand; and this impression was deepened by a misunderstanding of the Apostle's language. When he says that " we that remain shall be caught up together with the rising dead in the clouds to meet the Lord in the air,"[i] the Thessalonians did not see that he was associating himself with the Church of all ages, but supposed that he

---

[a] I Thess. i. 9, 10.      [b] Ps. cxi. 10.      [c] I Thess. i. 10.
[d] Ib. ii. 19.      [e] Ib. iii. 13.      [f] Ib. iv. 13–17.
[g] Ib. v. 2.      [h] Ib. 23.      [i] Ib. iv. 17.

was describing something that would certainly happen to
themselves. So, again, the warning that the day would
come as a thief in the night, was understood to mean
not only that it might come at any moment, but that it
would certainly come soon. And when this idea had once
taken possession of the minds of the readers, every allusion to the subject seemed to illustrate it anew; the
Apostle never would have said so much about the Second
Coming unless it was going to happen in a very short
while.

What was the consequence of this illusion?

It is clear, from the Second Epistle to the Thessalonians,
that they were " shaken in mind and troubled," probably,
by addresses of other teachers based upon the language of
the First Epistle. They were in danger of " not standing
fast," and " holding the traditions " as to steady conscientious work "which they had been taught," whether by word
of mouth or by the Apostolic Epistle.[a] Some of them, at
any rate, walked disorderly, and not after the tradition, as
to the true lines of Christian conduct, which had been
received from the Apostles.[b] They would not work at all,
but were busybodies;[c] they forgot the Apostolic command, that " if any man would not work, neither should
he eat." [d] In short, the effect of this belief at Thessalonica in a near approach of the day of God had been to
unfit men for their daily duties; to make them think
that, as all would end so soon, it did not in the meanwhile much matter what was done or what was left
undone.

St. Paul corrects the error which lay at the root of
this disorder. He warns the Thessalonians against un-
authorized uses which were actually made of his name
and authority. He explains that in any case our Lord

<hr />

[a] 2 Thess. ii. 15.    [b] *Ib.* iii. 6.    [c] *Ib.* 11.    [d] *Ib.* 10.

will not come until after the coming of the Antichrist; [a]
and, as the Antichrist had not yet appeared, the greater
event which was to follow was thrown into a more distant future.    He prays that the hearts of his readers
might be directed into the love of God, and the patient
waiting for Christ. [b] Love would teach patience, if nothing
else could ; love would be too sure of its Divine Object on
the Throne of Judgment, to lose its head while its path
yet lay amid the duties and the things of time.

This mistake has been repeated in later ages. Some
modern preachers, more bold than wise, have not seldom
foretold the end of the world at a given date. Sometimes, indeed, they and their hearers have acted as if in
reality they thought nothing less probable than the fulfilment of their predictions ; but sometimes, also, when
they have been sincerely believed, great unsettlement has
resulted. Such unsettlement, or "disorderly walking," [c]
as the Apostle calls it, is in any case inconsistent with the
law of duty and the law of love. Duty prescribes that
what we have to do should be done, whatever may or may
not be coming. The men of the *Birkenhead* knew that
she was sinking, but they never thought of breaking rank ;
since to keep rank was their duty for the moment. And
love is at least a match for duty, in producing this sort of
unselfishness. Disorder and unsettlement are the product
of aroused self-consciousness ; and love forgets self in the
thought of its Divine Object, and lets Him, or rather
begs Him, act as seems best to Him. Love knows that
in quietness and confidence are its strength [d] as well as
its joy.

We are sometimes tempted to think of the last great
day as of some earthly catastrophe ; of a fearful storm,
foretold from some Transatlantic observatory ; or of a

[a] 2 Thess. ii. 8-10,     [b] *Ib.* iii. 5,     [c] *Ib.* 6,     [d] Isa. xxx. 15.

political revolution, which those who are accustomed
to note the signs and causes of popular agitation tell
us is inevitable within a certain limit of time.    In
these cases, no doubt, excitement and unsettlement,
exactly proportioned to the anticipated violence of the
catastrophe, is what we should expect.    The eve of a
revolution has been described more than once ; some of
us may have witnessed it.    You feel that explosion and
disaster are in the air ; that hidden forces are sensibly
at work, and will presently assert themselves.    No one
knows exactly what to do, or what not to do ; there is
pervading uneasiness visibly expressed on the countenances
you pass in the street.    At any moment something un-
toward may be announced as happening ; a rising in the
streets ; a resignation of the Government ; a flight, which
will be historical, perhaps tragical ; an appeal to popular
passions ; and then all the scenes of bloodshed and violence,
whether sudden or premeditated, which are at least possible amid events of this description.    At such a time
settled devotion to work is, to say the least, very difficult ;
no one can say who will be spared or who will escape.    We
are dealing with forces, the effects of which, apart from
the Providence which permits them to operate at all, are
beyond calculation.

Such-like catastrophes are insignificant indeed in comparison with the awful day when God will judge the
world.    And yet on the Day of Judgment there will be
a reason for calmness and self-possession which can never
be so powerful before.    Everything that takes place at
the Day of Judgment will be the direct expression of
a Will That is perfectly loving and holy ; nothing will
be an evil, which such a Will only tolerates for its own
high ends.    And love, expecting the future Judge, pierces
this heart and secret of the judgment ; knows that all

will be well, even though much will be inevitably and
unspeakably awful. Of one thing love is quite sure,
that no real hasting towards the day of the Lord is to be
achieved by a temper which neglects the plain commands
of duty.

## II.

Again, a true love of our Lord, in view of His coming
on the Day of Judgment, is greatly concerned to be doing
the best it can with what He has given in the way of
ability or opportunity. This is our Lord's teaching in
the Parable of the Talents.ᵃ In that parable there are
many lessons for all of us, but there is one in particular
which we cannot lay too seriously to heart. It is the
temptation to do nothing to which the man with one
talent yielded, and because he had one talent only. The
parable is true to nature in its account of the inequalities
which distinguish human beings; inequalities of natural
character, of surrounding circumstances, of distinctive
endowments and gifts; but there is nothing in it which
comes so home to many of us as the conduct of the man
with one talent. For, in truth, we most of us are precisely
in this case; we have just one talent and no more. And
because we have only one, we think, like the man in the
parable, that there is nothing useful to be done with it.
And our Lord, knowing as He does that this is the average
error of a majority of human beings, deals with it with
plain and loving severity. It almost might seem to us
as if for the moment He was taking the side of the well-
to-do against the poor, whether in the things of body or
spirit; as if He were implying that the well-endowed
always make the best use of their gifts, while the poorly
endowed always misuse them.

ᵃ St. Matt. xxv. 14-30.

But this is, of course, a very superficial way of considering what He really does teach in the parable.  No
teacher ever lived who was less likely to flatter the
well-endowed than our Lord.  We know what stern
language He held towards the governing and educated
classes of His time.  We know how He told them that
Tyre and Sidon, with only the opportunities of pagan
cities, would be better off in the Day of Account than the
highly favoured Chorazin and Bethsaida.[a]  If He had any
partialities, it was for the poor, the unfortunate, the unen-
dowed; yet it is to them that He addresses the warning
of this searching parable.  The failings of the well-to-do
are conspicuous and proverbial; their abuse of splendid
gifts and opportunities needs no prophet to point the
moral; they fail in the full glare of publicity, and the
world which notes the failure has no mercy on the fallen.
But it is otherwise with those whose natural endowments,
physical and intellectual, whose education, position, means,
connections, opportunities for action, are all on a small
scale.  They fail as they succeed, in comparative privacy;
they gain as they lose, but little at the best; and they
think too often that their real responsibility is to be
measured by the notice which, whether in failure or
success, they attract from the public, that is to say, from
their fellow-creatures.  And there are passions and temptations to which they are especially likely to yield.

Of these, the worst is envy.  If the man with one talent
had been created alone, it is conceivable that he might
have made the best of his talent.  But he sees around
him others who have two talents, and others with five.
Why should he have less than they?  What is the
principle of this award, so unequal in its decisions?  If
he had had what they have, he would have been capable,

[a] St. Luke x. 13, 14.

he thinks, of doing magnificently well; but as it is, why should he trouble himself, where there is little to waste and little to win? He does not ask himself whether, in view of his capacities, his one talent is all that he can properly administer; he does not ask whether he would not break down under the strain of the greater responsibility; he never considers whether a man who, as it is, is not faithful in that which is least is likely to be faithful also in much.[a] He is too occupied with others to be true with himself; he feels that the endowments which God has given to others and has denied to him are somehow an outrage and an insult to him; and the passion of envy darkens his eye, and stiffens his arm, and freezes his heart.

A great Athenian sage once said that envy was the curse of democracies; and the world, as we all know, is getting more democratic every day. Where all enjoy equal rights, and all are impatient of the idea of superior merit, men forget how much they have, and think only of that which others have and they have not. And thus each stratum in rank or fortune, or mental accomplishments, or influence, or reputation, is regarded with a certain implacable jealousy by the class immediately below it; and, when all ought to be working for the common good, men are separated by fear or hatred; every form of real superiority feels itself menaced; and hearts which should be free and bright are so poisoned as to be unable to enjoy God's good gifts, or to avoid abusing them.

My dear brethren, if we have not this talent, we have that; if we are denied those advantages, we escape the responsibilities which attach to them. Why will the last be first, and the first last, in the future world, but because so often in this the responsibilities of pre-eminent endow-

<hr>

[a] St. Luke xvi. 10.

ments are fatal to its possessors ? The question is not how
many or what talents we have, but the use which we
make of those which we have. Mary of Bethany was not
a wealthy woman, but when her one great opportunity
of service came, she did her little best; she broke her
one precious alabaster box of ointment in honour of our
Lord; and He has made her act and name a praise in His
Church to the end of time.[a] The poor widow had only
two mites for the sacred treasury, but she cast them in;
and no precious thing that has since been contributed
to the cause of God has received such a mark of His
approval.[b] If we have only one talent, it is our all; if
we have five, they are our all; and the man who has five,
and gives only four to God, is infinitely lower, in His
sight, than the man who has one and gives it. Before
Him the highest and most ample gifts are insignificant.
But " the offering of a free heart "[c] is never insignificant;
it is the fulfilment by a moral being of the high purpose
for fulfilling which he was endowed with the privilege of
life.

Here, then, a true love of our Lord, acting in full view
of the Day of Account, imperiously guides the course
and conduct of life. It hustles and turns out of the
windows of the soul the poor and miserable passions of
envy and ingratitude; it concerns itself, not with the
question how much it has to give, but with the joy of
giving whatever it has to give. To be found making the
most of what He has lent, be it much or little; to be
found trimming the lamp, whether it burn with a faint or
with a brilliant flame;—this is the concern of love. It is
by such love as this that the Church was built up; it was
built up, not by the powerful, or the learned, or the
wealthy, but by thousands of poor men and women, whose

[a] St. John xii. 3-8.        [b] St. Luke xxi. 1-4.        [c] Ps. liv. 6.

hearts were filled with the love of our Lord, and who
spent their lives in giving their little all to the cause of
His kingdom and His glory. They lived in the unseen
world rather than in this, in the future rather than in the
present; but by doing this they transformed the present
and visible world into something higher than it had ever
been before: they transformed it by the persistent inten-
sity with which, in life and in death, they were "looking
for and hasting unto the coming of the day of God."

### III.

One other result of the love of our Lord, while "looking
and hasting for the coming of the day of God," will be to
make much of prayer, private and public, as a preparation
for it.

It has been said, more sharply than wisely, that worship is one thing and religion is another. Religion, we
are told, is the investment of practical duty with the glow
of emotion; whereas worship is the mere indulgence of
sentiment, and so is quite alien to the practical character
of true religion. Now, to begin with, both parts of this
description are faulty; it is difficult to say which is more
faulty of the two. Religion is the practical acknowledgment of the rights and claims of God; it cannot exist at
all unless God be sincerely acknowledged to be what He
is; a Moral Being of boundless Power and Wisdom. And
when people talk of a religion of nature, a religion of art,
a religion of poetry, a religion of friendship, and the like
—as if friendship, and poetry, and art, and nature, could
take the place of God in the life of the soul—they are
using insincere language, or they are talking nonsense.
Religion may exist with very little emotion indeed; and
religion covers a much wider field than duty. Nor is

worship truly described as the mere indulgence of sentiment. On the contrary, worship is a most practical employment, into which, as a matter of fact, a great many
people, who have not a particle of sentiment in their
characters, enter with all their hearts. Worship is before
all things a recognition of the rights of God over the
human soul, but it is also an occasion of procuring from
Him benefits which are not otherwise obtainable. And
in public worship we satisfy, after our poor fashion, His
claim to our common thanksgiving and praise. We listen
to His instructions and warnings, conveyed to us, as we
believe, through His written Word; and we obtain from
Him temporal and spiritual blessings, which He gives in
answer to prayer. What is our purpose here to-day, unless
it be "to render thanks for the great benefits that we
have received at His hands, to set forth His most worthy
praise, to hear His most holy Word, and to ask those
things which are requisite and necessary, as well for the
body as the soul"? To a man who really believes in the
existence of a Moral God, Who has made Himself known
to His reasonable creatures, all this is a very practical
proceeding indeed; it cannot be called the indulgence of
sentiment, any more than can any daily duty which conscientious men perform regularly towards their fellow-
creatures or themselves.

But there is an aspect of worship which may easily escape
us, and which should be insisted on in this connection. It
is a preparation for the day of God. It is a rehearsal, to
so say, in view of that great meeting, at which we must
all one day appear and take our parts; it is a method of
accustoming the eye of the soul to sights, and its ear to
sounds, with which after death it will be perforce familiar.
Worship in all its forms is before all things the placing
ourselves in the Presence of God; it is worse than worth-

less if it be not that. God is everywhere; but the essential feature of true worship is that it begins with solemnly recalling this simple but often-forgotten truth. The soul sets God before it; it remembers that God has searched it out and known it; that it cannot go from His Presence,[a] but that it can forget what it cannot escape. And then some one of God's attributes—His Almightiness, or His Mercy, or His Omniscience—is singled out and placed before the soul's eye, just as at the beginning of each of our Collects, and in the strength of this attribute, in other words, because God is what He is, He is asked to grant some petition which the worshipper urges. Now, what is this initial act of prayer, if it be true, and not merely a piece of half-conscious lip-service, but a rehearsal for the day of the Lord? Exactly in the degree in which we understand what we are doing in thus challenging the attention of the Almighty and Infinite Being, do we prepare for that solemn moment when we shall meet our Lord visibly face to Face. And this applies especially to the celebration of the Holy Sacrament of our Lord's Body and Blood, when we approach Him more intimately than at any other time in our earthly pilgrimage, and may learn more easily and thoroughly than on any other occasion how to bear ourselves in the world to come.

Certainly it would greatly help us to offer sincere prayer, if we could always remember that prayer is our best way of training for the world which will open before us on the Judgment Day. At that day, as we fall before our Lord on His Throne of Judgment, we shall, none of us, be tempted to think of anything else than the awful scene before us. How different from now, when so many of us lounge, body and soul, into the presence-chamber of Heaven; and while we obey the conventional postures

[a] Ps. cxxxix. 1-11.

—if we do obey them—of devotion, allow our minds to
dwell continuously on the pleasures, the annoyances, the
efforts, the failures, the personages, the long array of
elaborate trifles, which, except in connection with our
sins, or for purposes of intercession, we ought to have
forgotten utterly as we crossed the threshold of the Temple
of Jesus Christ! If only a true love of Him; a love which
longs for His Advent, and prays to be conformed to His
likeness, could obtain possession of all our hearts; how
would the whole act of prayer become supernatural in
its downright sincerity! How should we not in prayer,
beyond any other occupation, be "looking for and hasting
unto the coming of the day of God"! It may, indeed,
be asked how, strictly speaking, we can hasten towards
the day of God in any of the ways described. Certainly,
my friends, we cannot abridge the interval of time which
parts us from it; but we can, in another sense, make it
nearer to us. Time has no real relation to the life of a
spirit; we must all of us be conscious that at some
periods of our lives time seems to double or treble its
length, while at others long tracts of time pass by without our being aware of it. It is the state of our consciousness by which our nearness to or distance from the
day of God must be practically measured; and this is
profoundly affected by the deliberate calmness, by the
earnest devotion to work, by the use of talents, by the
increased instancy and solemnity of prayer, on which I
have been dwelling. Love is the soul of these things;
and love, as it gazes on its object, forgets the lapse of
what we call time, and we approach, though at a still im-
measurable distance, the secret of His Life, with Whom
one day is as a thousand years, and a thousand years is
but as one day."

" 2 St. Pet. iii. 12.

Already the great Festival has well-nigh overtaken us;[a] and as we listen to the Alleluias of Christmas, the anticipations of the Second Advent seem to be out of place. But let us not forget them, while we kneel before Christ's Altar to-morrow morning. Let us ask Him to make His first Coming to us in the flesh a means whereby, at His second Coming to judge the world, we may be found, through His wonder-working grace, an acceptable people in His sight.

"Even so, come, Lord Jesus."[b] They are the last words of the Apocalypse; the last words in our New Testaments; the last words of our Bibles. They are unintelligible save to the soul which loves our Lord, and which, in its eagerness to see Him, forgets all that intervenes. It forgets the sorrows that may yet await it in time; the last illness; the death-agony; the waiting in the intermediate place of the departed; the long watching, it may be, for that moment, so blessed, yet so awful, which will come at last. It almost forgets, for the instant, how much there is in itself which He cannot approve; how little it can bear the fire of His judgment; or how, although His servant, it can hope to be justified if He enter into judgment with it.[c] But it is thus confident, because He is already not only its Judge but its Saviour, and has "covered" what else He must condemn with His "Robe of Righteousness."[d] One who was present with St. Bernard in his last hour tells us how, when almost at his last gasp, he seemed to himself to be set before God's Judgment-seat, while Satan stood by, loading him with heavy accusations on the score of the sins of his whole life. And then he uttered these his last and often-repeated words: "I confess, Lord, I am not worthy; by my own merits I

---

[a] In 1882 the Fourth Sunday in Advent fell on Christmas Eve.
[b] Rev. xxii. 20.          [c] Ps. cxliii. 2.          [d] Isa. lxi. 10.

cannot win the Kingdom of Heaven. But Thou, my Lord, Who hast a double title to it, one by inheritance from the Father, and the other by the merits of Thy Passion, dost forego the latter and makest it mine. On Thy gift, therefore, I rest my claim, and I am not confounded."

It is in this conviction that we may still say, " Even so, come, Lord Jesus." It is thus that, though filled with a sense of our own unworthiness, and of the awfulness of meeting the All-holy on His Throne of Judgment, we may yet be constrained by a love which in the end will cast out fear, and which even now bids us "look for and hasten unto the coming of the day of God."

# SERMON XXXVIII.

## THE CLOSE OF OPPORTUNITY.

St. Matt. xxv. 10.

*And the door was shut.*

OUR Lord groups His parable of the ten virgins around a metaphor which belongs to all climes and times; the metaphor of a closed and open door. The five wise virgins, you will remember, took oil in their vessels with their lamps. The five foolish virgins took their lamps, but took no oil in them. The ten virgins were thus in their different ways awaiting the marriage-feast; but until the great moment came they all slumbered and slept. Then was heard the midnight cry, "Behold, the bridegroom cometh!" All the ten arose; all the ten trimmed their lamps. But here a tragical difference became apparent. The lamps of the wise burned brightly and strongly; the lamps of the foolish, having no oil, forthwith went out. Just at the critical moment, when all was eager hurry to do fitting honour to the advancing bridegroom, the foolish virgins asked the wise for some of their oil. To have given it at any time would have been hard; to give it then was impossible. The foolish virgins must do what they ought to have done before; they must "go to them that sold, and buy for themselves." There was nothing else to do; but meanwhile the marriage procession could not tarry; the great pageant went incessantly, inexorably forward. Every one who could fell into his appointed place; every one who was ready passed on into the supper-chamber. The five wise virgins passed on, but without their companions; "and the door was shut."

"The door was shut." There are metaphors which belong not to one age, or people, or literature, or phase of mind, but to the human family; they are always intelligible, always welcome, always popular. Of such a character is the figure of a door, which our Lord makes much of in this parable and on other occasions. A door guards and it excludes; it suggests something beyond it which is worth protecting; it denies or it affords access to some scene of happiness or comfort, to some home of earthly or heavenly blessing, which it guards against assault and intrusion. The word had this wider figurative sense already in Hosea's time. Hosea speaks of the "valley of Achor as a door of hope."[a] Achor, you will remember, was a valley in the territory of Jericho, near the entrance of Canaan from the side of the desert. And when the tired and disheartened Israelites had so far ended their long wanderings as to reach this valley, the hope that they were already near the final moment of victory and possession was actually breaking on them; that valley of Achor was a door through which they entered into hope. Therefore, in a later time of discouragement and trouble, it was natural for the Prophet to associate the rising hope that God would once again bless and visit His people, with that little valley near

[a] Hos. ii. 15.

Jericho that had meant so much for the men who followed Joshua into Canaan.

So, at the close of his first missionary journey, St. Paul, in company with Barnabas on their return to Antioch, gathered the Church of that place together, "and rehearsed all that God had done with them, and how He had opened the *door of faith* unto the Gentiles."[a] The "door of faith" meant entrance into the enjoyment or possession of faith; just as the "door of hope" means entrance into the possession and enjoyment of hope. This door was opened to the heathen by the preaching of the Apostles. By this door the heathen could enter into that great region of truth which we call the Gospel of Christ, or the Catholic Faith; that truth, of which Christ our Lord, in His Divine Person and in His redemptive work, is the central Subject, and which is only and really apprehended by a new spiritual sense, namely, the Divinely given faculty of faith. So St. Paul bids the Colossians pray that he, prisoner as he was in Rome, might yet be vouchsafed what he calls a door of utterance;[b] an opportunity, that is, of proclaiming, with courage and freedom, Christian Truth in its completeness to the Jews and heathen around him. These doors, you observe, severally open upon the enjoyment of hope, upon the truths of faith, upon the scene and opportunities of missionary action; but the Bible speaks of another door which gives admission into the dark, unexplored recesses of the human soul. "Behold," says our Lord from Heaven, "I stand at the door, and knock: if any man hear My Voice, and open the door, I will come in to him, and will sup with him, and he with Me."[c] And the state of salvation here, which, if it be not forfeited, leads on to the state of glory hereafter;—it, too, has a door. "I," says our Divine Lord,—

Incarnate, Crucified, Risen—"I am the Door: by Me if
any man enter in, he shall be saved." [a]

Once more there is a door, which includes all these and
more, since it opens into the life everlasting. This door is
not always open. It is the door of present opportunity. It
is the door to which our Lord refers in the warning words,
"When once the Master of the house hath risen up, and
hath shut to the door, and ye begin to stand without, and
to knock at the door, saying, Lord, Lord, open unto us;
and He shall answer and say unto you, I know you not
whence ye are." [b]  And it is the door in the parable
before us. The hour has struck; the Bridegroom has
come; the five wise virgins with their lamps burning
have entered; the five foolish virgins with their lamps
gone out have not entered; and the door is shut. Yes!
that door is the door of opportunity.

Let us dwell on this point, brethren; it is always
practical for living and dying men; it is especially in
season on Advent Sunday.


# I.

"The door was shut." Consider, first, how easily this
may happen with respect to the outward blessings and
opportunities of life.

Take education. Only a minority of young people,
while they are being educated, understand, we will not say
what an advantage education is, but that it is an advantage at all. You are, perhaps, born in a well-to-do family,
and you do not give a thought to the thousands of un-
educated children around you;—children whose minds
often furnish raw material that might be chiselled into
the highest intellectual beauty, while too often they lie

---

[a] St. John x. 9.                          [b] St. Luke xiii. 25.

neglected in the gutters of our great cities. Children of well-to-do parents feel the strain and discomfort of prolonged exertion. They know that they have to make some exertion or they will get into trouble. But they chafe at the constraint and exaction of regular hours, at obedience to masters and mistresses, at confinement to the house when the weather is bright and their spirits are high, and they would like to be out and enjoying themselves. They often spend almost as much vital force in regretting, if not in resisting, the circumstances in which they find themselves, as would suffice to make those circumstances welcome by turning the cultivation of their minds into a pleasure and a success. And so the years pass, and they leave school, having successfully spent much labour and ingenuity in contriving to avoid being much benefited by it; and they find themselves, whether they will or not, involved in the struggle, perhaps overwhelmed by the business of life. The days, the weeks, the months, the years, are devoted to labours which leave no margin, or almost none, for other things; to labours which, however good and necessary, are monotonous, mechanical, for general purposes unimproving. And then they wish that they could have their time over again; that precious time of the first years of life, when their outlook was so narrow; when they thought only of the playground and the half-holiday, and rarely or never of the coming years. "How I wish," it has been said to me, "I could only go to school again, with my present sense of its value!" How natural a wish! how impossible its fulfilment! Long years ago, that door of education, securing for the mind the material and the habits which would permanently improve it, was finally shut.

Take friends. We Christians do not look at friendship quite in the light in which it was regarded in the ancient

world. The ancients looked upon a friend as an integral
part of the outfit or decoration of a well-appointed life ;
not to have one friend, in the technical sense, was to be
in very poor circumstances. Friendship was considered,
not so much a natural and instinctive result of the
affections, addressing themselves incidentally to something
sympathetic in the mind or character of another man, as
a more deliberate and, indeed, artificial creation ; as a
thing achieved by assiduous cultivation ; as, in short, a
work of art. And so in ancient times there were famous
treatises on friendship, such as Cicero's ; which corresponded to other treatises on poetry or on gardening. The
selection and adoption and maintenance of a friendship
was made a matter of rule and method ; and the risks and
diseases to which it was liable, and the catastrophes which
might conceivably destroy it, were discussed and classified.
Behind this old heathen, artistic idea of friendship, there
lay the assumption that men generally were the natural
enemies of each other; and that friendship, while selecting
one individual from among the many and welcoming him
to the fireside and to the heart, did but leave the rest of
the world in an outer atmosphere of more emphatic and
forbidding separation. Christianity, as we know, is based
on a conception the very inverse of this. For a Christian,
every man is a possible friend until events have shown him
to be in fact an enemy ; and even then he can never be
thought of but as an enemy who is only such because he
has for the moment lost his way, and may be again won
back to friendship. And therefore Christianity cannot set
forth friendship with a background so terrible and so
picturesque as was possible for the old heathens. There is
no such dark foil to Christian friendship as there was for
friendship in the ancient world ; nay, Christianity must
whisper a gentle but clear warning against any such devo-

tion of the affections to a single individual as should make
the Christian forget the supreme claims of the Friend of
friends, the many claims of every brother in Christ, and
indeed of every member of the vast human family.

Thus much may be said by the way on a very large
subject, if only to prevent misunderstandings as to what
may be meant by friendship. But with this reserve a
friendship, in the mellowed and Christian sense, may often
be a very great blessing, especially if the friend be endowed
with great gifts of mind and character, or if he be older,
and so an adviser and an authority as well as a companion.
And as friendships with us more often arise, as we say, out
of circumstances instead of being diligently cultivated
and forced, there is always a probability of their being
enjoyed without being reflected on and made the most of.
What a friendship might have been to us we often discover
for the first time only when it has been withdrawn. What
might not have been gained from that clear intellect, that
warm heart, that true and intrepid will! Jonathan has
been slain in Mount Gilboa, ere David sings—

> "I am distressed for thee, my brother Jonathan:
> Very pleasant hast thou been unto me;
> Thy love to me was wonderful,
> Passing the love of women." [a]

The *In Memoriam* of the modern poet expresses the heart-
ache which follows the sudden close of a great friendship
in early life; and of this, in most cases, not the least ingredient consists in the self-reproach which is felt on the
score of its wasted opportunities. But those years have
glided by; death has done his work; the door is shut.

Take wealth. This, too, is an external blessing, the
real value of which is often missed until it is too late.
The first, crude view of property is, that it is something

[a] 2 Sam. i. 26.

to be spent in whatever way upon the owner, whether
directly as ministering to his enjoyment, or indirectly by
procuring him the good will and approbation of his fellow-
men. Not seldom has the question been asked, What is
the good of having anything, if a man may not do what
he likes with it? This notion of property is so natural
and so seductive, that a lifetime may pass without its being
questioned. Questioned it is quite certain to be in every
case, when life is over; but it is sometimes questioned,
alas! to no purpose, while life still lasts. A series of bad
harvests, a bad debt, a thoughtless investment, an unsuspected liability, a financial crash, may break in on that
placid, selfish life like the waves into the cabin of a sinking
steamboat, that has come into collision with a vessel of
greater tonnage at the dead of the night. And then,
when the vivid language of Scripture has become fact,
and riches "make themselves wings and flee away,"ᵃ and
have, in point of fact, entirely effected their flight; then
comes the thought, the depressing thought, What might
not have been done with them? What might they not
have been made to do for God's glory, for the well-being
of souls, for the solace of human poverty and suffering, for
the promotion of many a cause of public or private benevolence? What might not have been done with them?
But, alas! all is over; the door is shut.


II.

"The door was shut." What is true of outward advantages—wealth, friends, education—is not less true of various
forms of personal capacity, whether of body or soul. A
day comes, not seldom, in life when we can no longer

ᵃ Prov. xxiii. 5.

command them; when the door, which they keep open
for us, has closed.

We know it is so with bodily health. A young man,
who, as the Bible says, rejoices in his youth,[a] and deems
himself able to do almost anything, can hardly as yet
understand this. Of course, if he is told that his health
will some day be forfeited, he assents to the incontro-
vertible; he does not run a tilt against common sense.
But, at the same time, his daily habits of thought and
feeling bear him strongly in a direction opposed to the
truth which he admits. He is full of animal self-reliance,
and he looks down more or less on the weakly and the
decrepit; he cannot tax his imagination sufficiently to
depict to himself a time when he too will perhaps be full
of aches and pains, and will walk abroad with difficulty;
when he will wish at night that it were morning, and in
the morning that it were night.[b] His present working
stock of robustness and vigour takes such possession of
him that he cannot habitually look beyond it, and treat it
as a blessing which is, in fact, already on the wing. To
be thankful for the great gift of good health is one thing;
to assume that it is ours by right, and that we are somehow meritorious for having it, and not likely to lose it, is
another.

Certainly bodily strength is not the highest of God's
gifts; it is not in fact, as it might seem to be in the
imaginative writings of the school of Healthy Animalism,
almost a kind or department of moral excellence; but it
is a condition of usefulness which powerfully affects both
the mind and the character. It passes away; and then,
on the bed of weakness or pain, we say to ourselves,
What might not have been done with it? It passes away;
and we find ourselves, like Samson when his locks had

<hr/>

[a] Eccles. xi. 9.          [b] Deut. xxviii. 67.

been shorn,[a] surrounded by the difficulties which make exertion imperative, yet powerless to deal with them. Yes, health passes; and, if we can do so, we try medical advice, and physic, and change of air; we visit the watering-place which is recommended by the most modern science; we make magnificent plans for employing recovered health to the best advantage, to the glory of God and to the good of mankind. Alas! the Angels are looking down with what would in fallen man often be amusement, but what in them is the tenderest pity. The door is shut.

So, too, with the powers of the mind, which reach their perfection in average men when those of the body are on the wane. When a powerful and cultivated mind is in full activity, its buoyancy and vigour inspire it with an almost boundless self-confidence; it will even take offence at the suggestion that its capacities are limited, and that one day they may be less effective than they are. So that mind lives in and for itself; finding its full satisfaction for the time being in the exercise and play of its energies, and never raising the question whether they have not been given for some higher purpose beyond. For many a year the illusion may hold on; the mind may even seem to be all and more than it has been; while all else decays around, its powers may subsist in strength and even freshness. But the years still pass; and at last the mental faculties give way—first one, and then another, and then a third. It is a pathetic sight, the break-down of a great intellect before the eyes of those who have watched and measured and admired its force and splendour. But a day comes when the memory can no longer be depended on, even for subjects which it had completely made its own; or when the judgment, which had been so calm

[a] Judges xvi. 15–21.

and clear, is felt to have lost its balance; or when the fancy
has no longer any relish for the masterpieces that used to
charm it; or when the power of observation is seen to be
altogether less keen and scrupulous than in bygone years.
The critical faculty, perhaps, still survives, but without
breadth and equitableness; it survives as the instinct of
finding fault rather than as the power of wise correction;
it is petty, querulous, captious, feeble, trembling into
confusion when it attempts to become emphatic. Ah!
it is already in ruins—that mind; yet it retains clear-
sightedness enough to take the measure of what it is and
of what it was, of what it might have been once and can
no longer be. Before its dimmed and failing sight there
rises the vision of what might have been achieved by it in
the noonday of its power; of the truths which might have
been investigated or defended; of the great causes which
might have been advocated and promoted; of the work,
the one piece of mental work, given it to do, and which
none else had the means of doing, and which now must
be for ever undone. Surely this is one of the saddest
forms of not uncommon regret. But it avails not. The
door is shut.

### III.

Thus, as the years pass, we listen to the sound of the
closing doors as, one after another, they strike upon the
ear of the soul and the conscience; we hear them proclaiming that something which has been ours, and for
the use of which we have to answer, is ours no longer; we
hear them more often and louder as time flies past, while,
in their frequency and urgency, they lead us up towards
a time when will be heard the closing of a door beyond
which there is no other; the door of our probation in this
life, or, of all probations, at the Last Judgment.

Place the Last Judgment in the light of that aspect of life on which we have been dwelling, and it is seen, in its essential character and principle, to be not an innovating catastrophe so much as the result to which the lesser catastrophes of life steadily point forward. It is the final term of experiences which lead up to it by a continuous analogy; it exhibits visibly, and on a scale of unimagined vastness, that judgment of God which is ever going forward invisibly and with individuals; bringing to a close first one and then another sphere and department of responsibility, until each account is sufficiently made up to be closed, by whatever means and in whatever sense; until at length all accounts are closed, and the last hour for all who are on their probation has clearly sounded.

The life of a man may be looked at in many ways. It is the life of a highly organized animal; it is the life of a being with social instincts; it is the life of a mind which, under the disguise and protection of an odd physical form, can think and reason, and claim its share in an intellectual world. But it is more—much more than all these; it is the life of an imperishable spirit during the stage of its probation. All other aspects of human life are of small account compared with this; for this discovers at once man's greatness and his peril; it stamps his present existence with a paradoxical union of insignificance and import. Our life is insignificant because it is the briefest preface to the volumes of an eternity that must follow; it is of infinite importance because it will determine, beyond recall, their unchanging character.

The time of probation. Yes! that is the true and adequate description of human life, to which all other descriptions are utterly subordinate. Why have we these bodily frames, with their various functions? Why are we spirits, with these several endowments of mind and affec-

tion and self-determining will? Why is your life or
mine cast in such and such circumstances, with such
advantages or without them, with or without friends, or
education, or health, or property? Why, but because He
Who made each one of us wills that in the particular
circumstances which are of His appointment, the spirit
which He has made, and which He sees through and
through in its inmost essence of thought and purpose,
should freely choose Himself as its End and Portion, and
should in that choice be utterly and for ever blessed?

The acceptance or rejection of this destiny is the meaning of probation. God tests us by all that we are, by all
that surrounds us, each in his individual, inalienable life.
He will discover whether we will choose Himself, or something else than He; and whether, having so chosen, we
will adhere to the choice. And as life passes, the time
during which this momentous issue is decided passes
also; and at last it is closed, and the door is shut.

The door is shut for each of us as we draw our last
breath. While there is life, there is hope. While there
is life, though all other doors may have closed, the door
of mercy, of full and abundant mercy, is open. None
may say that on this side the grave the will of man ever
reaches such a point of self-determined fixedness in evil
as to be inaccessible to grace; none can limit the possibilities of a recovery which the wonder-working grace of
Him Who was born in Bethlehem, and Who died on
Calvary, and for Whom time does not exist, may achieve
in the last moments of conscious responsibility. But
when once the soul and body have parted company, the
door is shut. There is no repentance in the grave, nor
pardon offered to the dead. None cross the line which
separates those who die in God's grace from those who die
out of it; although there may be on the one side an ever-

increasing obduracy of the lost will, and on the other a continuous discipline and growth in all that is needed for the endless vision of the All-holy. What is certain, is that at death probation closes ; the door is shut.

And Advent Sunday points to a day which will, so far as man is concerned, close all the doors, whether of opportunity or capacity, that yet are open. Beyond the failure of powers and the loss of friends, and the withdrawals and forfeitures that come with years, beyond our own death and the death of all around us, there rises that overwhelming sight—the Throne of Judgment. "And I saw a great white throne, and Him that sat on it, from Whose Face the earth and the heaven fled away. . . . And I saw the dead, small and great, stand before God ; and the books were opened : and another book was opened, which is the Book of Life : and the dead were judged out of those things which were written in the books, according to their works." [a]  "Behold, He cometh with clouds ; and every eye shall see Him, and they also which pierced Him." [b]

How, dear brethren, can we do better than imprint on our memories, and if it may be, by God's grace, on our hearts, those words of the Advent Epistle, which the short dark days seem each year to invest with a pathetic setting all their own, and which, familiar as they may be to our ears, are exhaustless when we reflect on their unspeakable solemnity ?—" Now it is high time to awake out of sleep : for now is our salvation nearer than when we became Christians. The night is far spent, the day is at hand : let us therefore put off the works of darkness, and let us put on the armour of light." [c]

Whatever else in life may have been closed for any of us, whatever of outward blessing or of personal and

[a] Rev. xx. 11, 12.    [b] *Ib.* i. 7.    [c] Rom. xiii. 11, 12.

inward capacity is now of the past, one thing remains, one door is still open. It is the door of opportunity; the door through which we may pass to be washed through repentance in the cleansing Blood of the Immaculate Lamb, and to feed the dim lamp of our souls with the oil which He supplies through His Spirit and His Sacraments.

That door is still open; but who shall say how soon it may not be closed for any one of us?

> "See how occasion calls thee, while the sand
>     Of hurrying life admits of no delay,
>   And mounts the steep of the eternal land!
>     One step o'ercome, more easy the essay,
>     While o'er thy conquered self thou gainest sway.
>   Haste to arise, and on the destined road,
>     In arms bright-burnished with the heavenly ray,
>   Thou shalt meet Him Who came to bear thy load,
> And guide thee gently on to Light's serene abode." [a]

[a] Rev. I. Williams, *The Baptistery*, pt. i. p. 24.

# SERMON XXXIX.

## THE TRUE USE OF THE BIBLE.

### (SECOND SUNDAY IN ADVENT.)

Ps. cxix. 105.

*Thy Word is a lantern unto my feet, and a light unto my paths.*

TO-DAY we are led by the Collect and the Epistle to
think of the Bible; and of the Bible under one particular and most important aspect, namely, as a means of
enabling us to prepare for another life. The Epistle,
indeed, speaks only of the Old Testament when it refers
to "things written aforetime as written for our learning,"
and written that we "might have hope." For St. Paul
is thinking of his application to our Lord Jesus Christ of
David's words, "The reproaches of them that reproached
thee fell on Me;" [a] and, indeed, when St. Paul wrote to
the Romans, there were not more than two, or at most
three, books of the New Testament as yet in existence.
Still his words hold a large principle, which warrants us
in giving them a wider range of meaning. We may apply
them to the New Testament as well as to the Old, and
not least to that glorious Epistle of his to the Romans, in
which they actually occur. And thus to-day's Collect
refers these words to the whole Bible. In it we pray to

[a] Ps. lxix. 9; Rom. xv. 3, 4.

Him " Who has caused *all* holy Scriptures to be written
for our learning," that we may make such a use of this
precious gift that, by the " patience " which it teaches
and by the " comfort " which it affords, we may have a
" blessed hope of everlasting life." In the passage before
us, " Thy Word," which meant, in the Psalmist's mouth,
the Mosaic Law, has for us Christians a like range of
meaning: " Thy Word is a lantern unto my feet, and a
light unto my paths."

The 119th Psalm is a hymn of one hundred and
seventy-six verses in praise of the Mosaic Law, which,
whether as God's Law, or His statutes, or His commandments, or His testimonies, or His precepts, or His ceremonies, or His truth, or His way, or His righteousness, is
referred to in every single verse of it except two. There
is no other Psalm like it, for its varied power of expressing
all that is deepest and most affectionate in the human
soul when in communion with God as revealed to us in
His Word and Will ; and, like many of the most beautiful
things in the moral and spiritual world, this Psalm is the
product of sorrow. There is not much reason for doubting
that it was written quite at the close of the Jewish Captivity in Babylon by some pious Jew, who had felt all the
unspeakable bitterness of the exile ; the insults and persecution of the heathen ; the shame, the loss of heart,
the " trouble above measure," [a] which that compulsory
sojourn, in the centre of debased Eastern heathendom,
must have meant for him. The writer was a man for whom
sorrow did its intended work, by throwing him back upon
God, His ways, and His Will ; and so in this trouble, when
all was dark around, and hope was still dim and distant,
and the heathen insolent and oppressive, and the temptations to religious laxity or apostasy not few nor slight, he

[a] Ps. cxix. 107.

still could say, "Thy Word is a lantern unto my feet, and
a light unto my paths."

And this witness of the captive Jew who wrote the
Psalm, thinking only of the Mosaic Law, has been echoed
again and again by Christians, with reference to the whole
Bible of the Old and New Testaments, and in a deeper
sense. They have found this Book a lamp unto the feet,
and a light unto the paths. They have found that the
two parts of the verse are not different ways of saying
the same thing. The Word of God is a lamp or lantern to
the feet by night. It is a light, as that of the sun, by day.
It makes provision for the whole of life; it is the secret
of life's true sunshine; it is the guide when all around is
dark. It thus throws light on "the path" and "the feet;"
on the true course which thought and conduct should
follow, and on the efforts which are necessary in order to
doing so. With the Word of God at hand, we should be
in no doubt about the greatest practical question which
man has to deal with; the true road to everlasting happiness in another life.

Here, however, we are met by the fact that, in an age
and country like ours, the Bible is everywhere to be met
with; it is more easily to be had, at any rate in England,
than any other book. Of the millions who possess, and
who now and then read it, how many can say sincerely,
"Thy Word is a lantern unto my feet, and a light unto
my path"? And if it be the case that, in a great proportion of cases, the Bible fails of its true purpose, and
men read it, if at all, without securing the gift which it is
meant to bestow, what is the reason? The answer is, that
certain conditions are attached to this guiding and illu-
minating office of the Bible, and that, if it fails to guide
and enlighten, these conditions are not complied with.
What are they?

# I.

The first condition is that the Bible should be diligently searched for those truths, those precepts, those examples, which will directly guide us through life to our eternal home. No doubt every line of the Bible has some bearing on man's future destiny; but in some cases this bearing is direct and obvious, in others it is indirect, and only perceived after long reflection. For instance, St. Paul desires Timothy to bring with him from Ephesus to Rome the cloak which was left at Troas, "and the books, but especially the parchments." [a] This verse has its use and interest; it shows the spirit in which service may be asked and rendered by fellow-labourers in the cause of Christ; it illustrates the use of literature as an agent in the propagation of the Faith. But no one would compare it, in point of direct religious or moral teaching, with such words of the same Apostle as "Bear ye one another's burdens, and so fulfil the Law of Christ;" [b] or, "This is a faithful saying, and worthy of all acceptation, that Christ Jesus came into the world to save sinners;" [c] or, "Christ in you, the Hope of glory." [d]

And this distinction between the direct and indirect bearing of different parts of Holy Scripture, on those moral, spiritual, and doctrinal truths, which are of the first importance to man, as a moral being on his probation, journeying towards the eternal world, is even more applicable to the Old Testament. Thus, for example, in the Book of Esther the directly religious element would seem at first sight to be almost entirely wanting. The Name of God does not once occur from the beginning to the end of the book. Nothing is said in it about Jerusalem, or the Holy Land, or the Priesthood, or the Temple, or the sacrifices,

[a] 2 Tim. iv. 13.    [b] Gal. vi. 2.    [c] 1 Tim. i. 15.    [d] Col. i. 27.

or the general features of the religious life of Israel. The book does, indeed, give an account of the circumstances under which the Feast of Purim was instituted; but that is its only point of connection with the religious institutions which characterized Israel as the people of Revelation. For Israel as a nation, and for the nobler characters as distinct from the baser who are depicted in it, the book does undoubtedly enlist our sympathies; but, taken by itself, it would not lead an ordinary reader to such truths as would guide him towards another life. A knowledge of Scripture, at once more comprehensive and deeper, does indeed place this book in its true setting; exhibits it as an integral portion of a larger whole, the broad scope and intent of which is beyond dispute; and we thus learn to see, beneath the tragic vicissitudes of life at an Eastern court, that greater cause which was really in question, and at a critical stage of its history. But this does not lie on the surface; and the same may be said of other portions of the history recorded in the Old Testament. On the other hand, there is much in Isaiah, and the Psalms, and the later Prophets which at once speaks to us of a higher life, and of the truths and motives which should lead to it, even if we should know nothing of the historical circumstances under which the words were first uttered. A first effort, then, clearly should be to search for the more directly religious elements in Scripture, that we may understand the bearings of the indirectly religious elements; to look out for that which speaks of God and to conscience, of the future and to the sense of duty; to trace it in book after book, in age after age, as it becomes clearer and more distinct; to keep the eye of the soul well fixed on this, whatever else it may or may not take notice of. Thus will the Bible be "a lamp unto the feet, and a light unto the paths."

Now, it requires resolution to do this. The many-sidedness of the Bible; its immense resources; the great diversity of its contents and character; its relations with ages so widely apart as are the age of Moses and the age of St. Paul; its vast stores of purely antiquarian lore; its intimate bearings upon the histories of great peoples in antiquity, of which independently we know not a little, such as the Egyptians and the Assyrians; the splendour and the pathos of its sublimer poetry;—all these bristle with interest for an educated man, whether he be a good man or not. The Bible is a storehouse of literary beauties, of historical problems; of materials for refined scholarship and the scientific treatment of language; of different aspects of social theories or of the philosophy of life. A man may easily occupy himself with one of these subjects for a whole lifetime and never approach the one subject which makes the Bible what it is. And, indeed, much of the modern literature about the Bible is no more distinctly related to religion than if it had been written about Homer, or Herodotus, or Shakespeare, or Gibbon. It deals only with those elements of the Bible which the Bible has in common with other and purely human litera-tures; it treats the Bible as literature simply, and not as the vehicle of something which distinguishes it altogether from all merely human books. And, therefore, a serious effort is needed to set these lower aspects and interests of the Bible sufficiently aside in order to study its true and deepest meaning—the message which it conveys from God to the soul of man.

Do I say that the purely literary interests which cluster round the Bible, and which are set forth in so many of the books which are written about the Bible, are value-less? Far from it. Nothing can be valueless which enables us better to understand the first and greatest of books. But what is wanted is a sense of proportion; a perception of the relative importance of things; of the subordination in which the earthly and the human must always stand to the spiritual and the Divine. Thus the life of David is not without high political interest. But how insignificant is this interest when we compare it with David's language and conduct as a great penitent! The case is parallel to that of the relation which the externals of worship bear to its essential spirit and life. The architecture of churches, the beauty and character of music, the order and accuracy of ceremonial,—these things are not without their value, since man is led, by his imagination and his ear and his sense of beauty, towards the frontier of the invisible world. But the essential thing in worship is the communion of the living soul with its Maker and Redeemer. And a man who should imagine himself a true worshipper of Christ because he was well versed in sacred music, or in the details of ritual, would exactly correspond to a man who should think himself a true student of Scripture, merely because he was a keen Biblical archæologist, or a good Hebrew scholar, or an authority on the critical questions which have been raised as to the date and authorship of the Gospels. Both in the case of worship and in the case of the Bible the essential thing is beyond.

Here, then, we see the necessity for a serious effort to keep the eye and will intent upon that which is of primary importance in the study of Scripture. It eludes us, most assuredly, if an energetic effort be not made. In Scripture, as in nature and in thought, the highest truth is hidden if it be not sought after. God tells us that He reveals Himself to those who seek Him early ᵃ and diligently, in Scripture as in prayer, or in nature, or in the means of

ᵃ Prov. viii. 17.

grace. He hides Himself from those who would saunter with easy off-handedness through the pages of the Bible, as though they were taking a stroll up and down a back garden, and languidly noting the Immensities as if they were daisies or dandelions growing on either side of the path ; as though, forsooth, nothing were so easy of comprehension at a glance as the Self-unveiling of the Eternal Mind ! No, we find in the Bible what we seek in it ; we find that which we can find as well in other literatures if that is all for which we search ; but we find depths and heights, glories and abysses, which language can but suggest, and thought can but dimly perceive, if we are indeed, and with earnest prayer, seeking Him Whose Word the Bible is. Only to those who sincerely desire and labour to have it so, is the Bible "a lamp unto the feet, and a light unto the paths."

## II.

Again, in order to succeed in this search for the true import of Scripture, we need method, order, regularity, purpose—above all, purpose—in reading it. Here it is natural to take the Daily Lessons, as an arrangement offered to us by God's Providence, and to let no day pass without reading them through—if in church all the better —with earnest prayer to God the Holy Ghost that He would enable us to understand them. But, besides this, we shall soon feel, if we are serious on the subject, that something more is needed in the way of independent study. It has been said by a great student that every man who is really interested in a book sooner or later makes his own index to it ; and most Christians who have lived much in their Bibles have, in whatever way, marked and compared and collected the passages through which God has spoken to

their souls at critical times in life. But this principle
may with great advantage be acted on regularly; we
may resolve never to begin a new reading of the Bible
without placing distinctly before our minds some truth or
duty to be searched for, from the beginning to the end.
Supposing we apply this at first to the New Testament.
During one reading we may look out for all allusions,
direct or indirect, to the doctrine of the Holy Trinity,
or the Attributes of God; in another for statements and
traces of our Lord's Divinity; in another for references
to the character and results of His Death; in another
for anything that bears on the work of the Holy Spirit,
whether in the constitution of the Church, or in the
Sacraments, or in the hearts and characters of individuals;
in another for references to the nature and work of those
unseen and blessed intelligences, the Angels; in another
for traces of the activity of evil spirits; in another for
illustrations of some one grace or virtue, such as charity,
or the love of God and of man for God's sake; or faith, its
nature and its duties; or hope, considered as a moral lever;
or peace, as describing the state of mind produced by a
sincere and practical reception of Truth; or, again, the
moral basis of wealth, and the duties imperatively attaching to it; or the dignity and claims of poverty; or the
moral and religious aspects of sickness and death. There
will be no difficulty as to subjects if we are serious; and
it is astonishing how much that generally escapes notice
is seen to bear more or less remotely upon the subject in
hand when once we are looking out for traces of it.   Just
as a single purpose in life, steadily pursued, lights up
surrounding interests, and quickens energy for a hundred
objects besides itself; so, in reading the Bible, the mental
intentness which is necessary to the steady pursuit of one
truth sheds rays of intelligence on other truths which

sparkle round it. The keen searcher for diamonds tells
us that he often finds, over and above that for which he
is looking, crystals and precious stones which intrude
themselves on his gaze in the course of his search.

If we are trying to do God's Will so far as we know it,
the interest of the Bible, read with a view to its encourage-
ments and examples, is exhaustless. Each servant of God
has so much to teach us, that the difficulty is how to
leave him and go on to the next. The devoutness of
Abel; the isolated and persevering goodness of Noah; the
faith which Abraham exhibited in his obedience; the
confidence and patience of Jacob in the dark hour of
adversity; the meekness, the fidelity, the courage, of
Moses; the zeal of the sons of Levi; the saintly passion
for justice which ennobled Samuel; the affectionate piety
and deep self-abasing penitence of David; the heroic
endurance of Job; the austere life and fearless courage of
Elijah; the fervour of King Josiah for the honour of God;
the abstinence, the tact, the wisdom, of Daniel—to cite
only a few of the worthies of the pre-Christian time;—how
much have not these to teach us! And still more when
we cross the threshold of the New Testament, and mark
the earnest longing for coming Truth in Simeon and
Anna, and the faithfulness of the Wise Men to very indistinct guidance, and the splendid asceticism and heroic
courage of the Baptist, and the perseverance of the poor
Canaanitish woman under apparent discouragement, and
the strong faith of the ruler and of the centurion, and the
humility of the publican who could only cry for mercy;
when we look higher to the saintly band of the Apostles,
and to that Virgin Mother whom the generations of men
were to call blessed [a] to the end of time, and above her
and above all to Him, in Whom alone evil found no place,

[a] St. Luke i. 48.

and in Whom every form and shade of human goodness
had its archetypal representation,—why, here still more, if
we have only a motive and plan of study, the difficulty
is, as I have said, how to move on; each example is so
suggestive, so seductive, so full of spiritual wealth; the
moral radiance around us has so many rays and such
diversified hues of beauty, that it seems almost little to
say, "Thy Word is a lantern unto my feet, and a light
unto my paths."

## III.

Once more, if the Bible is to light us on the road to
eternity, we should surely welcome the guidance of the
Church of Christ in reading it.

Some good people fear that the claim of the Bible to
contain God's Revealed Will is disparaged if we avail
ourselves of the services of a guide to its main purpose
and meaning.  But if any outward guidance to the
meaning of the Bible is advisable, this is due to the
magnificence and vastness of the Bible.  The Bible is a
great repertory of the highest truth; but, then, it is so
intricate and varied and far-reaching, that we, being such
as we are, may easily lose our way in it.  Certainly we
do not need a guide for ordinary books; we have no
difficulty in finding our way through them, and making
up our minds about them, in whatever sense, without
assistance from without.  But as books rise in the scale
of excellence, they do need this supplementary assistance.
Few thoughtful men would say that it was better to read
nothing but the text of Dante or Shakespeare, and to pay
no regard whatever to the immense explanatory literature
which has in the course of centuries gathered round each
of these great poets, setting forth with various success

the characteristics of their thought, their leading purposes, their philosophy of life, their place in the history of the human mind.  And when we come to the Bible, which towers far more loftily above the highest works of human genius than do these above the lowest, this necessity of a guide is felt proportionately.  We do not require a compass on Loch Lomond or Loch Katrine; but we do need a compass in order to cross the Atlantic, and we do not disparage the Atlantic by saying that we need a compass in order to cross it.  We do not apply to a guide in order to visit Greenwich or Richmond Park on a summer afternoon; but if we are strong enough to think of ascending the Matterhorn, we engage the strongest and most skilful guides who are to be had in the valley below.  There is much in the Bible so plain that he that runs may read it.  But because the Bible is so solitary in its magnificence, so like Nature in that it is constantly suggesting the illimitable; because it lifts us, again and again, above the merely local, the human, the particular, the easily intelligible, into those regions of thought where all is tinged with the glow of the Infinite; therefore we need some friend who shall come to us, as St. Philip once came to the Ethiopian eunuch,[a] with the credentials of sympathy and of authority, to assist us in our endeavours to make it "a lamp unto our feet, and a light unto our paths."

Such a friend is the Church of Christ.  She has a peculiar claim to tell us something about the drift and meaning of Scripture, since, so far as the New Testament is concerned, it is on her authority that we accept it as Scripture, that we reject the claim of other books written at the time to be part of Scripture, and that we attribute to those which we receive supreme and decisive authority in the things of God.  For the Bible nowhere says itself

a Acts viii. 26–39.

that it consists of so many books and no more, or that those books of which it does consist have a character attaching to them which makes them unlike all other books. These truths we receive on the authority of the Primitive Christian Church; and if the Church is to be listened to when she says what is Scripture and what Scripture is, she surely may be listened to with advantage if she has anything to tell us as to what Scripture means. In point of fact, when we look closely into the matter, we see that God committed His Revelation of Himself and of His Will, not to one recipient or factor, but to two; not to a book only, not to a society only, but, in different senses, to a book and to a society; to the Bible and to the Christian Church. The Church was to test the claim of any book to be Scripture; she took nearly four centuries before she recognized the claim of the Epistle to the Hebrews. And Scripture in turn was to be the rule of the Church's teaching. History shows that neither Scripture nor Church can be thrown into the background with lasting impunity. If the Church be forgetful of the supreme claims of Scripture, she soon becomes a prey to superstitions and follies which fatally discredit her message to mankind; if Scripture be not interpreted by the original and general sense of the Church, it comes in time to be treated as the plaything of individual fancy, as a purely human literature, as so much material to be torn to shreds by some negative and anti-religious criticism, for the amusement, if not exactly for the improvement or edification, of the world.

To us of the Church of England, the old Primitive Church of Christ, from which we claim lineal descent, still speaks in the language of our Prayer-book: first and most clearly in the three Creeds, and next in all those doctrines of the Faith, which are taken for granted in the Prayers, and especially in the Collects, bequeathed to us by the Christendom of fourteen or fifteen centuries ago, and representative of the mind of still earlier times. The old rule is that *lex supplicandi lex credendi*; we must at least believe what we dare to say in prayer to God. This rule makes the whole Prayer-book a rule of faith ; and as such it may guide us to the true mind of Scripture. Left to ourselves, we should not have known, perhaps, how to reconcile what Holy Scripture says, on the one hand, about the Unity of God, and, on the other, about the Divinity of the Son and of the Spirit as well as of the Father. But the Church offers us the doctrine of the Holy Trinity, and the apparently opposed truths fall, each into its true place, as teaching us to know Him Who is Three in One. Left to ourselves, we might have been perplexed by the fearless explicitness with which Christ our Lord is spoken of in Holy Scripture—sometimes as a Man sent, commissioned, raised from the dead, exalted by God ; sometimes as " One Being with the Father," [a] as " God over all, blessed for ever," [b] as " the only begotten God "—such is the true reading—" Which is in the bosom of the Father," [c] as " the Great God, even our Saviour Jesus Christ." [d] But the Church tells us that He is " equal to the Father as touching His Godhead, and inferior to the Father as touching His Manhood ; Who, although He be God and Man, yet is He not two, but one Christ." Left to ourselves, we should have thought, perhaps, that what the Bible says about the sovereignty of the Divine Will is inconsistent with its demand of personal obedience ; or that its exaltation of faith, as the faculty which receives God's gift of righteousness in Jesus Christ, cannot be harmonized with the value which it also places on those good works by which we shall be judged. But all this ground has been traversed

[a] St. John x. 30.　　[b] Rom. ix. 5.　　[c] St. John i. 18.　　[d] Tit. ii. 13.

by the Church, and she is at hand with her rich store of
authoritative experience and explanation.

We may observe, with joy and thankfulness, that some
of those who in words reject altogether the authority of
the Church do, in fact, within certain limits, however unconsciously, accept it. They accept it in accepting the
Canon of the New Testament Scriptures; they accept it
in that they often bring to the interpretation of Scripture
a firm belief in those doctrines of the Trinity, the Incarnation, and the Atonement, which the Church first teaches
us to see, and which we do see, in Scripture; and if, after
this, they break away from their guide, and refuse to
recognize other truths which she would bid them see in
Holy Scripture, we can but rejoice that they have followed
her thus far and in matters of such vast import, and trust
that in the coming time they will be led to see their way
to do so with more entire consistency. No; Scripture is
not disparaged because God has given us this providential
guide to bear before us and to exhibit the lamp of His
Word, lighting us, if we will, at each step of our road
towards our everlasting home.

## IV.

But above all, if the Bible is to do its work, we must
be careful to act upon each truth which it teaches us as
we learn it. For there is one great difference between
moral or religious knowledge on the one hand, and purely
secular knowledge on the other—a difference which we
cannot lay too closely to heart. It is that while secular
knowledge is, as a rule, remembered until the memory
decays, moral and religious knowledge is soon forgotten
if it is not acted on. The reason for this is that in the
one case the will is interested, and in the other it is not.

The will is interested in our losing sight, as soon as may be, of a precept which we disobey, or of a doctrine which we have professed, but which as we feel condemns us ; and so the will exerts a steady, secret pressure upon the mind—a pressure which anticipates the ordinary decomposition and failure of memory, and extrudes the unwelcome precept or doctrine, gradually but surely, from among the subjects which are present to thought. The will is passive when the intellect learns that any two sides of a triangle are greater than the third ; what does that matter to conduct ? But the will is not passive when the understanding is told that Jesus Christ, the Eternal Son of God, died for our sins upon the Cross,[a] or that "after death comes the judgment,"[b] or that in Baptism we have "put on Christ,"[c] and shall have to answer for it if our robe has been soiled or lost. In these matters the will is keenly interested, and unless we act at once on what we know to be true, thus enlisting the will on the side of truth, it will surely undermine and finally expel the truths which we have learnt from the Bible about the Mind of God. Suppose, for example, that we have happily learnt to be thoroughly dissatisfied with ourselves on the score of our past lives, and that we are conscious of a moral glow when we read of the justification of the publican who cried for mercy ;[d] or of the opening the well of living water to the Samaritan woman ;[e] or of the salvation brought to the house of Zacchæus ;[f] or of the absolution of the woman taken in adultery ;[g] or of the sins of St. Mary Magdalene, forgiven because she loved much ;[h] or of the tears shed by St. Peter when our Lord looked at him ;[i] or of the promise made

[a] Rom. v. 8.        [b] Heb. ix. 27.        [c] Gal. iii. 27.
[d] St. Luke xviii. 13, 14.        [e] St. John iv. 10-26.
[f] St. Luke xix. 1-6.        [g] St. John viii. 1-11.
[h] St. Luke vii. 47.        [i] Ib. xxii. 61, 62.

from the Cross to the penitent thief." Yet these beautiful scenes will not help us unless they are followed up by
our sincerely turning to Him Who thus came " to seek
and to save that which was lost ; " ᵇ Who " wills not that
any should perish, but that all should turn to repentance;"ᶜ
Who " was Himself made a Propitiation for our sins;"ᵈ and
Who still pardons and raises up from the death of sin to
the life of righteousness those who in His Church come
unto God by Him. Or we are in sorrow, and we read over
that wonderful passage in the Epistle to the Hebrews,
which tells us at length that affliction is a proof of the
love of God, Who will not leave us to ourselves, but Who
" scourgeth every son whom He receiveth." ᵉ Good ; but
this passage will not help us unless we co-operate with its
teaching ; unless we welcome the Divine Instructor ; unless
we pray and strive to be "not conformed to this world,
but transformed by the renewing of our mind ; " ᶠ to
" crucify the flesh with its affections and lusts ; " ᵍ to put
on the armour which God gives us, " that we may be able
to stand against the wiles of the devil ; " ʰ to " work out our
own salvation with fear and trembling." ⁱ Or we have reason
to think that our last hour is possibly not very far off,
and we echo Balaam's wish, " Let me die the death of the
righteous, and let my last end be like his ; " ʲ or David's
prayer, " Lighten mine eyes, that I sleep not in death ; lest
mine enemy say, I have prevailed against him." ᵏ Or we
linger wistfully over St. Paul's words about " having a
desire to depart and to be with Christ ; " ˡ about "living,
if we live, unto the Lord, and dying, if we die, unto the
Lord ; " ᵐ about "living being Christ to us, and dying

ᵃ Luke xxiii. 43.          ᵇ Ib. xix. 10.          ᶜ 2 St. Pet. iii. 9.
ᵈ 1 St. John ii. 2.          ᵉ Heb. xii. 3-11.          ᶠ Rom. xii. 2.
ᵍ Gal. v. 24.          ʰ Eph. vi. 11.          ⁱ Phil. ii. 12.
        ʲ Numb. xxiii. 10.          ᵏ Ps. xiii. 3.
        ˡ Phil. i. 23.          ᵐ Rom. xiv. 8.

gain ; " [a] about " the house not made with hands, eternal in the heavens," which will remain " when this earthly tabernacle is dissolved." [b] But all this language is a call, not merely to feeling, but to action ; to redeeming the time by prayer, self-examination, confession of sins, a good Communion, while yet we may. The danger is lest the vigour of the soul should evaporate in expressions of admiration which are morally worthless, or even productive of moral weakness. The Word of God is a light to us, not because we say so, but when we carefully observe everything on which its rays are falling ; the path we tread, the objects we pass, the companions of our journey, the view it gives us of ourselves ; and when we forthwith rouse ourselves into action. An example which we have striven to follow, a precept which we have honestly endeavoured to obey, and is by the effort indented on the soul, means much more than it could have meant if we had read it with cheap admiration and passed on. Just so far as the will is exerted in order to make Truth practically our own, does Truth become to us present and real ; not merely a light without, but a light within us ; a light transferred from the pages of the Bible to the inner sanctuary in which conscience treasures up its guiding principles ; a light which illuminates the humblest path with the radiance of the just, " shining more and more unto the perfect day." [c]

[a] Phil. i. 21.          [b] 2 Cor. v. 1.          [c] Prov. iv. 18.

# SERMON XL.

## THE SEEN AND THE UNSEEN.

### (THIRD SUNDAY IN ADVENT.)

2 COR. IV. 18.

*We look not at the things which are seen, but at the things which are not seen :
for the things which are seen are temporal ; but the things which are
not seen are eternal.*

THIS is one of those pregnant sayings which, if St. Paul
were not the inspired Apostle that he was, would be
felt to stamp his writings with the note of genius. In a
few words, so simple that all can understand them, so profound that none can ever hope to exhaust their meaning,
he traces, as with the touch of a master, a leading feature
of the Faith which he preached, and for which he gave his
life. He tells us first what is the Christian way of looking
at existence ; and then why Christians look at existence
as they do. And his words arise naturally out of the
account which he is giving of himself to his Corinthian
readers. In this Second Letter to the Church of Corinth,
we see him at the very height of his struggle with the
misguided and indefatigable men, who at Corinth, as
in Galatia, were bent upon discrediting his mission and
undoing his work. They too were preaching a Gospel of
their own ; a Gospel with a merely human Christ, and a

Mosaic Law of universal obligation, and a Mosaic ministry of lasting validity; a Gospel in which Christ's Death and Resurrection and Ascension, although not denied, yet practically went for nothing, since His obedience to the Law, which was misinterpreted, was held to be the only point in His Life about which men need really care. As for St. Paul, these teachers denied that he had any true knowledge at all of God's Revealed Will, or any true mission as an Apostle from our Lord Jesus Christ. He was, they said, a mad visionary, who had created a Gospel out of his own diseased imagination, and who then preached, not it, but himself. Nay, they went further; they said that his personal character would not bear inspection; that he was ambitious; that he was a mere vulgar partisan; that he indulged personal animosities; that he was at heart a coward; that his letters betrayed the turbulence of his temper; that he could not even be trusted with the public funds of the Church, since he had misapplied them.

This, and much else to the same purpose, they said; we gather the exact form of their charges from a study of the Apostle's replies. Certainly he, in turn, describes them as they were. They were sophists, false apostles, deceitful workers. They lived for the outward and the showy; their secret practice was marked by craft and wickedness. There was no limit to their arrogance and self-complacency; they plundered, devoured, enslaved the Churches which welcomed them; they claimed the fruit of other men's labours, not least of his own; they were blinded by the god of this world; they were servants of that dark spirit who could appear at pleasure as an angel of light, since they too disguised themselves as ministers of righteousness and Apostles of Christ.

It was a desperate struggle. We follow its phases, more

or less, throughout the whole of this Epistle, but especially
in its fourth, fifth, and eleventh chapters; and we see
how, more than the opposition of the heathen, nay, more
even than the grave evils which he has to rebuke among
his flock at Corinth, it wounded the tender heart of the
Apostle. It was wearing him out; as he knew full well.
And yet he is able to rise out of and above it into a serener
atmosphere, where all that touches this life is seen in its
true proportions. If his outward man was perishing, his
inward man was being renewed day by day.[a] If for the
moment he must suffer an affliction which he has already
learnt to call "light," he knows that it is "for a moment,"
and that it "works for him a far more exceeding and
eternal weight of glory."[b] And this places him in harmony with that Gospel which, in its unearthliness, was
so opposed to the outward and worldly religion of his
opponents, and which was not more constantly on his lips
than in his heart. " We look not at the things which are
seen, but at the things which are not seen : for the things
which are seen are temporal ; but the things which are not
seen are eternal."

## I.

" We look not at the things which are seen, but at the
things which are not seen." Here is an authoritative
account of the Christian point of view in respect of two
worlds ; this and the next, the seen and the unseen. So
far as we are true Christians, we do not look intently, or
as at objects which we have mainly in view, at those things
which are discerned by the bodily eyesight; but at those
other things which are at least as real, and which are not
discerned by it.

[a] 2 Cor. iv. 16.          [b] *Ib.* 17.

"The things which are seen"—what are they? Are
they simply whatever meets the eye of sense in this
present life; the furniture of this earthly home of man's
existence? Are they the ever-changing spangles of the
robe which Nature wears—the sky, the clouds, the sunlight, the stars, the successive appearances of the surface
of the earth as the seasons pass; the animals around us,
the houses in which we live, the faces of the friends we
know, the rooms, the haunts in which we pass our time,
the dresses we wear, the outward trifles on which long
habit has, perhaps, taught us to depend for our comfort?
Yes! the phrase means all this; but it means more than
this. It includes much that grows out of this visible
scene and is connected with it, yet is not itself properly
discernible by the senses. Along with the things we see,
go naturally our associations with them; our impressions,
and judgments, and hopes, and fears about them. "The
things that are seen!" This present life, and all that
properly belongs to it; its happiness, its troubles, its
outward trials and the conditions of mind which they
create, its pomps and splendours, its miseries and humiliations, its ceaseless activities, its astonishing efforts, its
failures, its tragedies, its degradations. "The things that
are seen" mean the complex life of the society in which
we live; the life of the great community or state of which
we are members; the life of our neighbourhood, of our
immediate friends, of our family. We are surrounded by
characters, persons, objects, causes, employments, upon
which, or upon the outward signs of which, the eye naturally
falls; and in ordinary men, who see no further, these
"things which are seen" occupy the whole of the attention. A Christian, St. Paul says, is in the position of
a man who is aware of the presence of the visible world,
while his gaze is fixed upon the invisible. He is mentally

in the position of a traveller passing through scenery
which is interesting, but who is absorbed in a discussion
arising out of it, which makes him concentrate his mind
on something beyond it.   Or, to put it otherwise, we may
have remarked the effect which is sometimes produced
by the entrance into a small company of a stranger, whose
presence is so commanding, or his words so striking and
original, that the gaze of every one is immediately fixed
on him.   They still take in, as it were, by a side glance,
and listlessly, the general features of the room, the furniture, the different members of the company, the social
characteristics of the occasion, but they are occupied—
eye, and mind, and imagination, and heart are occupied
—with the interesting stranger.   And such an apparition
in the midst of the human family was the revelation of
the invisible world by Christ our Lord and His Apostles.
It took possession of men's minds; it drew them away
from the world of sense; it made this passing scene, by
comparison, tame and uninteresting.   St. Paul condenses
this experience in the passage before us.   " We look not
at the things which are seen, but at the things which are
not seen."

   " The things which are not seen "—what are they?
Doubtless they are, in part, those moral and spiritual
truths and virtues which are obscured or crowded out of
view in the present life of multitudes, but which are,
nevertheless, beautiful and standing realities.   They are
justice, charity, truth, sanctity.   We see approximations
to these things in the conduct of God's servants here on
earth.   But we do not see the perfect and abstract qualities
themselves; they lie beyond the ken of sense; they are
perfectly seen, and seen only, as attributes of the Most
Holy, of the Self-existent.

   " The things which are not seen! "   We do not see

God. "No man hath seen God at any time."[a] The King, Eternal and Immortal, is also the Invisible.[b] But we shall see Him as He is;[c] and meanwhile we look by faith, which is a second sight, at Him—the Almighty, the All-wise, the All-good, Who made and keeps all else in life; Who is, in His awful, unapproachable Essence, eternally Three and yet One, Blessed for ever.

"The things which are not seen!" We do not see the Angels. We know, on the highest authority, that they exist in multitudes which can hardly be expressed in numbers; that in their nine ranks of ordered excellence—cherubs, seraphs, thrones, dominations, virtues, principalities, powers, archangels, and angels—they serve God incessantly day and night; that they reach heights of moral and intellectual beauty to which we men can lay no claim at our very best; and yet that they are all ministering spirits, sent forth to minister to those of us which shall be the heirs of salvation.[d] What a vast world of unseen life is that of the Angels; close around us no less than in the highest heavens; worthy, most assuredly, of the gaze of our souls, if only we have the spiritual faculty which can discern its surpassing beauty!

"The things which are not seen!" We do not see the souls of the departed. We know that all whom we have loved and lost exist still beyond the veil; that they are waiting for us, and perhaps watching our steps as we draw nearer and nearer to the time of meeting them. But they are now, as we ourselves soon shall be, among "the things which are not seen."

"Spirits departed ye are still,
And thoughts of you our lonely hours will fill,
As gales wake from the harp a language not their own;
Or airs autumnal raise a momentary moan,

---

[a] St. John. i. 18.　　[b] 1 Tim. i. 17.　　[c] 1 St. John iii. 2.　　[d] Heb. i. 14.

Till all the soul to thoughts of you is sighing,
And every chord that slept in sadness stern replying,
Where are ye now in regions blest,
On shores of land unknown, in silence and at rest!" ᵃ

## II.

Yes! " We look not at the things which are seen, but
at the things which are not seen; " " Our citizenship is in
Heaven; " ᵇ " We walk by faith, and not by sight; " ᶜ " Ye
are come unto Mount Zion, and to the city of the Living
God, and to an innumerable company of Angels, and to
the spirits of just men made perfect;" ᵈ "If in this life only
we have hope in Christ, we are of all men most miserable;" ᵉ
" The sufferings of this present time are not worthy to be
compared with the glory that shall be revealed in us." ᶠ
Such is the general tenor of St. Paul ; the present and the
seen, when contrasted with the future and the unseen, is
insignificant. And what is the reason for this? "The
things which are seen are temporal ; the things which are
not seen are eternal." That which meets the eye of sense
is here only for a season, and will pass away. That which
meets the eye of the soul, illuminated by faith, is seen to
belong to another order of existence ; it will last for ever.

It is this distinguishing quality of enduring and un-
limited existence, which makes the Christian look so much
more intently at " the things which are not seen," than at
" the things which are seen." This quality suffices to outweigh the advantages which at first sight might seem to
be on the side of the world of sense and sight. That
world is here, close to us ; we see, feel, touch, handle it.
It is not discovered by argument, or perceived by an in-
tuitive faculty which others may not share ; it is obtruded

ᵃ *The Baptistery,* pt. iv. p. 101.   ᵇ Phil. iii. 20.   ᶜ 2 Cor. v. 7.
ᵈ Heb. xii. 22.   ᵉ 1 Cor. xv. 19.   ᶠ Rom. viii. 18.

on our five senses, with engaging or brutal importunity,
as the case may be.   The old saw, which reminds us
that a little of that which we have in our hands is worth
a great deal at a distance, seems to express human
judgments on the subject, and, as far as matters of this
world are concerned, it has much to say for itself.   But
it is outweighed by the fact that the world which we
hold in our hands is passing.   This present life is like one
of the acidulated drops, which melt in the mouth as we
enjoy it; and because it does thus "perish in the using," [a]
because it presents itself only to begin to disappear, it is
worth much less attention than that which lasts, since
it belongs to another order of existence.   In this world,

"Change and decay in all around I see."

Friends die off; neighbourhoods lose their old character;
-society around us wears a new face; our powers of body
and mind become modified and weaker: we are not the
men we were ten or twenty years ago.

How different England is to-day from the England of
George IV.; or the England of Pitt and of Nelson; or
the England of the Stuarts, or the Tudors, or the Plantagenets, or the old Saxon kings!   But Almighty God is
now exactly what He was at each of these periods; and
the great moral virtues, and the ever-blessed Angels, and
the conditions of the unseen world, are just what they
were; and then as now, now as then, souls who here
desire to escape from the torrent of change and decomposition around, and to lay strong hold on the Alone Unchangeable, must, with St. Paul, "look not at the things
that are seen, but on the things that are not seen: for
the things that are seen are temporal; but the things
that are not seen are eternal."

To St. Paul this aspect of truth was constantly present.

[a] Col. ii. 22.

As he had written in his earlier Letter to the Corinthians, "This I say, brethren, the time is short : it remaineth, that they that have wives, be as though they had none; and they that weep, as though they wept not ; and they that rejoice, as though they rejoiced not; and they that buy, as though they possessed not; and they that use this world, as not using it to the full : for the fashion of this world passeth away."[a] It was the transitoriness of the seen which made him fix his gaze on the unseen.

And this had been the teaching of our Lord. The Kingdom of Heaven which He founded upon earth was but a vestibule to that Kingdom in Heaven, in which the Apostles were to sit on thrones, judging the twelve tribes of Israel ;[b] in which the Patriarchs Abraham, Isaac, and Jacob were to be the companions of believers who had sprung from among their descendants ;[c] in which Lazarus was to lie in the bosom of Abraham ;[d] in which all that is best and that is unattainable, even in the best organizations of society on earth, was to be more than realized. Our Lord had bidden men look onward before St. Paul, and, as we know, with Divine Authority. To those who thought that this world would be the main scene of the new kingdom, He addressed the solemn parable of the man who would pull down his barns and build greater, and to whom it was said suddenly, "Thou fool ! this night thy soul shall be required of thee."[e] And to His own servants and disciples He delivered the never-to-be-forgotten instruction, "Lay not up for yourselves treasures upon the earth, where moth and rust doth corrupt, and where thieves break through and steal : but lay up for yourselves treasures in Heaven, where neither moth nor rust doth corrupt, and where thieves do not break through nor steal."[f]

[a] 1 Cor. vii. 29–31.  [b] St. Matt. xix. 28.  [c] *Ib.* viii. 11.
[d] St. Luke xvi. 23.  [e] *Ib.* xii. 20.  [f] St. Matt. vi. 19, 20.

## III.

To these considerations an objection has often been made which is worth noticing, as it has been repeated quite recently by an accomplished representative of the one form of materialistic thought which endeavours to make provision for the religious instincts of man. "See how you Christians," it is said, "with your faith in eternity, forget the duties that belong to time. If you are true to your Creed, you are so absorbed in the contemplation of what does or may await you beyond the grave, that you are in great danger of leaving this world in the hands of those who live avowedly for themselves, and care nothing for man's higher interests. See here," it is added, " how much more Positivism can do for man than does Christianity." Christianity makes religion only a part of life; "the Church would restrict the things of the Spirit to certain ontological problems; she would limit religion to the utterance of prayer and the assertion of certain propositions of teleology." Whereas Positivism, which does not trouble itself with anything that does not rest on a basis of sense, "is conversant with all that concerns man's daily life; with his home, and his duty to his neighbour, and his work as a useful member of society, and his zest for all that is beautiful and tender and true." Its influence is to extend until "every common act of existence is a religious act; and the rule of man's spiritual existence shall be acknowledged in industry, in art, in politics, in every social institution and habit."

Certainly, language has to be connected with new meanings when we thus hear of religion—the virtue or passion which links the soul to God, the only Perfect

Being—as existing somehow without God; and it will
surprise you, my brethren, to be told that you must go
beyond the circle of even Theistic beliefs to find a creed
which can make the whole of life religious, and which
knows how to triumph where Christianity has failed.
But let that pass, and let us at once acknowledge that
Positivism has endeavoured more than once, within the
last score of years, to apply to national conduct and to
international relations some of those maxims of self-sacrifice, and of returning good for evil, which it had learnt
in reality from our Lord, and has retained after discard-
ing the Creed of Christendom. Whether the lives of
Positivists contrast favourably with the lives of average
Christians, is not a question for profitable discussion;
it is more practical for us Christians to take shame to
ourselves for the contrast which our own lives so generally present to the ideal which is set before us in the
Gospel. For to say that Christianity leaves the greater
part of man's life without religion, while it concentrates
attention on the future and the unseen, is surely untrue.
It is contradicted by such maxims as "Whatsoever ye do
in word or deed, do all in the Name of the Lord Jesus;"[a]
or, "For every idle word that men shall speak, they shall
give account thereof in the day of judgment;"[b] or, "In
everything give thanks, for this is the Will of God in
Christ Jesus concerning you;"[c] or, "Whatsoever ye do,
do it earnestly, as unto the Lord, and not unto men;"[d]
or, "We shall all appear before the judgment-seat of
Christ, that every one may receive the things done in his
body."[e]

Indeed, the question whether Christianity is of the
character which is thus attributed to it was raised, at

[a] Col. iii. 17.     [b] St. Matt. xii. 36.     [c] 1 Thess. v. 18.
[d] Col. iii. 23.     [e] 2 Cor. v. 10.

least indirectly, in the age of the Apostles. In his First
Epistle to the Thessalonians, St. Paul had insisted, with
great earnestness, on the possible nearness of the Second
Coming of our Lord, and on the relative insignificance of
all that belonged to this state of existence when contrasted with that which is to follow it. The Thessalonian
Christians so far misunderstood him as to neglect their
business, their families, their duties as members of society,
in their absorbing interest in a coming end of the world.
The Second Letter to the Thessalonians was intended to
correct this mistake. It pointed out, first, that the end
of the world would not come until after the appearance
of the Antichrist; and next that, as the Apostle himself
had worked for his daily bread, so should his Thessalonian
converts. The heavens had been opened to them; but
their life here was to be ruled by the law that, if any
man would not work, neither should he eat.[a] This was
the Apostolic tradition which they had been taught from
the first, and by which they were to rule their lives. The
disorderly walkers who worked not at all, but were
busybodies, were to be noted, admonished, if necessary,
shunned.[b] The Apostle does not withdraw one word
which he had taught as to the relative importance of the
future and the present. But the greatness of the future
does not cancel the duties of the present; "patient
waiting for Christ "[c] means duty in all the relations of life,
and not only in those acts of worship and contemplation
which more directly prepare men to meet Him.

There is, indeed, an admission which ought, in honesty,
to be made at this point. Our energies are finite, and
that which is given to the unseen may be withdrawn from
the world of sense. It may well be that a man who is not
interested by a sight of the eternal future can get through,

<hr>

[a] 2 Thess. iii. 10.        [b] *Ib.* 11.        [c] *Ib.* 5.

after his fashion, more manual or intellectual work, having reference only to this life, than a man who believes in that which the Christian Revelation tells us about the life after death. But this admission is counterbalanced by the moral enrichment of this life which is due to belief in another. The ground which might be apparently won for this world, by securing thought and time against the demands which the future world must make upon them, would be lost by the absence of those commanding and constraining motives which belief in another life supplies. " The things that are not seen "—Almighty God, and the eternal future—make large demands upon the head and heart; but they also, or rather thereby, make the humblest duties of this life serious and noble, since all are a preparation for that which is to follow. There is one scene in the Life of our Divine Lord which is narrated by the last Evangelist, apparently with the view of impressing this upon us. St. John tells us how Jesus, " knowing that the Father had given all things into His hands, and that He was come from God, and went to God," with His thought resting on these vast and limitless truths—does what ?—" riseth from supper, and laid aside His garments; and took a towel, and girded himself. After that He poureth water into a basin, and began to wash the disciples' feet, and to wipe them with the towel wherewith He was girded." [a]

No duty is too humble to be inspired by the grandest convictions as its ruling motive. No faith is too sublime to consecrate any portion of a life-work that is meant for eternity.

We do not, then, admit that to live mainly for the unseen world is to inflict, upon the whole and in the long run, damage on man's life in this. It is rather a parallel

---

[a] St. John xiii. 3, 4.

case to that which many a parent has to consider, in the matter of education. The parent is tempted sometimes to grudge the years that are spent at school, perhaps at college, when his boy might be earning his bread and doing something for his family. But, if the boy is worth his salt, the delay will justify itself. The larger cultivation of the mind will bring with it, in due time, its full reward; in wider views of life, in keener and more practised faculties, in a power of acting with and upon other men which could not otherwise have been secured. Positivism may say, if it will, as we Christians kneel before the Altars of the Eternal and the Crucified, "See how these men waste the time which might be given to social, economical, sanitary, political improvements!" Never mind; if man does not cease to exist at death, we are working upon a basis of fact which Positivism ignores. Let us kneel on! Let us kneel on; for, most assuredly, the time is not lost. We gain more in moral force than we lose in minutes, or quarters of hours, or hours; Heaven irradiates with a meaning not otherwise to be had the monotonous drudgery of many an earthly lot; and it is better, in the long-run, "for the things that are seen," that we should thus look mainly at "the things that are not seen."

## IV.

If this truth, as to the relative importance of the seen and the unseen, be really held, it will affect our lives in a great many ways.

It will, for instance, govern our disposal of our income, whether that income has been earned by daily toil, or has come to us from a previous generation. If we look only at "the things which are seen," we shall spend it mainly upon ourselves; reserving perhaps some little portion for objects of a public character which it is creditable and popular to support. If we look mainly at "the things which are not seen," we shall spend at the least a tenth, probably more, upon some agencies that shall bring the eternal world, and all that prepares men for it, home to our fellow-creatures. No man can seriously believe in the reality of the life after death, and not ask himself the question, What am I doing to help others to get ready for this momentous future?

And while that which directly prepares for eternity has a first claim on the help which a Christian can give it, he will not forget much that prepares indirectly; such as the providing better homes for the very poor; homes in which vice is not forced upon them by the cubic space within which they are forced to live. It is needless to go into details; but "a man's private account-book is generally the most accurate commentary on his deepest convictions." None of us give our money for that which, in our real belief, is not bread; but we may easily take for bread "the meat which perisheth," instead of "that which endureth unto everlasting life." [a] We of the Church of England are sometimes too forgetful of the privilege of giving to Christ and His poor; the privilege— for such it is—of thus expressing in act our true estimate of the relative value of "the things that are seen," and "the things that are not seen." It might be advisable that some of us should ask ourselves what we shall wish we had done with the means that God has given us, ten minutes after our hand has become unable to sign a cheque, and while the eternal world is just breaking upon us?

[a] St. John vi. 27.

Again, our estimate of the importance of the seen and the unseen, respectively, will affect our whole view and practice in the matter of education. If our horizon is confined to this life, we educate our children for this life, and for this life only. If we look with the Apostle to "the things that are not seen," we educate our children primarily for that endless existence which awaits them beyond the grave, and secondarily for this life, which is but a preface, though a most important preface, to that which will follow. If we are in the not-uncommon state of mind which holds this life to be certain, and the next possible, but only possible, we make education in the things of this life primary and obligatory; and education in the truths and duties which prepare for the next, secondary and optional. If we are parents, we say to our children, "Be sure, at any rate, that you learn your Latin and Greek, your mathematics and chemistry, your history and modern languages; these things secure success in life; and no harm will be done if you also make some decent acquaintance with the Bible and the Church Catechism." If we are schoolmasters, we perhaps announce that we teach religion to those who like it, but that for others we have a conscience clause; a conscience clause —that eloquent proclamation of a conviction that while education in the things that are seen is indispensable, education in the things that are not seen may be dispensed with; that characteristic commentary which an age of half-belief has learnt to make on the commission of our Lord, "Preach the Gospel to every creature," [a] and on the resolution of the Apostle to "know only Jesus Christ and Him crucified." [b] Nay, this is not all; we may sometimes meet with parents who do not scruple, both in public and private, to express—doubtless at the time

<hr>

[a] St. Mark xvi. 15.          [b] 1 Cor. ii. 2.

with entire sincerity—their dread of unbelief; while yet they send their children to places of education where the teachers have a deserved reputation for information and ability, but which a young man will probably not leave without having forfeited the faith in God and Jesus Christ that was learnt at his mother's knee. No! next to our expenditure, our practice in this matter of education is a pretty accurate commentary on what we really hold for certain as to the relative value of "the things that are seen" and "the things that are not seen."

So, again, in moments of prosperity, our real view of existence instinctively asserts itself. If we are looking only to "the things that are seen," we abandon ourselves without reserve to the ecstasy and delight of a sense of triumph or success. We pocket the new accession of wealth; we welcome the unwonted incense of flattery; we gloat over the tinsel of each scene which ministers to our self-love. Existence lasts but for a few years, and we make the most of each passing sensation while it is still ours to do so. But if we are looking to "the things that are not seen," we cannot but regard times of great prosperity here with serious apprehension. They may wean our affections from our true home; they may make us forget that "here we have no continuing city."[a] Things visible may twine themselves round our hearts until we lose sight of "the things that are not seen;" until our spiritual sense becomes dull and obtuse, and the eye closes to everything that is not of the earth, earthy. This was our Lord's manifest reason for pronouncing a woe on the rich; they might so easily forget the true riches.[b] This is His reason for pronouncing a woe on those of whom all men speak well;[c] they are, like the false prophets, in a fair way to forget

---

ᵃ Heb. xiii. 14.    ᵇ St. Luke vi. 24; xvi. 9-11.    ᶜ *Ib.* vi. 26.

VOL. II.    Q

the true and awful standard of real excellence. In days
of prosperity a Christian's prayer will constantly be, "O
turn away mine eyes lest they behold vanity, and quicken
me in Thy way." [a]

There used to be in bygone centuries, perhaps there
still is, a custom at the enthronization of a Pope which
embodied this truth with a vivid effect. When, at the
most solemn moment of the occasion, the procession, of
which the new Pontiff was the central figure, was advancing
along the nave of the great church, while all around contributed something to the idea of associated ecclesiastical
and civil magnificence, a master of the ceremonies lit a
torch, which slowly died away and went out. As he bore
it aloft at the head of the procession, he chanted the
words, " Pater Sancte, sic transit gloria mundi "—" Holy
Father, thus does this world's glory pass away." That
was a word of solemn truth in a scene not unlikely to
overlay spiritual realities by temporal pomp; that is a
stern warning which any of us might do well to remember
at the proudest and brightest moments of life; when
friends surround us with kind, or even flattering words,
such as self-love might easily weave into a robe that
would hide our true self and circumstances from our gaze.
"Thus does this world's glory pass away." It is a commonplace, no doubt ; but each generation of men forgets
the accumulated teaching of experience, and has to learn
for itself the old lesson, as though it were strictly original,
over again. Only when the evening of life is coming on,
and the shadows are lengthening, do most men, who are
not deeply influenced by Christianity, repeat such a warning with entire sincerity.

So, again, in the dark days of trouble. How could we

[a] Ps. cxix. 37.

bear them if this life were indeed our all? If there is nothing beyond "the things that are seen," pain is a weird mystery from which man naturally escapes in the easiest way open to him. But if suffering has a purpose in it which will be made clear in eternity; if each stone of the great temple of souls must be chiselled until it exactly fits the place reserved for it; if each blow that falls upon it is aimed by the unerring Hand of the Divine Sculptor, and if more blows are needed when a place of conspicuous honour is destined to receive a form of more than wonted beauty;—then we may suffer in silence, and may hope. "If in this life only we have hope in Christ, we are of all men most miserable." [a] If we look at "the things which are not seen" by the eye of sense, we "reckon that the sufferings of this present life are not worthy to be compared with the glory that shall be revealed in us."

Advent is a time for careful inquiry into our true state of mind in respect of the two worlds with which the Apostle is here concerned. God grant that we may employ it as He wills, in a matter of such vast importance.

> "O lead us unto Thee, the hidden Well,
>   Who art alone Immutable!
> With Thee alone, there hidden are on high
>   The joys that satisfy:
> And they who drink of joys Thy Hand supplies,
>   They shall be satisfied." [b]

[a] 1 Cor. xv. 19.    [b] *The Baptistery*, pt. iv. p. 102.

# SERMON XLI.

## THE PURPOSE OF DISORDER.

(FOURTH SUNDAY IN ADVENT.)

Ps. CXLVIII. 8.

*Wind and storm fulfilling His Word.*

IN this Psalm, written for use in the Jewish service immediately after the return from the Captivity in Babylon, all the works of God, both on earth and in Heaven, are summoned to praise the Creator as best they may. The heavenly bodies, the spiritual intelligences who inhabit the heavens, the earth with its various forms of life, culminating in man, are to praise Almighty God by unconscious obedience to the law which governs them, or by conscious acknowledgment of its Author, as the case may be. The sun and moon, the stars, the fire and vapour, the snow and hail, the wild beasts and the cattle, the birds and reptiles, and, in their magnificent freedom, so perfect in its obedience, the holy Angels,—these all do obey the law of the Creator. There are fallen spirits who yield Him no obedience; whilst man lives on the frontier between obedience and rebellion.

It might at first sight seem that there are forces in Nature which have escaped from God's rule, and are in insurrection against it, since they bring upon His world destruction and death. And therefore, when the Psalmist names "storm and wind," he carefully adds, "fulfilling His Word." The storm and wind, he maintains, although somewhat against appearances, do obey God's Will; but appearances may point so much the other way that the fact can hardly be taken for granted, and requires an explicit statement. Wind and storm, seemingly the outbreak of anarchy in the midst of the realm of order, are yet in reality the expression of the same Perfect Will as that on which they violently innovate. " Wind and storm fulfilling His Word."

## I.

"Fulfilling His Word!" We may remember, some of us, a walk through a park on the morrow of a hurricane. Leaves, twigs, branches, wrenched violently from their trunks, strew the soil in every direction. Oaks which have stood erect, perhaps since the days of the Plantagenets, now lie prostrate. Nor is vegetable life the only sufferer. The eye rests on what may remain of young birds dashed from their shattered nests upon the ground, or perhaps, here and there, of an animal which had run for shelter beneath the cover of a tree already tottering to its fall. Everywhere we are met with a scene of ruin, which Nature, with her patient energy, will take years to repair.

Or we are on the sea-coast. The angry waves are subsiding; and as we watch them, they presently lay at our feet the timbers of what a few hours ago was a home of human beings; and then one and another fragment of a ship's furniture is floated up; and then perhaps, at last, a human body, so bruised and gashed by its rude contact with the rocks as to be barely recognizable. And then, as we walk on, we meet a bewildered mother, with her infant child. She is going to find that her fears are too well grounded. That corpse which we have just left will tell her that she and her infant are alone in this world, and that she will never again hear the voice or look into the eyes which have made her young life so bright and joyous.

"Fulfilling His Word!" Somehow or other, then, His Word is fulfilled in this devastation and disfigurement of that which His Hands have made; and the agent which inflicts it obeys some law, as regular as that which governs the motion of a planet, although with more complex conditions. In its early history this earth seems to have been the scene of a series of catastrophes; each of them the product of existing laws, tending to prepare a home for higher forms of life. God—we may dare so to speak of His works in Nature as distinct from His action in the moral world—God might have ordered it otherwise; but He has, in fact, made death the precursor and the servant of life, at least almost everywhere in Nature. Alike in the vegetable and the animal worlds, the dead furnish nourishment for the living; and the storm which seems to be the antagonist of life, is such only on a relatively small scale and incidentally; it is, in the main, a great fertilizer of that which, but for it, would be inert and unproductive. For, in the view of Him Who sees all that is or will be, there is, beyond the immediate present, the illimitable future; and in some way this present ruin is preparing for it. Yet more; behind the seen and physical world is the invisible and moral world, and, in ways we do not suspect as yet, its high requirements may be thus provided for. But the Bible occasionally does lift the veil, and shows us how the destructive forces of Nature have been servants of the will of a Moral God. It was so when the waters of the Red Sea returned violently on the Egyptian pursuers of Israel.[a] It was so when, at the prayer of Elijah, the messengers of Ahaziah were killed by lightning.[b] It was so when, as Jonah was fleeing to Tarshish from the Presence of the Lord, " the Lord sent out a great wind into the sea, and there was a mighty tempest in the sea, so that the ship was like to be broken." [c] So, again, it was when there arose a great storm on the Sea of Galilee, that the disciples might learn to trust the power of their sleeping Master; [d] or when St. Paul, a prisoner on his Romeward voyage, was wrecked on the shore of Malta.[e] In all these cases we see the " wind and storm fulfilling God's Word," because the Bible leads us to understand how God's Word or Will was fulfilled; but there is much in modern history, perhaps in our own lives, which seems to us to illustrate the matter scarcely less vividly. Our ancestors saw God's Hand in the storm which discomfited the Great Armada; and a century later, the wind which buried the intruding successor of the saintly Ken beneath the chimneys of his own palace at Wells, seemed to pious Churchmen of that time to be not improbably a messenger of the Divine displeasure. There are serious difficulties, as our Lord implies in His allusion to the loss of life at the fall of the tower of Siloam,[f] in pressing such inferences too confidently or too far. But we may see enough, and may have reason to suspect more, that enables us to be certain of this—that Nature is in the Hand of the Ruler of the moral world, and that we may be sure of a moral purpose, whether we can exactly trace it or not, in the use which He makes of natural occurrences.

It is, indeed, an old persuasion, which is not at once to be dismissed as belonging to the world of discarded super-

---

[a] Exod. xiv. 26-30.  [b] 2 Kings i. 10-14.  [c] Jonah i. 4.
[d] St. Matt. viii. 23-27.  [e] Acts xxvii. 14-44.  [f] St. Luke xiii. 14.

stitions, that the forces of Nature have been at times, by
permission, under the control of evil spirits, who thus
have turned the resources of His own handiwork against
the good and All-merciful God. This opinion has seemed
to be partly warranted by St. Paul's phrase, when describing the evil spirit as "the prince of the power of
the air."[a] And the same inference has been gathered
more confidently from the account of the origin of Job's
troubles at the beginning of the book which bears his
name. Satan had ascribed Job's uprightness to the fact
that God had set a hedge about him, and had blessed the
work of his hands. Satan had maintained that Job would
curse God to His Face, if only the happiness and prosperity
of his life were withdrawn. Upon this "the Lord said unto
Satan, Behold, all that he hath is in thy power ; only upon
himself put not forth thine hand. Then Satan went forth
from the Presence of the Lord;"[b] and Job's troubles began.
First the Sabeans stole his oxen, and slew the herdsmen.[c]
Then the lightning killed his sheep, and the shepherds
who were tending them.[d] Then the Chaldeans stole his
camels, and killed the camel-drivers.[e] Then a hurricane
from the wilderness smote the house in which Job's sons
and daughters were eating and drinking, and killed the
young people on the spot.[f] Here Satan is at work in the
moral and physical world at the same time. Not merely
the violence of the Sabean and Chaldean robbers, but
also the lightning and the hurricane which killed Job's
sheep and his children, are ascribed to the agency of the
evil spirit ; and if it should be said that this is quite
inconsistent with what we know at the present day about
the invariable operation of the laws of Nature, let us consider for a moment what is our own relation to a great

[a] Eph. ii. 2.　　[b] Job i. 12.　　[c] *Ib.* 14. 15.
[d] *Ib.* 16.　　[e] *Ib.* 17.　　[f] *Ib.* 18, 19.

many of these natural laws. There they are all around us, and it depends, within limits, upon the exercise of our free wills whether we will put them in motion or not, or whether, for certain purposes, they shall lie dormant. If I drop a stone upon the ground I put the law of gravitation in motion, so far as that stone is concerned, and it is strictly within the province of my free will to decide whether I will do so or not. In the same way, and on a much larger scale, evil spirits and good angels, of vast intelligence and capacity, may surely have it in their power, not to modify God's laws in Nature, but to decide, within limits, whether or not to precipitate those laws, or some of them, into active energy. In this sense Satan may have been concerned with the lightning and the hurricane. In saying that he can hurry on a thunderstorm, we do not ascribe a greater power to him than belongs, in certain states of the atmosphere, to the discharge of a pack of artillery. But it is always to be observed that he can only act by permission, and within strictly defined limits. "All that Job hath is in thy power; only upon himself put not forth thine hand." [a] If the hand which for the moment and immediately directs the storm is evil, the storm nevertheless fulfils God's Word, because it is by His permission alone that any such limited empire over nature is possible to any creature, and is only allowed for purposes wise and vast, of which from the first and always He has due cognizance.

## II.

As we pass from the physical and inanimate world and enter the human, the spiritual and the moral, we find new and rich applications of the words before us. The storm

[a] Job i. 12.

and wind become metaphorical expressions, having real counterparts in the passions and agency of man. And here too, as elsewhere, we watch the "wind and storm fulfilling God's Word."

This is the case in societies of men, whether immediately founded by God for purposes higher than and beyond this present life, such as the Church of Christ, or instituted by Him through the medium of human wills, and the causes which work in human history, with a view to man's well-being in this present phase of his existence, such as the Civil Government or State.

Let us begin with the State. Every reflecting person must know how intimately the well-being of mankind is bound up with the maintenance of social order, with the stability and vigour of existing institutions, with good government, with the due security of life and property. It is the State which organizes and combines the conditions of well-ordered human life; the State answers in the social life of man to physical nature in his animal life: its strength and unvarying order are the guarantee of man's well-being. And yet the State is exposed to destructive storms which rival in their sphere the most violent catastrophes of Nature; and the question is how such storms are fulfilling God's Word.

There is the storm of invasion—the extreme and most dreaded result of the storm of war. Never, probably, before the establishment of the Roman Empire, were such blessings as well-ordered Government can secure, secured for so large a proportion of the human family as was then the case. Upon the subjugation of a number of petty states, continually at war with each other, the Romans established a vast system of law and police, which was almost conterminous with the then civilized world. It extended from the Euphrates to the Straits of Gibraltar, and from the

Grampian Hills to the great desert of Africa. This wonderful political edifice, which was begun by the soldiers of Rome, was built up and completed by her lawyers and her administrators; and such was the seeming strength and compactness, and such the practical wisdom of their work, that men believed it would and must last for ever. " The Roman peace "—that was the proud and attractive description of this magnificent system of ordered human life, the general blessings and advantages of which were not forfeited by the absolute power wielded by its rulers, or by the hideous vices for which some of them were, unhappily, notorious. We Christians certainly cannot forget that it was under this great system of law and government that the inspired words were written: " Let every soul be subject to the higher powers. For there is no power but of God: the powers that be are ordained of God. Whosoever therefore resisteth the power, resisteth the ordinance of God : and they that resist shall receive to themselves damnation. For rulers are not a terror to good works, but to the evil. Wilt thou then not be afraid of the power ? do that which is good, and thou shalt have praise of the same: for he is the minister of God to thee for good." [a]

There is, then, good authority for saying that, upon the whole, the Roman Empire was an institution which promoted the temporal happiness of mankind. And so it lasted on century after century, not through attachment to a dynasty, since its rulers were perpetually changing ; not through the combining power of race, since almost every division of the human family had representatives within its frontiers ; but because, upon the whole, it justified itself as a great home and instrument of civilization, thereby conferring immense benefits upon a vast

[a] Rom. xiii. 1-4.

number of human beings. But the centuries passed, and
moral corruptions, imported chiefly from the East, eat out
the heart and fibre of Roman strength; and then came
the storm of the barbarian invasions. On they came;
Goths and Huns and Vandals; on they came, wave after
wave, breaking upon the enfeebled defences of decaying
civilization; on they came, wrecking cities, devastating
provinces, breaking up altogether the old fabric of society,
and establishing in its place a state of things from which
Rome had delivered the world; a number of petty states,
constantly at war with each other, and lacking, in not a
few instances, the primary conditions of social order.

And yet this " wind and storm " was " fulfilling God's
Word." Rome had done its work, and the evil which
festered under its ordered splendour at last greatly outweighed the good that could be secured by its longer continuance. It left to the world its great conceptions of law
and rule; they were never better appreciated than they are
in our own day. It had to make way for new and vigorous
nations, instinct with a healthier spirit, and guided from
the infancy of their existence by a Divine religion; and
the scenes of ruin in which it perished had a sanction
which has been justified by the event. They were described, rather than foretold, by the inspired seer of the
Apocalypse. The merchants of the earth cried, " Alas,
alas! that great city, wherein were made rich all that had
ships in the sea by reason of her costliness ! " [a] But that
was not the true voice of the moral world. " Rejoice over
her," cries the Evangelist in ecstasy—" rejoice, thou
Heaven, and ye holy Apostles and Prophets; for God
hath avenged you on her ! " [b]

Then there is the storm of revolution, more dreadful,
in its extreme phases, than the storm of invasion; just as

[a] Rev. xviii, 19.          [b] *Ib.* 20.

cruelty or wrong at the hands of relations is more unendurable than at the hands of strangers. Such a storm was that which burst upon France in the closing years of the last century. We may go far indeed to find a parallel to the Jacobin Terror, in point of deliberate ferocity indulged in the name and in the midst of an advanced civilization. The brutalities of the Committee of Public Safety are the more revolting, from the contrast which they present to the lofty professions of a sensitive philanthropy, amid which the Revolution was ushered into being. And yet, as we look back upon those terrible years which occupied the whole attention of our grandfathers, we can trace in them, too, the " wind and storm fulfilling God's Word." The old society which was thus destroyed was inconsistent with the well-being of the greater part of the French people; and the agonies of the Revolution have been counterbalanced by the exchange which millions have made of a life of much'hardship and oppression for a life in which all are equal before the law. He " Who makes the clouds " of human passion " His chariots," and " Who walks upon the wings of the wind " [a] of human violence, permitted a company of pedantic ruffians, who for the moment controlled the destinies of France, to work their will, because He had in view a larger future, which would show that, however unconsciously, they were fulfilling His own high purposes of benevolence and justice.

And here a word of caution is necessary. It is one thing to look back upon social convulsions, whether war or revolution, and reverently to trace what may have been God's reasons for permitting them ; it is another to take a part, however indirect and humble a part, in letting loose these scourges upon the human family.

[a] Ps. civ. 3.

Satan, no doubt, furnished the circumstances which aided to perfect the patience of Job; but that does not show that it is well to be Satan, or to be in any way associated with him. There may be cases in which, even in the judgment of good men, war or revolution have become unhappily inevitable. But the presumption—the immense presumption—must always lie in the opposite direction; since it does not rest with us to control and shape the gigantic forces of active evil, and to make sure that the wind and storm, for which we may be in our measure responsible, do fulfil God's Word.

## III.

In the Church—the Divine Society—we trace the operation of the same law. The Church is exposed to storms which, in her higher life, correspond to the storm of invasion and the storm of revolution in the life of the State.

Thus there is the storm of persecution, which is distinctly ascribed to Satan's agency in Holy Scripture. "We wrestle not," cries St. Paul, "against flesh and blood, but against principalities, against powers, against the rulers of the darkness of this world."[a] "Be vigilant," cries St. Peter; "because your adversary the devil walketh about as a roaring lion, seeking whom he may devour: whom resist steadfast in the faith."[b] "Behold," says our Lord to the Angel or Bishop of the Church of Smyrna, "the devil shall cast some of you into prison, that ye may be tried."[c] "I know"—our Lord again speaks to the Angel or Bishop of the Church of Pergamos—"I know thy works, and where thou dwellest, even where Satan's seat is: and thou holdest fast My Name, and hast not denied My

[a] Eph. vi. 12.      [b] 1 St. Pet. v. 8.      [c] Rev. ii. 10.

faith, even in those days wherein Antipas was My faithful martyr, who was slain among you, where Satan dwelleth."[a]

How sorely the storm of persecution battered the infant Church of Christ it would take long to tell. It might well have seemed to the first Christians hard and almost unintelligible, that the Almighty and Loving Father should have called into existence the Society of His true children and worshippers from among the sons of men, only to expose it to the fierce trial which beat on it with such pitiless and well-nigh incessant fury for the first three centuries of its history. And yet, as we look back, we can see that this education in the school of suffering was not needless, nor thrown away. If the Head of the new Society had been crowned with thorns, the members could not expect to be crowned with roses, and withal to be in true correspondence and communion with their Head. If the storm of persecution had swept round without touching the Cradle of Bethlehem, while the Holy Innocents were sent to their appointed thrones by the sword of Herod ; if it had beaten with relentless fury upon that Cross whereon hung the Infinite and the Eternal, expiating human sins in pain and shame; it could not be that His members would be perfected except through sufferings. And thus, as a matter of fact, the blood of the martyrs was the seed of the Church, even more than were the ablest writings of the Apologists. Pagans thought that the detestable superstition, as they called Christianity, would be stamped out, if only they could persecute long enough ; and it seemed at times to Christians, in those darker hours, as if these persecutors might almost be right, and that the Name of Christ would disappear from among men. But, in her moments of deepest depression, there came to the Church across the centuries the great promise which had

just been made to Israel in Babylon, and which taught
our fathers in the faith of Christ that the storm of persecution was fulfilling God's Word by hastening the impending triumph.

"O thou afflicted (cries Isaiah), tossed with tempest, and not comforted,
    Behold, I will lay thy stones with fair colours,
    And lay thy foundations with sapphires.
    And I will make thy windows of agates,
    And thy gates of carbuncles,
    And all thy borders of precious stones.
    And all thy children shall be taught of the Lord ;
    And great shall be the peace of thy children.
    In righteousness shalt thou be established :
    Thou shalt be far from oppression ;
    For thou shalt not fear :
    And from terror ;
    For it shall not come nigh thee.

   .     .     .     .     .     .     .     .

    No weapon that is formed against thee shall prosper ;
    And every tongue that shall rise against thee in judgment
    Thou shalt condemn." [a]

Then there is the storm of controversy. Between the
sacredness of Divine truths and the angry passions which
rage around them, when the floodgates of religious discussion have been opened, there is a painful contrast,
which we feel most deeply in our best moments. And yet
the wind and storm of controversy has its place and use in
God's providential government of His Church. If St. Paul
had not withstood St. Peter to the face at Antioch,[b] it
may be surmised that, humanly speaking, the Church of
Christ might never have exceeded the dimensions of a
Jewish sect. If St. Athanasius had not opposed Arius
at Alexandria, it is difficult to see how, but for a miracu-
lous intervention, the Christian Church would have continued to teach the Divinity of Jesus Christ. If Augustine
had allowed Pelagius and his coadjutors to be uncon-

[a] Isa. liv. 11–17.        [b] Gal. ii. 11.

tradicted, Western Christendom would have ceased to believe that we are saved by grace. The controversies of the sixteenth century plunged a large part of Europe into spiritual anarchy; but they cleared away mists which else must have hung in ever-thickening corruption on the face of Christendom. Our own age has not been wanting in its full share of religious disputes, and we have not escaped the heart-burnings and other evils which always accompany it. But these winds and storms have fulfilled God's Word, by rescuing from oblivion some neglected truths; by reminding Christians of a truer and higher standard of practice which they had well-nigh forgotten; by bringing out into the sunlight the unity which often underlies apparent differences, as well as the deep differences which may traverse specious agreement; by persuading men of good will to combine courage in defence of truth with chivalrous and charitable bearing towards opponents; by deepening the sense of the preciousness of that Will and Word of God, which is itself attested by our misunderstandings, our struggles, our very faults of temper, accompanying the effort which is made to recognize and proclaim it. Yes, even controversy may have its blessings—

> " As if the wilderness between
>    Of waves and clouds all cold and drear,
>  A Form benign were seen,
>    All calmly treading on the storm,
> With blood of human life and human kindness warm." [a]


## IV.

Not less applicable are the words to the experience of individual life, which is assailed by storms that, in their various ways, fulfil the Word or Mind of God.

[a] *Baptistery*, pt. iv. pp. 142, 143.

There are the outward troubles of life; loss of means, loss of friends, loss of reputation, the misconduct of children, the inroads of bad health, the slow decay of hopes which were once bright and promising. These things are what men generally mean by the metaphor in common talk. The storms of life represent its disasters and failures of this external kind; and no doubt, when they fall upon us in quick accumulation, they do break down nerve and spirits, and lay us low, as the Psalmist says, even to the dust.[a] But these storms, most assuredly, are not seldom our best friends, if we only knew it. They break up the close alliance which the soul, despite her higher origin and destiny, is too ready to make with the outward world of sense; they throw us back from the realm of shadows upon that other kingdom, which is so close to us, which we forget so easily, but where all is real.

Life is full of illustrations of the truth that these storms are meant to fulfil, and often do fulfil, God's Word by promoting the conversion and sanctification of souls. Thousands in every generation echo that experience of the Psalmist, "It is good for me that I have been in trouble, that I might learn Thy statutes."[b] Only a few days since there came to me a man whom I had known many years since as a person of good character, and who had made and saved money in business. He had been led to invest his savings in a partnership which had every guarantee of respectability and trustworthiness, but which within a few weeks became bankrupt, and left him without a penny, and responsible for heavy debts. This happened some two years since, and for some time it was a question whether he and his large family must not go to the workhouse. In order to feed and clothe

    <sup>a</sup> Ps. xliv. 25.                <sup>b</sup> Ib. cxix. 71.

them, he had to do manual labour day and night, at a
very small remuneration. Since then things have somewhat bettered with him, though he is still a very poor
man, instead of being, as he was, in easy circumstances.
But he said to me, " I would not have it otherwise, sir.
My troubles have been the greatest blessing of my life."
And then he told how he had had a religious education,
and had forgotten God altogether in his years of prosperity; and now had been driven back upon God as his
Hope and Refuge, and had found in Him much more
than he had lost in earthly things. Prayer, the Bible,
the Holy Communion; all had been forgotten; all had
been resumed, and were a source of the truest support
and strength. Never was there a more striking case of
" wind and storm fulfilling His Word."

Then there are inward storms of difficulty and doubt as
to religious truth. In days like ours, when every other
magazine in a reading-room or on a drawing-room table
may tell us, in scarcely veiled and very cultivated language, that our faith in Jesus our Lord is untrue, we
cannot be surprised that this trial presses sorely upon
many minds. Sometimes, no doubt, it is welcomed.
Some men do not wish the faith to be true, for reasons of
their own; and supposed difficulties find a ready acceptance and sympathy, where the stern facts of revealed
religion bode no good for conscious disobedience to the
Law of God. Sometimes, too, men bring doubt upon
themselves, like children who play with hot embers upon
a hearth till their clothes catch fire. They know little or
nothing of the world of thought to which a fashionable
doubt belongs; they are excited by a novel and brilliant
exhibition of it; and they have no adequate idea, and
therefore no adequate distrust, of their own powers. Who
can wonder that they fall out with the Bible and the

Creed? They have invited their difficulties, and have no reason to complain.

But there are cases of a very different kind, where good and faithful believers are exposed, through circumstances which they cannot control or modify, to trials of faith which press them very sorely. Perhaps a young man, who has come up to a great office or house of business in London, hears for the first time, and cannot help hearing, truths called in question which are the very principles that have hitherto shaped his life. Or a young woman brought up in a Christian home is obliged by circumstances to make her living as a governess, and she finds herself in a clever family where religion is only referred to to be made the subject of epigrams, whether jocular or malignant. She is at a disadvantage, social as well as intellectual; the storm of polite criticism and elegant invective, directed against all that she holds most dear and sacred, beats pitilessly upon her; each act of social intercourse, each meal, each walk, each drive, only exposes her to new assaults upon her faith. She has no sympathy with the assailants; she resents, in her inmost soul, the dishonour which is done to the Adored Master to Whom she owes all that makes life endurable; she finds it difficult always to keep herself under due restraint, and to refrain from saying things that would wound or exasperate in turn. Still the storm and wind beat on, and she feels at times as if she must lose heart; as if, in an atmosphere so cold and bleak and biting as that in which she is forced to live, her faith must at last give way. Let her persevere in the conviction that in some way, which she discerns not as yet, the wind and storm are fulfilling God's Word. Let her think of the Israelitish maiden in the house of Naaman the Syrian, to whom it was given to do a good turn to her pagan master.[a]

[a] 2 Kings v. 1–14.

Let her remember Esther at the heathen court of
Persia, who lived on in faithful silence, till a day came
when she was able to save her countrymen from the
vengeance of their enemies.[a]   Let her reflect on the condition of many a Christian slave in Roman households in
the first ages of the Church, who witnessed, whether he
would or not, the foulest infractions of the Law of Christ ;
who listened, whether he would or not, to the most blas-
phemous attacks upon His Holy Name and His honour,
but who lived to bring a mistress or a master, before death
came, in loving penitence to the feet of the Crucified,
" that they might receive remission of sins, and an inheritance among them that are sanctified through faith in "[b]
Him.[c]

There are, no doubt, souls who are exposed to fierce
intellectual trials, because in no other way would they
themselves learn the patience, the courage, the humility,
the self-distrust, which are so essential to the Christian
character.   There is the dreadful risk, no doubt, lest the
violence of the storm should wear them out, and they
should sink disheartened, and lie down and die.   But
the struggle need not thus be given up in any case.
God's grace is sufficient for all who will.   His strength
is made perfect in man's weakness.[d]

Much, indeed, depends upon the issue of all such trials.
But when the storms of life beat upon us, and when our
thoughts rest on that last tempest, which may precede or
accompany our passing hence, and which Advent brings
so prominently before us, let us recall those solemn words
of our Lord which He uttered at the end of His Sermon

---

[a] Esth. ii. ; vii.                    [b] Acts xxvi. 18.

[c] Compare, *e.g.*, St. Ambrose's account of the martyrdom of Agricola
immediately after his slave Vitalis ; *De Exhortatione Virginitatis,* i.

[d] 2 Cor. xii. 9.

on the Mount: "Whosoever heareth these sayings of Mine, and doeth them, I will liken him unto a wise man, which built his house upon the rock: and the rain descended, and the floods came, and the winds blew, and beat upon that house; and it fell not: for it was founded upon a rock. And every one that heareth these sayings of Mine, and doeth them not, shall be likened unto a foolish man, which built his house upon the sand: and the rain descended, and the floods came, and the winds blew, and beat upon that house; and it fell: and great was the fall of it." [a]

So it is ever in the spiritual world. Loyalty to known truth is our warrant of endurance under the trials which may await us; that endurance which transforms the fiercest blasts into tender fulfilments of God's Word of promise to those who are the special objects of His love.

[a] St. Matt. vii. 24-27.

# SERMON XLII.

## THE DAY OF JUDGMENT AND MORAL COURAGE.

### (SECOND SUNDAY IN ADVENT.)

#### St. Luke ix. 26.

*Whosoever shall be ashamed of Me and of My words, of him shall the Son of Man be ashamed, when He shall come in His own glory, and in His Father's, and of the Holy Angels.*

THE teaching of our Lord and Saviour is for all nations and for all time ; but some of His words are especially needed at one period of the Church's history, and some at another. It is with the Christian Church as with the individual Christian. The sides of truth which arrest attention, which touch conscience, which mould character, vary, within limits, as we pass from childhood to manhood, and from manhood to old age. To one age, whether of the Church or the man, this passage of the Bible is most needful and useful, to another that; to one this aspect of a doctrine, to another that. Let us see how this bears on the solemn truth referred to by our Lord in the passage before us—the truth of the Last Judgment. And observe that we are not now discussing the Day of Judgment in its relation to the heathen or unbelieving world. That is, indeed, a tremendous subject; full of solemn and unfathomable mystery ; traversed by bright gleams of light, traversed by awful shadows; but, practically, less immediately important to you and me than the relation of the Day of Judgment to Christians.

If we consider our Lord's sayings on this last subject, we shall find that there are three main failures for which Christians will be condemned at the Day of Account.

## I.

Of these failures, if we may so gently describe them, the first is disobedience; conscious, wilful disobedience to the Gospel Law. I say to the Gospel Law. We are naturally so attracted by the Gospel as a Revelation of grace and mercy, that we forget another aspect of it; we forget that it too, after its own manner, is a Law. Jesus Christ is a higher and greater Lawgiver than Moses, and His Gospel is a more exacting, because a more spiritual, code than that contained in the Pentateuch. It is a law of liberty,[a] no doubt, because the Christian soul, illuminated and fortified by grace, may freely and joyfully embrace and obey it; because, in Christ's household, obedience is not wrung out of unassisted and reluctant nature by the mere force of penal sanctions. But it is not a law of licence. The Christian, justified freely, is not free to be and to do whatever human nature may desire; the Christian may not sin that grace should abound.[b] For the Sermon on the Mount is as much a part of the Gospel as the Parable of the Prodigal Son;[d] and the twelfth chapter of the Epistle to the Romans as the third, or fourth, or fifth. Now, this lofty, pure, spiritual Law is the standard by which we Christians are and shall be judged; all the more certainly because, unlike the ancient Jews, we have been endowed with

[a] St. James i. 25.    [b] Rom. vi. 1, 2.
[c] St. Matt. v.–vii.    [d] St. Luke xv. 11–32.

grace, that is to say, with infused spiritual light and strength, for the very purpose of enabling us to obey it.

Surely it greatly concerns us Christians to bear in mind how our Lord teaches that all judgment is relative to the opportunities which men have enjoyed; that to whomsoever much is given, of him will much be required;[a] that "that servant which knew his lord's will, and prepared not himself, neither did according to his will, shall be beaten with many stripes; while he that knew not, but did commit things worthy of stripes, shall be beaten with few stripes;"[b] that in the Day of Judgment it will be better for Tyre and Sidon than for Chorazin and Bethsaida.[c]

Some of the early Christians, at Corinth and elsewhere, who had been under St. Paul's teaching, and had misunderstood it, could not believe that they were thus under a law of any kind. They thought that the new law of liberty consisted in licence to do and be what they liked, provided only that they experienced the emotions which are right and, indeed, indispensable in a Christian. The Apostle will not let them dream their dream undisturbed. "Know ye not that the unrighteous shall not inherit the Kingdom of God? Be not deceived: neither fornicators, nor idolaters, nor adulterers, nor effeminate, nor thieves, nor covetous, nor drunkards, nor revilers, nor extortioners, shall inherit the Kingdom of God."[d] Again, to some Galatians who shared the illusion, "Be not deceived; God is not mocked: for whatsoever a man soweth, that shall he also reap. For he that soweth to the flesh shall of the flesh reap corruption."[e]

So, also, our Lord foresaw, that because works of mercy had been catalogued and manipulated among the later

---

[a] St. Luke xii. 48.    [b] *Ib.* 47, 48.    [c] *Ib.* x. 13, 14.
[d] 1 Cor. vi. 9, 10.    [e] Gal. vi. 7, 8.

Jews, as if they could be weighed and measured by a mechanical formalism, therefore they would afterwards be disparaged by the selfishness and sloth that is always lurking in human nature, under the pretence of loyalty to a lofty spirituality. When, then, He describes the Last Judgment, who are, according to His representation, the lost? They are simply Christians who have failed to obey the Gospel law of charity; they have not tended Christ present in the various forms of human suffering. "I was an hungred, and ye gave Me no meat: I was thirsty, and ye gave Me no drink: I was a stranger, and ye took Me not in: naked, and ye clothed Me not: sick, and in prison, and ye visited Me not." [a] "Depart, ye cursed, into everlasting fire." [b]

## II.

A second failure for which Christians will be condemned at the Day of Judgment is that of false or merely outward profession. Our Lord's teaching is full of warnings on this score; we may take, as a sample, the great passage in the Sermon on the Mount, in which He contrasts the practical religion of many a Jew in His day with that of the sincere servant of God. He reviews the three main departments of religious effort; duty to other men, duty to God, duty to self.

He begins with almsgiving, which stands here for all duties of charity towards our neighbours. "Take heed that ye do not your alms before men, to be seen of them: otherwise ye have no reward of your Father Which is in Heaven. Therefore when thou doest thine alms, do not sound a trumpet before thee, as the hypocrites do in the synagogues and in the streets, that they may have glory

---

[a] St. Matt. xxv. 42, 43.      [b] Ib. 41.

of men.   Verily I say unto you, They have their reward.
But when thou doest alms, let not thy left hand know
what thy right hand doeth: that thine alms may be in
secret: and thy Father Which seeth in secret shall reward
thee openly." [a]

Then He goes on to prayer, which here stands for all
the kinds of worship, reverence, and devotion that are due
to Almighty God.   " When thou prayest, thou shalt not
be as the hypocrites are: for they love to pray standing
in the synagogues and in the corners of the streets, that
they may be seen of men.   Verily I say unto you, They
have their reward.   But thou, when thou prayest, enter
into thy closet, and when thou hast shut thy door, pray
to thy Father Which is in secret; and thy Father Which
seeth in secret shall reward thee openly." [b]

Lastly, He takes fasting, which here represents every
effort to place the lower instincts of our nature under the
control of the illuminated conscience, so as to preserve
in a composite being like man that settled, ordered, and
harmonious subordination of matter to spirit in which
human excellence consists.   " When ye fast, be not, as the
hypocrites, of a sad countenance: for they disfigure their
faces, that they may appear unto men to fast.   Verily I
say unto you, They have their reward.   But thou, when
thou fastest, anoint thine head, and wash thy face; that
thou appear not unto men to fast, but unto thy Father
Which is in secret: and thy Father Which seeth in secret
shall reward thee openly." [c]

Here we note, in each instance, that an act, good in
itself, is rendered hollow and worthless by an unworthy
motive.   One motive only befits true Christian action,
the glory or Will of God; the true Christian gives alms,
prays, fasts, because God wills it, and simply with an eye

[a] St. Matt. vi. 1-4.        [b] *Ib.* 5, 6.        [c] *Ib.* 16-18.

to His Will. When this motive is lost sight of, and the
desire to have praise of men takes its place; when alms
are given to secure a reputation for liberality, and prayers
are said to secure a reputation for piety, and fasting is
practised to secure a reputation for self-denial;—then, let
us be sure of it, all is radically bad; the heart is eaten
out of the good action by this impure and vicious desire
for the praise of men. At the same time, those who
thus give alms and pray and fast, do get a certain return
for their expenditure; they get exactly what they seek.
They seek human praise, and they have it; they have
nothing further to look for, and have no right to complain
if nothing further awaits them. As our Lord says, more
pathetically than severely, "they have their reward."

And this suggests a distinct view of the effect and
operation of the Day of Judgment. It will be a great
day of discovery; it will unveil before all eyes secret
and unsuspected excellence, and secret and unsuspected
hollowness. As the Apostle says, "Some men's sins are
open beforehand, going before to judgment; and some
men they follow after. Likewise also the good works
of some are manifest beforehand; and they that are
otherwise cannot be hid."[a]

Now, this aspect of the Day of Judgment is especially
needed in times and places when religion confessedly
enjoys social ascendancy, and when, therefore, the motives
for insincere profession are particularly urgent. Look at
Italy, for instance, in the latter half of the fifteenth
century, when the literary and intellectual movement
which is known as the Renaissance had eaten out all
true Christian faith in the souls of numbers of educated
Italians. These men thought, felt, and, so far as they
dared, talked and wrote like pagans; but the Church

---

[a] 1 Tim. v. 24, 25.

was everywhere around them, strong with the strength
of centuries; reigning, to all appearance, in an unshaken
and unassailable supremacy; too secure to be much
alarmed at sundry faint and distant mutterings of a
coming storm, which in the next century would break
with awful emphasis beyond the Alps; too secure to be
anxious at the disintegrating influences which surrounded,
nay, which deeply penetrated and pervaded her; careful
to insist upon the traditional proprieties, the etiquette,
as we may call it, of religious language and action, and,
for the most part, letting other things take their course.
That was a situation in which insincere religious profession abounded as a matter of course; in which money
was given, and prayers were repeated, and austerity was
paraded, with a view to satisfying a conventional standard
of requirement, and thereby securing the favourable, or
at least escaping the unfavourable, verdict of contemporary society. All such professors had their reward in
personal safety and comfort, if not in social consideration
and applause; they had their reward, but they also had
to await the final verdict of Him Who seeth in secret.

And the same thing is observable in our own day
within the limits of many a small and compact religious
clique, every member of which is known to and carefully
watched by all the others. The members of such a clique
are associated upon the basis of and in loyalty to a certain
religious standard, whether of faith or conduct; and profession of this standard, whether by word or deed, is indispensable as a condition of membership. How often in
such a situation are not words used, or observances conformed to, only to avoid scandal, to set a good example,
to encourage others, when there is within distrust, ques-
tioning, perhaps aversion, certainly not joyous compliance
with what is believed to be the Divine Will!

Nor may I forget here to remind myself of what is, in fact, a standing danger for all who wear Christ's livery, as ministers of His Church. By the very terms of our profession, we, the clergy, are bound to use in public sacred language, and to perform sacred rites, and to maintain before men a certain language and demeanour. St. Paul says at least as much as this in his instructions to Timothy. And a clergyman is expected, even by those who reject what he has to teach, to be true to this requirement of his sacred office. Yet who that knows anything of human weakness can fail to see how easily this outward bearing and language—so necessary, so indispensable—may become a mask to which nothing truly corresponds within? Great, indeed, is our need to fix our minds less on the standard which the Church exacts, and which the world expects from us, than on the motives of sincere and generous love which should inspire and prompt it, and on the secret faults of will and temper and indulgence which may so soon render it worthless before God. Great need have we, great need have all, whose duty it is to maintain an outward standard of conduct and language before the eyes of others, to think often and anxiously of that Day, when nothing that is covered shall not be revealed, and hidden, that shall not be known.[a]

### III.

And this brings us to the third failure for which Christians will be condemned at the Day of Judgment, namely, the failure to profess the truth, of which they are secretly convinced. Of this our Lord speaks in the passage before us. "Whosoever shall be ashamed of Me and of My words, of him shall the Son of Man be ashamed, when He

[a] St. Matt. x. 26.

shall come in His own glory, and in His Father's, and
of the Holy Angels."

This is the failure which men make at times when
Christians are in a minority, or when earnest Christianity is
powerfully opposed. There is no temptation to be ashamed
of Christ when all the world around you is, at any rate
professedly, praying to Him, praising Him, and generally
devoted to Him. But the temptation was a very formidable one when the Church was still young, and when
Christians carried their lives in their hands; when the
authority of all that has weight among mankind—of rank,
of wealth, of learning, of power—was ranged in opposition
to the Faith; when, in order to make a stand, a man had
to be very sure of his ground; sure of the truth and the
vital import of the convictions which sustained him.
Wonderful it is how, in those first ages of the Faith, men
and women, and boys and girls, in all conditions of life,
joyfully accepted a painful death rather than be disloyal
to their Lord and Saviour. Of the extant records of those
early martyrdoms, some, no doubt, are the work of the
collectors of vague and decaying traditions in a later age;
but others bear on them the unmistakable stamp of
genuineness—as rough reports drafted at the time; so
brief are they, so simple, so rude of expression, so indifferent to everything like literary effect. It is the same
story over and over again: first the popular suspicion of
the " crime" of Christianity; the denunciation; the arrest;
the trial before the Imperial officer; the summons to
sacrifice to the genius of the Emperor; the refusal; the
official expostulation; the second refusal; the threats,
more and more terrifying, in order to break down what
seemed an irrational obstinacy; the final triumph of conscience, which calmly and deliberately would accept the
worst rather than be false to truth;—and then the last

dark scenes of agony, until all had closed in death. So it was with many a humble Christian, whose name yet lingers in the Calendar; with deacons like Laurence, and virgins like Agnes, and youths like Pancras, and soldiers like Sebastian. Jesus their Saviour had trodden the way of sorrows; and these bright souls, clothed in the white robes of His Righteousness, follow the Lamb whithersoever He goeth;[a] follow Him on that path of suffering which is the road to glory. It was otherwise when the Church had conquered society, and when general opinion had rallied to the side which it had lately persecuted and denounced. And then there were long ages during which, however Christians might differ from one another, none would have been ashamed to own the Name, which on earth, as in Heaven, was now set above every name.[b] But the wheel of time brings strange revolutions; and we live in circumstances when this can no longer be said with entire truth. In every country of Christendom—our own not excepted—there is now a section of the people which rejects the Name and words of Christ, not merely in practice, but professedly. Those of us who can remember anything of educated society, even thirty years ago, in England, must be alive to the change which has taken place in this respect. It may not be all loss; it may be that hollow and enforced profession has but revealed itself as what it really was all along, in this rejection of truths which it is no longer socially worth a man's while to profess. But, however this may be, such a change clearly imposes on Christians the duty of confessing Christ before men, more explicitly than in days when there were none who openly challenged His claims. It throws out into sharper relief the meaning of the saying, "Whosoever shall be ashamed of Me and of My words, of Him shall

---

[a] Rev. xiv. 4.        [b] Phil. ii. 9, 10.

the Son of Man be ashamed, when He shall come in
His own glory, and in His Father's, and of the Holy
Angels."

Ashamed of Christ! Who of us, in his higher, better
moments, does not indignantly repel the thought that
such a perversion of the moral emotion of shame should
ever be possible? How could it be that a feeling which,
in a healthy condition of the soul, never emerges except
when conscience reports, or when others detect in us some
voluntary association with evil, is called forth by the
association of our faith and hope and love with Him Who
is the Perfect Moral Being, the very Prince and Flower
of the human family? There are moments of elevated
feeling, of unusual insight, when many a man can say
with the ecstatic Apostle, "Though I should die with
Thee, yet will I not deny Thee!"[a]  It seems, at these
times of lofty and pure enthusiasm, that no pressure
exerted on the heart or will, no bodily torture, no anguish
of soul, should avail to make a Christian, whom Christ
has washed with His Blood, and sanctified. by His Spirit,
and enriched with His Divine Example, ashamed of Him.
At such times it is easy to exclaim with the Apostle,
"God forbid that I should glory, save in the Cross of our
Lord Jesus Christ."[b]

And yet what is the fact? Are there no workshops,
no offices, in this metropolis, where young men meet day
by day, and where to avow serious faith in Jesus Christ,
God and Man, our Example, our Crucified and Risen
Saviour, requires a courageous effort? Are there none
where such an avowal would be encountered, if not put
down, by a fierce scowl, almost by violence? And are
there no drawing-rooms, no clubs, where men of cultivated
minds meet and converse, and where a frank confession

[a] St. Matt. xxvi. 35.          [b] Gal. vi. 14.

that a man believed what St. Paul believed would provoke
a gesture of measured surprise, a delicate curl of the lip,
a gentle shrug of the shoulders, a scarcely perceptible
raising of the eyebrows, more terrible to a sensitive
young man than it would be to lead his regiment across
a plain which is swept by the enemies' cannon? "You
don't mean to say that at this time of day you believe
that?" That is the language of the gesture—so tentative,
yet so implacable; and too often it does its work with
fatal effect.

Why should it be so? What does the sneer represent?
Not superior knowledge; for Christianity has a good
account to give of itself, as a faith in the Supernatural.
Not high moral principle; for this, most assuredly, is
more generally on the side of simple faith. Not that
complex superiority which cannot be resolved into anything merely moral or merely intellectual, but which
confers distinction—undefinable but indisputable distinction—on its possessor. No; they who enjoy this high
distinction know too much of the difficulty and the pathos
of the realms of thought, to sneer, even when they detect
most surely the presence of error. What, then, does the
sneer represent? It represents a sort of abstract or
essence of a certain form of class-opinion, the opinion of
the particular class which has weight with the man to
whom it is addressed; his own class, or the class just
above or just below his own. A certain section or sub-
section of opinion, not necessarily the best informed,
thinks, or wishes others to suppose, that it thinks that
Christ our Lord has had His day; and the sneer is an
endeavour to enforce this prescription without incurring
the responsibilities of patient discussion.

Look at St. Peter in the palace of the High Priest.
Even then, before Pentecost, Peter, in his fervid love

of his Master, would not have shrunk from death had
he been suddenly forced to choose between death and
apostasy. But in that ante-chamber of the High Priest
his fervour has cooled down; the situation is threatening;
his Lord is already a Prisoner on His trial. He meets a
maidservant, and it is impossible not to be astonished
at the impertinence with which this maid ventures to
challenge him. What is it that makes her so formidable?
She represents a body of class-opinion; the opinion of
the class among which Peter moved, and, such is human
nature in its weakness, that he who was to be Christ's
First Apostle succumbs in an agony of cowardice and
shame. "I know not the Man." [a]

We have heard and seen a great deal during the last
few years of the Salvation Army, as it is called; and
there is no doubt of its having achieved results which
are, to say the least, very remarkable. Its creed, certainly, would appear to be only a fragment of that body
of truth which was taught to mankind by the Apostles
of Christ; but to proclaim a truncated edition of the
Apostolic Creed is not peculiar to the Salvation Army.
Many of its methods, also, however excellent their motive,
are in practice inconsistent, as it must seem, with the
laws of that awful reverence with which all that touches
the Name and Honour of the Infinite and Supreme Being
should surely be handled. But there can be no question
that this movement has roused a sense of religion among
classes of our countrymen who are too generally beyond
the influence of the Church; and it is better for us to ask
ourselves the secret of this success than to criticize too
hardly the machinery which has secured it? What is
that secret? Is it not that the Salvation Army, when
it has once brought a man to know ever so little of Christ

[a] St. Matt. xxvi. 69–72.

our Lord, lays on him this precept, " Do not be ashamed
of Him ; do something, say something, which proves to
yourself and to others that you are not ashamed of Him.
Wear a livery ; walk about the streets, sing hymns as
you walk ; organize yourselves into bands and companies ;
and do all with this one object, to proclaim to the world
that you are not ashamed of the Lord That bought you"?
Say what we may about the methods, the inspiring motive
is a noble one ; it lies deep in the very heart of the
Eternal Gospel. No truth is truly held until we dare,
when occasion requires, to own it ; to exult in owning it ;
and the poor men and women who join the Salvation
Army, often to their honour, and, as we may hope, to their
endless gain, endure much for the sake of whatever truth
they own. That is the real secret of their strength ; they
are not ashamed, after their own fashion, to confess Christ,
so far as they know Him, before men.

Is it meant, you ask, that we are to parade our religious
convictions on all occasions, in all places, in all societies,
without regard to the proprieties which are dictated alike
by usage and by forethought ? Is there no risk of irri-
tating, of exasperating, by such an undiscriminating pro-
pagandism ? Are there no swine before whom our Divine
Master would not have us thus cast His pearls,[a] quite
unthinkingly ? Certainly, brethren, one precept or
principle is never to be insisted or acted on in forgetfulness of others which guide, or limit, or in any way
interpret its application. Every duty has its appropriate
opportunity ; and the opportunity for owning before others
our allegiance to our Lord Jesus Christ, occurs when we
are challenged to do so, or when not to do so may give
others a false impression as to what we believe, or may
forfeit our chance of helping them by our example or our

[a] St. Matt. vii. 6.

sympathy. The exercise of the duty is to be determined by Christian prudence; but it is not to be determined by self-interest, or by the fear of man. If we have not been playing tricks with conscience, conscience may be depended on to tell us when and how we ought to own our Christian Faith; and if we do own it firmly, modestly, tenderly, God will bless the effort to His glory, and to the good of other souls and of our own.

Somewhat more than fifty years ago there was a small dinner-party at the West End of London. The ladies had withdrawn, and, under the guidance of one member of the company, the conversation took a turn of which it will be enough here and now to say that it was very dishonourable to our Lord. One of the guests said nothing; but presently asked his host's permission to ring the bell, and when the servant appeared, he ordered his carriage. He then, with the courtesy of perfect self-command, expressed his regret at being obliged to retire, but explained that he was " still a Christian "—mark the phrase, for it made a deep impression — " still a Christian." Perhaps it occurs to you that the guest who was capable of this act of simple courage must have been at least a Bishop. The party was, in fact, made up entirely of laymen. And the guest in question became the great Prime Minister of the early years of the reign of Queen Victoria; he was the late Sir Robert Peel.

There is much which makes many a perfectly sincere man unwilling to say anything, except under great provocation, about his religious belief. He fears that he may discolour, or exaggerate, or distort what he means to say. He distrusts his own moral fitness to say anything at all. He reflects that those to whom he is speaking, although not Christians, may be, according to their light and opportunities, better men than himself. He doubts whether he

will not do more harm than good, through unskilfulness,
or impetuousness, or inaccuracy, or some faults of expression or taste. As he thinks the matter over, he becomes
less and less courageous, more and more fastidious and
unwilling to speak. Meanwhile, every variety of blasphemy and folly has its apostles; every negation, however
audacious and desolating, has its defenders on the platform
and in the press; every superstition, however grotesque
or discredited, has its fanatical devotees; error, moral and
intellectual, stalks abroad everywhere around us, now
loudly advertising, now gently insinuating itself—violent,
moderate, argumentative, declamatory, all by turns. And
is the Religion which our Lord has brought from Heaven
alone to be without advocates or defenders? Are Christians to be the only people who so weigh and mince their
words, who are so fearful of saying too much or of being
too enthusiastic, that they will say little or nothing for
their Master's Name and cause?

You reply that it is the distinguishing prerogative of
Truth that it needs no human supports, and can take care
of itself. Reflect that God, Who might have ordered it
otherwise, has made the propagation and defence of Truth
depend on human effort. No Christian who has the Faith
in his heart can keep it to himself with entire impunity:
a faith which is not communicated will soon shrivel up
within the soul that enshrines it. Even if a man holds
but feebly to a scanty and mutilated creed, his wisdom
is to do what he can to impress what he believes, so far as
his faith is positive, upon others. Like a flower in spring-
tide, his faith will thrive better in the open air than in
the hothouse of a cramped, narrow soul. You kill a conviction by saying nothing about it when occasion requires;
you strengthen it by proclaiming it firmly, modestly,
honestly, fearlessly. Thus, as in much else, the saying

becomes true, that " he that watereth shall be watered also himself." [a]

And if you still hesitate, under the influence of motives you are less willing to own, to do what you may, each within his appointed sphere, for the Person and Truth of our Lord, think of that day of which He speaks in the words before us. Think of the scene, transcending all words, all power of imagining, when He shall come in His own glory, and of His Father, and of the Holy Angels.[b] Think of the boundless exultation, of the unutterable woe; of the hopeless, inextricable confusion settling down, before Him and at His Word, into order— eternal order—the order of Eternal Day and of Eternal Night. How will it fare with us, with you and with me, if His Face, beautiful in its ideal humanity, beautiful in its superhuman glory, is turned away from us, as from those whom He is ashamed to own because in the days of time we were ashamed of Him!

" Lord, Thou knowest my simpleness, and my faults are not hid from Thee;" [c] " O give me the comfort of Thy help again, and stablish me with Thy Princely Spirit. Then shall I teach Thy ways unto the wicked, and sinners shall be converted unto Thee;" [d] " I will speak of Thy testimonies also, even before kings, and will not be ashamed." [e]

[a] Prov. xi. 25.     [b] St. Matt. xvi. 27.     [c] Ps. lxix. 5.
[d] *Ib.* li. 12, 13.     [e] *Ib.* cxix. 46.

# SERMON XLIII.

## THE MYSTERIES OF GOD.

### (THIRD SUNDAY IN ADVENT.)

I COR. IV. I.

*Stewards of the mysteries of God.*

THE Collect, Epistle, and Gospel for to-day all refer to the ministry of the Church, considered as one of the agencies which is intended to prepare mankind for the Second Coming of Christ. St. John the Baptist in prison is the subject of the Gospel; and St. John, as the fore-runner of our Lord at His First Coming, is a great example to be followed by those who have to prepare mankind for His Second. In the Epistle St. Paul discusses the functions and the responsibilities of the Apostolic ministry; while the Collect, which is addressed to our Lord Jesus Christ, combines the Gospel and the Epistle. After referring to the work of the Baptist, it chooses from St. Paul the pregnant phrase, "stewards of the mysteries of God," to describe the office of the Christian ministry. Grant that the "stewards of Thy mysteries may likewise so prepare and make ready Thy way, by turning the hearts of the disobedient to the wisdom of the just, that at Thy Second Coming to judge the world we may be found an acceptable people in Thy sight." Surely a most neces-

sary and wholesome prayer for all of us, during this
Ember-week, when we Christians are supposed, after the
manner of the Church of Apostolic times,[a] to be fasting
and praying before hands are laid next Sunday on those
who are to serve God in Holy Orders ; a prayer which we
shall use all the better if we devote this afternoon to considering the phrase of St. Paul, which is of such capital
importance in it,—"stewards of the mysteries of God."

## I.

"The mysteries of God." There can be no doubt that
this word "mystery" rouses a certain feeling of discomfort,
almost amounting to suspicion and dislike, in the mind of
an ordinary Englishman when he first hears it. In the
customary use of language, too, the word has got into bad
odour by the force of bad association. A "mystery" is
frequently understood to mean something which will not
bear the light ; something which is wanting in the qualities of straightforwardness and explicitness ; which belongs
to the region of charlatanism, intrigue, ignorance, superstition. When a crime has been committed—a theft or
a murder—the author of which has not been found out,
what is the phrase which rises involuntarily to our lips ?
"There is a dark mystery here," we say ; and, as we say
it, the word "mystery" seems to add a new element of
malignity to the crime ; to surround it in our minds with
that peculiar apprehension and dread which belongs to
undiscovered evil. In this sense you observe that hand-
bills published to-day refer to a "Mysterious Explosion
at London Bridge last evening,"[b] meaning, I presume,

[a] Acts xiii. 3.
[b] On Saturday evening, December 13, 1884, a fruitless attempt was
made to blow up London Bridge by means of dynamite.

that its origin and object are obscure.   In this sense a
modern poet speaks of the murderer who

> " On a lonely hill
> Shall do a deed of mystery." [a]

Thus the word is discredited by the force of association.
Shakespeare, indeed, after his wont, claims for it its nobler
sense, when he speaks of

> " Those mysteries which Heaven
> Will not have earth to know." [b]

But, like other words, it has lost caste in popular usage
since his day.

And thus, when we find the word " mystery " in the
Bible or Prayer-book, some of us, almost involuntarily,
turn away from it; we ignore its true force, or, at best,
we treat it as belonging to a state of mind which has
passed away.   It would be curious to ascertain the idea
which the word " mystery " suggests to the first five men
whom we meet in the street.   One man would probably
say, " I mean by ' mystery ' something confused and
unintelligible ; " another, " something involving a plain
contradiction ; " another, " a statement which is chiefly
distinguished by its defiance of reason ; " another, " some
physical or even moral impossibility ; " another, " that
which is believed to be true because there is no real
reason for believing it."   And if these, or anything like
these, are the ideas which are associated by us with the
word " mystery," what wonder that the word is regarded
with a certain dislike and suspicion when it intrudes into
the region of religious truth ?

[a] Praed.              [b] *Coriolanus*, act iv. sc. 2.

# II.

What, then, let us ask, is the true account of this word " mystery " ? As used in the Bible it is not to be confused with a word spelt in the same way, but having quite a different sense and derivation; I mean " mystery " when it stands for a trade, a calling, or even a miracle-play of the Middle Ages. This word is originally French, or, more properly, Latin ;[a] and it is applied to any pursuit, office, or performance which can impart instruction or advice. The word "mystery" in the Bible is a purely Greek word, the termination only being changed. In Greece, for many centuries, it meant a religious or sacred secret, into which, after due preparation, men were initiated by solemn rites. At Eleusis, near Athens, there were famous mysteries of this description. There has been much controversy in the learned world as to their origin and object: the most probable account being that they were designed to preserve and hand on certain tenets which formed part of the earliest religion of Greece, and which were lost sight of, or denied, or denounced by the popular religions of a later time.

A secret tenet thus partially disclosed was called a " mystery," because after disclosure it was still concealed from the general public; because it had been concealed even from the initiated man up to the moment of initiation ; and because, probably, it was of a character to suggest that, however much truth it might convey, there was more to which it pointed, but which remained unknown. This was the general sense which the word had acquired at the time when the New Testament was written.

[a] Magisterium.

Perhaps it will occur to you, as it has occurred to others, to ask, What business has a word with these pagan antecedents to appear at all in the phraseology of the Gospel, in the pages of the New Testament?

The answer is that the Apostles of Christ, in order to make their Divine message to the souls of men as clear as might be, took the words in common use which most nearly answered their purpose, and did the best they could with them; giving them, so to put it, a new turn; inspiring them with a higher significance. Thus, the word[a] which in the original language of the New Testament stands for "Church," had before meant the Athenian people in full deliberative assembly; and the word "liturgy,"[b] which is unhappily buried out of sight in our translation, but which is used in the New Testament of both Jewish and Christian offerings of prayer or sacrifice to God, originally meant some public service or work undertaken, at his own cost, by a private person for the good of the State. The Apostles found these words, as they found the word "mystery," ready to their hands, in the language which they had to use; they were guided to them by the Greek Version of the Old Testament; they, so to speak, blessed and baptized them, enriching them with a new and profound meaning, which yet was not wholly inconsistent with the associations that had already belonged to them for many centuries.

[a] The use of ἐκκλησία in St. Matt. xvi. 18; 1 Cor. xii. 28; Eph. i. 22; iii. 10; v. 23, etc.; Phil. iii. 6; Col. i. 18, 24; Acts xx. 28, etc., is derived immediately from the LXX. translation of קָהָל in Judg. xxi. 8; 1 Chron. xxix. 1; Deut. xxxi. 30; Josh. viii. 35, etc.

[b] Cf. Boëkh, *Athen. Stuatshaush.*, i. 480, *sqq.* The LXX. translate שֵׁרֵת, Exod. xxviii. 35; xxix. 30; Numb. xviii. 2; and עֲבֹד, Numb. iv. 39; xvi. 9, by λειτουργεῖν, which is used in its ecclesiastical sense in Acts xiii. 2, of solemn worship offered to God.

# III.

What, then, is the meaning of the word "mystery" in the pages of the New Testament?

It is used to describe, not a fancy, or a contradiction, or an impossibility, but a truth; yet a truth which has been or is more or less hidden.

Sometimes language itself, the meaning of which is hidden, is called a "mystery," as in the title on the forehead of the woman who typified the Pagan Empire,— Mystery, Babylon the Great, the mother of harlots; [a] or when some Corinthian Christians in their religious assemblies are said to have "spoken mysteries," [b] that is to say, language which was not understood by those who heard it.

Sometimes the word is used of the hidden drift, purpose, meaning, of institutions, or tendencies, or events; as when our Lord speaks of "the mysteries of the Kingdom of Heaven" [c] which it was given to the Apostles to know, or St. Paul of "the mystery of iniquity" [d] which does already work.

Sometimes, again, it is applied to Christian doctrines, which, after being hidden for long ages in the Divine Mind, were at last revealed by men taught by the Holy Spirit; as when St. Paul writes to the Romans of the preaching of Jesus Christ as "the revelation of a mystery, which was kept secret since the world began, but now is made manifest . . . for the obedience of faith," [e] or to the Ephesians, of the call of the Gentiles into the Church of Christ, as "the mystery which in other ages was not made known unto the sons of men, as it is now revealed unto His Holy Apostles and Prophets by the Spirit;" [f] or to

[a] Rev. xvii. 5.  [b] 1 Cor. xiv. 2.  [c] St. Matt. xiii. 11.
[d] 2 Thess. ii. 7.  [e] Rom. xvi. 25, 26.  [f] Eph. iii. 3, 5.

the Colossians, of Christ as an inward Presence in the soul of those who once were heathens, as "the mystery which has been hid from ages and from generations, but now is made manifest unto His saints." [a]

Once more, the word "mystery" is used of truth which has been revealed in outline, or partially, yet of which much is still beyond human comprehension; as when St. Paul bids the Ephesians pray that, while in prison at Rome, he may "make known the mystery of the Gospel," [b] that is, the Gospel which, though revealed, is still in many respects beyond our comprehension; or when he prays that his Colossian converts may be brought to an "acknowledgment of the mystery of God, and of the Father, and of Christ;" [c] or writes to them of "the mystery of Christ," [d] meaning the deeper truths about His Person and His Office; or to Timothy of the "mystery of faith," [e] which the Deacons should hold "in a pure conscience," meaning the partially hidden truths to which faith clings; or of the "mystery of godliness," [f] or piety, meaning especially the Divine Incarnation which Christian piety receives, without being able perfectly to comprehend it. And this sense of the word appears more clearly when St. Paul, foretelling to the Corinthians the instantaneous transformation of the mortal into an immortal body, says, "Behold, I show you a mystery; we shall not all sleep in death, but we shall all be changed;" [g] or when, after describing to the Ephesians that union of Christ with His Church of which marriage is a figure in the world of experience, he adds, "This is a great mystery." [h] Clearly, in each of these revealed facts, there is a great deal which eludes our finite comprehension; they are in this sense mysteries.

[a] Col. i. 26.     [b] Eph. vi. 19.     [c] Col. ii. 2.
[d] *Ib.* iv. 3.     [e] 1 Tim. iii. 9.     [f] *Ib.* iii. 16.
[g] 1 Cor. xv. 51.       [h] Eph. v. 32.

A mystery, then, is a truth, or a fact; the word is never applied to anything else or less; never to a fancy, an impossibility, a contradiction, any shadowy sort of unreality. But it is a partially hidden fact, a hidden truth. Truths are of two kinds; both of them truths, and as such equally certain, but they differ in that they are differently apprehended by us. There are some truths on which the mind's eye rests directly, just as the bodily eye rests on the sun in a cloudless sky. And there are other truths, of the certainty of which the mind is assured by seeing something else which satisfies it that they are there, just as the bodily eye sees the strong ray which pours forth in a stream of brilliancy from behind a cloud, and reports to the understanding that if only the cloud were to be removed the sun would itself be seen. Now, religious mysteries—as we commonly use the word—are of this description. We see enough to know that there is more which we do not see, and which in this state of existence shall not directly see. We see the ray which implies the sun behind the cloud. And thus to look upon apparent truth, which certainly implies truth that is not apparent, is to be in the presence of mystery.

Let us consider this more in detail.

We know, for reasons which need not here be entered on, that One Being only is Eternal; the One Eternal is the One God. If anything distinct from Him shared His eternity, there would be two Gods, not One. Hence it is certain to a serious Theist that matter cannot be eternal. Thus far the spirit of man gazes directly on apparent truth. But while doing so it infers, or rather is guided by Revelation to infer, that at some time there must have been an act on the part of the One Eternal Being whereby He summoned matter into existence out of nothing, and gave it form and organization, and even partially inspired it with life. We call that act Creation. We know that such an act must have taken place. But if we attempt to imagine it in detail; to picture to our minds this process of calling the material universe into existence out of nothing; we find ourselves in the presence of mystery. Creation is a truth, certain to us, but behind the cloud; it is a mystery.

Again, we know, from the testimony of the Evangelists, that our Lord Jesus Christ wore a bodily Form, and lived a true human life upon this planet eighteen centuries and a half ago; men saw Him, spoke with Him, touched Him, satisfied themselves by every ordinary test of His true Humanity. But we also know that He Himself claimed to be infinitely more than man; and that He claimed a homage from those around Him which was inconsistent, not only with the ideal perfection, but with the ordinary and reasonable modesty of mere manhood; that His character and His miracles were alike favourable to the supposition of His being superhuman in His real and deepest life; and that, accordingly, for very adequate reasons, His Church has from the first believed Him to be, and adored Him as being, God.

Thus far the soul is gazing on truth directly; but then comes the question, How can the same Being be both God and man, finite and Infinite, the Lord of Glory and the Victim who died on Calvary? We know it must be so; but here we are in presence of a mystery. It is a truth, but a truth behind the cloud.

Again, as believers in Revelation, we observe that not only the Father, but His well-beloved Son, and the Holy

Spirit, Who is sent both by Him and by His Son, are in
various passages of Holy Scripture spoken of as properly
Divine. On the other hand, no truth is more certain
to a believer in Revelation, or more insisted on in the
Sacred Scriptures, than the Unity and Indivisibility of the
Godhead. How are we to reconcile the two truths—on
the one hand, the true Divinity of each of the Divine
Subsistences, Father, Son, and Holy Spirit; and on the
other, the truth of the Divine Unity? We ask the question; and one answer only is possible, which the Church
gives us as she pronounces the sacred word "Trinity"—
Three in One, One and yet Three. Yet, as she pronounces
it, we feel that the truth, however certain to faith, is for
us, with our limited faculties, largely behind the cloud.
We are in the presence of mystery.

Once again, what do we mean by a Sacrament? We
mean an outward and visible sign of an inward and spiritual
grace, which accompanies the sign and is veiled and conveyed by it. The sign itself is patent to our bodily
senses; we see water, or bread and wine. If the sign is
only a symbol, and implies no inward accompanying Gift,
it is clearly not entitled to much attention. But if our
Lord's words are true, and the sign is an unfailing pledge
of a Divine reality accompanying it; if the water conveys
spiritual regeneration, and the bread and wine veils the
Body and Blood of the Immaculate Lamb, then that
which meets the eye is but as the ray of light which
tells us of the sun behind the cloud, and once more we
are in the presence of mystery. We understand the
Prayer-book when it speaks of "these holy mysteries," [a]
or St. Paul when he says that the Apostles are "stewards
of the mysteries of God."

[a] Communion Service.

## V.

Why, it is asked, should there be in religion this element of mystery? Why cannot everything about it be plain and obvious, lying well within the range of our observation, or at least the range of our reasoning capacities? Why should there be this outlying transcendental margin traced round the doctrines and rites of Christianity; this margin within which the Church whispers of mystery, but which seems to provide a natural home for illusion? This is probably what Toland, by no means the least capable of the English Deists, thought when he undertook the somewhat desperate enterprise of showing that Christianity is not mysterious. To strip Christianity of mystery was to do it, he imagined, a service; to bring it, in the phraseology of that time, within the conditions of nature; to subject it, if possible, to the rules of that world of sensible experience in which we live.

Is it, then, the case that the natural world around us is so entirely free from that element of mystery which attaches so closely to the doctrines and rites of Christianity?

Before very long spring will be here again; and probably some of you will try, in some sort, to keep step with it, even in London, by putting a hyacinth bulb into a jar of water, and watching, day by day, the leaves and bud unfold above, and the roots develop below, as the days get warmer and brighter, until at last, about Easter-time, it will burst into full bloom. Why should the bulb thus break out into flower and leaf and root before your eyes? Why? some one says, "they always do." Yes; but why do they? What is the motive power at work which thus breaks up the bulb, and almost violently issues into

a flower of such beauty, in perfect conformity to a general
type, but yet with a variety that is all its own? You
say, it is the law of growth. Yes ; but what do you mean
by the law of growth? You do not explain it by merely
labelling it ; you explain neither what it is in itself, nor
why it should be at work here or under these conditions.
You cannot deny its existence, and yet the moment you
endeavour to penetrate below the surface it altogether
eludes you. What is this but to have ascertained that
there is something hidden behind the cloud that is
formed by the surface-aspect of nature; what is this but
to be in the presence of mystery?

Or you have a fancy for astronomy, and one of the first
facts which you encounter in this wonderful subject is the
law of attraction, which keeps the heavenly bodies in their
orbits ; the law which governs all that is greatest and all
that is least in the world of matter ; the minutest atoms
and the most stupendous suns. The reign of attraction
is indisputable ; the ratio in which one mass attracts
another can be stated in mathematical language ; and we
live as we do upon the surface of the planet which God
has given us as our home, instead of flying into space,
because we are detained, gently but irresistibly, by the
law of attraction. We repeat the word " attraction " over
and over again, until we think that we know all about
it ; yet what do we know in reality? Attraction is something that none of us has ever seen, or heard, or touched ;
we know not whether it resides in the attracted masses
themselves, or is something distinct from them ; we
cannot say what in itself it is, or why it should exist at
all. The longer we consider it, the more convinced we
become, on the one hand of its reality, on the other of
its transcending all our powers of analysis and detection."

ᵃ *Caro. Essais.*

It is a truth, but a truth behind a cloud; we are in the presence of mystery.

Or when, a few minutes hence, you rise from your seats to leave this Cathedral, what will happen? You will make up your mind to go away, and you will go; that is all. Yes; but what does that mean? It means that an impalpable, immaterial force, be it thought or will, which you name "I," will put in motion, in each case, such and such material forms which you call limbs, and will make them do its bidding. Now, how can a purely spiritual, immaterial essence, of the existence of which you are or may be certain from experience, exert this influence upon matter? What known relation is there between spirit and matter which yields any approach to an explanation? The process is so constant and so familiar to all of us, that we are not alive to its intrinsic wonder; yet, if we will but think steadily about it, we shall see that here too is a truth, in itself certain, yet for us altogether behind a cloud; we shall acknowledge that we are in the presence of mystery.

And when you have passed beyond the doors of the Church, you will probably begin to talk to each other; and thus you will find yourselves face to face with another mystery of nature, if you can only break through the benumbing effect of long familiarity, sufficiently to recognize it. Think of what human language is. It is a variety of sound, produced by bodily, that is to say, by material organs; and, as sound, it belongs to the material world. And yet its value and significance connect it, not with the realm of matter, but with the realm of spirit. It is itself physical, yet it gives shape to so immaterial a thing as thought; it is only apprehended by sense, yet it is a messenger charged with the duty of communicating the most subtle variations of thought from one spirit to another. It bridges the gulf between these immaterial essences which, at the centre of our being, we, each one of us, are; it binds spirit to spirit by creating common convictions, feelings, resolves; or it flashes fire from one to another, kindling into fierce flame responsive passions, and leaving wounds, deep, perhaps ineffaceable, throughout an eternity. Why should such a petty physical incident as articulated sound be charged with these powers and attributes, having such effect and empire in the world of spirit? Ah! why? Think that question over and over; and the longer you think of it, the more surely will you be convinced that here too is a pregnant fact hidden behind the cloud, which as yet we cannot penetrate; you will know that you are once more contemplating a mystery.

The philosopher Locke laid down the doctrine, which has been so often quoted since, that we cannot acquiesce in any proposition unless we fully understand its terms; and hence he inferred that when a man tells us that any mystery is true, he is stating that to which we cannot assent, because a mystery is said to be a hidden, and therefore an uncomprehended, truth. This seems plausible enough at first; but, in fact, we may and do assent, reasonably enough, to a great many propositions respecting the terms of which we have only an obscure or incomplete idea. A man born blind may reasonably assent to the description of the objects which we who have the blessing of sight see with our eyes, although probably no description could give him an adequate impression of their reality. Locke himself, like the great thinker that he was, admitted, he could not help admitting, the infinite divisibility of matter. Yet had he, has any man, an adequate conception of what this means? Think of it steadily for a minute; think that an atom may be divided, and each division subdivided again and again, and that, although the continuously subdivided particles will soon become too minute to be obvious to sense, yet no particle will ever be so minute as to resist further subdivision, so that the process may be continued indefinitely. The imagination follows for a time, and then it fairly recoils from the task, as it does from the task of conceiving of limitless space, or endless duration of time. "The infinite divisibility of matter"—what is this but a truth, certain to reason, yet, for such as we are, with our limited faculties, a truth behind a cloud? It too belongs to the sphere of mystery.

Brethren, we are merely touching on the fringe of a vast subject, capable of almost illimitable expansion. Science does not exorcise mystery out of nature; it only removes its frontier, in some cases, a step further back. Those who know most about nature are most impressed, not by the facts which they can explain and reason upon, but by the facts which they cannot explain, and which they know to be certain, yet to lie beyond the range of explanation. To treat nature as not mysterious is to mistake a superficial, thoughtless familiarity with nature for a knowledge based on observation and reflection.

> "Whene'er the depths we trace, there opes beyond
> An inner world where Science lifts her torch,
> And glorious links we see of heavenly mould,
> But cannot track the chain. Thyself, unseen,
> Sittest behind the mighty wheel of things
> Which moves harmonious, though unheard below." [a]

And the mysterious creed of Christendom by its mysteriousness corresponds with nature, which is so constantly mysterious; while both are only what we should expect in a revelation—and nature, too, in its way, is a revelation [b] —of the Infinite God.

[a] Williams' *Cathedral*, 121.        [b] Rom. i. 20.

Suppose that a religion claiming to come from God were wholly divested of this element of mystery; suppose that it spoke of a God Whose attributes we could understand as perfectly as the character of our next-door neighbour, and of a government of the world which presented no more difficulties than the administration of a small joint-stock company, and of prayer and rules of worship which meant no more than the conventional usages and ceremonies of human society. Should we not say, Certainly, this is very intelligible; it is wholly free from the infection of mystery; but is it really a message from a higher world? is it not too obviously an accommodation to man's dwarfed conceptions? does it not bear the trademark of a human manufactory somewhere about it? After all, we may dislike and resent mystery in our lower and captious moods; but we know, on reflection, that it is an inevitable note of a real revelation of the Infinite Being, and that if the great truths and ordinances of Christianity shade off, as they do, into regions whither we cannot hope to follow them, this is only what was to be expected if Christianity is what it claims to be.

## VI.

"Stewards of the mysteries of God." That, then, is the idea of the Apostolic and ministerial office which St. Paul would have his Corinthian readers lay well to heart. Such an office has, undoubtedly, other sides and functions; but this aspect of it was well calculated to lift a great subject above the degraded level to which the personal and petty quarrels at Corinth had dragged it down; above the invidious comparisons and worthless discussions that were bandied about between his own especial adherents and those of St. Peter and Apollos. In this higher

atmosphere the man would be forgotten in the office.
It matters not who planted or who watered, or what are
the individual characteristics of the stewards; everything
merely personal shrinks away into its proper insignificance,
in presence of that sublime yet humbling relation to the
mysteries of God, which was common to all.

"Stewards of the mysteries of God." Guardians and
dispensers not of any store of merely human knowledge,
or of moral influences of human origin and compass, but
guardians and dispensers of truths which in their magnificence elude human comprehension and measurement;
which, while they touch man's life most searchingly and
intimately, reach far away into the distant heavens.
Guardians and dispensers of ordinances which are no
mere symbols of absent blessings, but instruments of
direct contact with the unseen but glorified Redeemer,
and so are charged with forces of incomparable value for
the souls and bodies of men. For, of a truth, all of these
mysteries of revelation gather in one sublime mystery,
which is the heart of all besides, which says less to our
speculative faculty, less to our sense of wonder, than to
our hearts and wills; the mystery that "God"—the
Almighty, the Infinite, the Everlasting, the All-wise—
"so loved the world, that He gave His only begotten Son,
that whosoever believeth in Him should not perish, but
have everlasting life." [a]

"Stewards of the mysteries of God." To this serious
and sacred work some scores of young men will dedicate
their lives, for this work they will be empowered from
on high, in this Cathedral and elsewhere, on this day
week. Few things in life stir in us a deeper interest than
the sight of a young man giving freely back to God the
life which God has given him, when it is at its freshest and

[a] St. John iii. 16.

its best; giving Him his thought and his memory, his affections and his will, to be disposed of as God shall see good in the coming years, for God's greater glory and for the well-being of souls. It is with the life of Christ's ministers as with the life of man; we may hope much from the promise of its bright morning, but we can be certain of nothing until the end has come.

In this perilous service the clearest and most powerful minds may go astray; the warmest affections may be perverted and degraded; the most vigorous and direct wills may become feeble or warped; the best and most deliberate intentions may be forgotten and laid aside; the disinterested may become self-seeking; and the humble, vain or even insolent; and the gentle, irritable; and the laborious, slothful; and the self-denying, self-indulgent; and the zealous, indifferent; and the reverent, profane; and the earnest of purpose, frivolous. Without God's sustaining grace in this scene of danger and weakness which we call life, any deterioration is possible; and mere natural aptitude or capacity guarantees nothing, and counts for nothing. Poor indeed and inadequate must any powers, whether of mind, or heart, or will, indeed appear, when the exacting claims of that awful stewardship are well considered; when it is considered how easy is failure in that virtue of faithfulness which is always a steward's first virtue; how easy to be wanting to the claims of God, the claims of truth, the claims of souls; how easy to forget that account, stern and certain, which of all men the steward of God's mysteries will one day have to give.

Surely, during this Ember-week, these young men have great claims on your sympathy and on your prayers; that they may, even amid failure, endure to the end, faithful in heart and purpose; and that, through the grace of our

Lord Jesus Christ, they may so prepare and make ready His way, that those to whom they shall severally minister, when we of an earlier generation have been gathered to our rest, shall, at His Second Coming to judge the world, be found an acceptable people in His sight.

# SERMON XLIV.

## THE END.

(SECOND SUNDAY IN ADVENT.)

REV. XXI. 6.

*And He said unto me, It is done. I am Alpha and Omega, the Beginning and the End.*

IN the passage before us, St. John hears the announce-
ment of a completed work. "It is done." He has
been gazing at the vision of the New Jerusalem. The
first Heaven and the first earth have passed away. The
proclamation has gone forth, "Behold, the tabernacle
of God is with men." [a] All tears are to be wiped away
from human eyes. There is to be no more death, nor
sorrow, nor crying, nor pain; since the former things are
passed away. As the seer listens, "He that sitteth upon
the throne saith, Behold, I make all things new." [b] And
then another brief utterance;—then another pause. "And
He said unto me, It is done. I am Alpha and Omega,
the Beginning and the End."

It is not within our purpose to inquire too narrowly
into the whole reference of these words in the Vision
of Patmos. This, at least, they do mean; that an old
state of things had ended; that a new world had begun.

[a] Rev. xxi. 3.      [b] *Ib.* 4, 5.

"It is done!" When, at an earlier stage of the vision, the seventh angel had poured out his vial into the air, there came a great voice out of the temple of Heaven, from the Throne, saying, "It is done!"[a] In either case, the close of an epoch is proclaimed; the knell of a dispensation, of a probation, of a struggle, sounds from a sphere which lies outside time. In either case, the Voice of God falls on the soul's ear with a solemnity all its own. "It is done!"

There are other moments in the Bible, two especially, at which God is represented as pausing, after bringing one great district of His work to a completion. Such a moment was that which closed the work of Creation. "On the seventh day God ended His work which He had made; and rested on the seventh day from all His work that He had made."[b] Such a moment was that on Calvary, when, hanging on the Cross, He summed up in one word His own everlasting purpose for our redemption, and the long series of humiliations and efforts, of teachings and examples, of acts and sufferings, whereby He had willed to work out that purpose to its very end. "It is finished!"[c] And as at the beginning of time, and as in its mid-career, so once more, when time is passing away, and all that has been is finally precipitated into its enduring form, the words sound from Heaven, "It is done!"

"It is done!" There is often a difficulty, not of the reason, but of the imagination, in thinking that anything will end; or, at least, anything in which we are actively interested. Reason, of course, knows that we are living on a passing scene; that nothing continueth in one stay; that memory and observation equally report changes which presage, if a remote, yet an inevitable end.

[a] Rev. xvi. 17.　　[b] Gen. ii. 2.　　[c] St. John xix. 30.

But imagination will often refuse to entertain and to dwell upon broad and importunate, but unwelcome facts; imagination is beset and possessed by the pressure of present interests, of hopes for the immediate future, of all that belongs to self. And let us remark that the world of thought has its fashions just as much as the world of poetry, or music, or dress; and just now, anything that can call itself evolution is as fashionable as it was of old, in the days of Lucretius. Men look out for a graduated sequence in the course of events; catastrophes, we are told, are discredited. Why events ever began to succeed each other at all, or to what they are tending as their final goal,—these vital questions are never raised. But a one-sided way of looking at the facts of life is seized upon by the imagination, which thus will clog and check the equitable action of reason; will throw unwelcome facts into an arbitrary background; will envelop plain conclusions in a cloud of mystical indefiniteness, and so will create an irrational confidence that, somehow or other, things will for ever go on very much as they do.

## I.

This appears, first of all, in the power we most of us have of putting aside altogether the thought of death. That other men may die—yes, that is intelligible; we see that they do die. But that I shall die; that a day will come when these senses, which for so many years have been the organs of the soul within, will have ceased to act; when these eyes will never see another sun, and these ears never hear another sound; when these hands and feet will lie motionless and cold, in the first stage of advancing decay;—this it is hard to imagine. Imagi-

nation, which can carry us off into some private dream-
land, in which fancy and caprice run unrestricted riot,
will at times be so paralyzed as to refuse to contem-
plate the plainest facts. And thus it happens that a
vast number of men never think seriously about the
most certain of all the events that await them in their
earthly life; the event that will bring it to a close.

The most certain, I say, of all the events that await
you and me is our death. You are a young man or
woman just entering life. Will you be admired and
well spoken of, or the reverse? You do not know. Will
your family life some years hence be a centre of warm
affection, or a scene of unspeakable discomfort and
misery? You do not know. Will your health be sound
and buoyant, or will you spend several years in a long
struggle with disease and pain? You do not know.
Will you sustain overwhelming reverses, or will you
float down the appointed years, enjoying an even tenor
of success? You do not know. Will you be the first
of your generation to die, or its last survivor? Will you
linger on, when all who knew and loved you in your
youth are withdrawn; will you linger on, perhaps with
a sore heart, longing for a summons which fails to come?
You do not know. You do not know how you will die,
or when, or where; in your bed, or in the streets, or in
a railway accident, or by a flash of lightning; to-night,
to-morrow, ten years hence, fifty years hence; in peace
and resignation, trusting in the completed work of our
Lord Jesus Christ, and strengthened for your last passage
by His Sacraments; or in terror and bewilderment, without
any light from Heaven to guide you through the gloom.
All these circumstances are unknown to you; but of the
inevitableness and certainty of death itself, you ought
to be as well assured as of your own existence. "It is

appointed to men once to die." [a] This is one of those sayings of Scripture which the wildest unbelief has not essayed to question. " It is appointed."

Yes! at a certain day, hour, and moment, we, each of us, shall die. The exact moment is known now, but not to us; we shall know it, first of all, by experience. We shall become aware of the approach, stealthy or rapid, of a sense of internal collapse and ruin; we shall experience the advancing, overwhelming darkness; the felt retreat of life, first from this sense or organ, then from that; the trembling hold upon the little that remains, and that must presently be forfeited; the last spasm, the last sigh; and then as another scene, strange and unaccustomed, beyond all that imagination can conceive, opens upon us, an utterance, as from the Throne, will sound through the depths of our being, " It is done ! "

There was an old custom invariably observed fifty years ago, when I was a boy living in a country parish, but now, I fear, increasingly if not generally disused; the custom of tolling the passing bell at, or as soon as possible after, the moment of death. It came down from days when men had a robust belief in the power of prayer; in its efficacy to bring help and strength to others at all times throughout life, but especially in the last agony. It was a summons which with each stroke of the bell seemed to proclaim, " A man is passing through the most awful of all the experiences that await us; pray for him, Christians—pray ! Already he sees sights and hears sounds which you too will one day hear and see. You may help him, you know not how much, on his road, if so it be, to light and peace; pray for him, Christians—pray ! "

[a] Heb. ix. 27.

But the passing bell had another meaning : it proclaimed that a soul had come to the end of its probation ; that all its sorrows and joys, its trials and advantages, its triumphs and its failures, its virtues and its sins, had reached their appointed term ; that it had crossed the line which parts time from eternity. It implied that already that life lay spread out in its completeness before the eye of the Infallible Judge ; like a river, tracked from its source in some remote mountain glen, flowing by villages and cities, receiving tributaries, watering pastures, and at last, in its full volume, burying itself in the ocean beyond. All is over now ; something more wonderful than the largest star or sun ; the moral probation of a soul. It is over ; each stroke of the bell echoes the voices of the angels and the judgment of God: "It is done ; it is done !"

## II.

The same difficulty of entering into the fact that that which exists now and here will come to an utter end, appears in our way of thinking about organized human life— about society. Many a man who looks forward to his own dissolution in a vague kind of way, falls back on the reflection that at least society will last on after him, as the home and stay of those who bear his name ; of those whom he loves and who love him. It is, indeed, difficult to see precisely what society will do for him, if it does survive him ; yet there is a touch of generosity in his care for it, mingled, however, with a somewhat cowardly unwillingness to recognize his real isolation in death. But we Christians know that one day human society, in its parts and as a whole, will come to an utter end. This is a sort of catastrophe

which many of you find it especially difficult to anticipate.
You study a section of human history; you mark man's
progress from a lower to a higher stage; you observe the
steps of social and political growth, the order and symmetry
of human progress. As society presses on along the path
of accumulating wealth, of scientific discovery, of enlarged
personal and political freedom, of nobler sense of all that
lies within the compass of associated human life, the task
of imagination in conceiving that it will all utterly end
becomes increasingly difficult. It looks so stable and so
strong; so vigorous and so justly self-reliant; so based
upon high courage, or keen sagacity, or hard common
sense, that nothing, it seems, could avail to shake it. So
thought the Egyptians under the kings of their ancient
monarchy, and the Tyrians whom Isaiah and Ezekiel
warned against trusting in the credit and range of their
commercial greatness, and the Persians under Cyrus, and
the Romans under the greater Cæsars, and the French
under Louis XIV. To the subjects of Vespasian and
Titus, and to the Roman people for many a day afterwards, the social structure of the empire seemed to be at
least as strong as the masonry of their Colosseum, which
has survived it for more than a thousand years. And the
old nobility of France never dreamt of breaking up in a
Reign of Terror, when it thronged the gardens of Ver-
sailles to make the court of the Great Monarch. It is
with human society as with individual human lives;
"the day of the Lord cometh as a thief in the night."[a]
It is, our Lord warned us, as in the days of Noah, when
"men ate and drank, and married and were given in marriage; until the day that Noah entered into the ark, and
the flood came and destroyed them all."[b] Certainly there
are symptoms which may be noted from time to time, and

---

[a] 1 Thess. v. 2.　　　　　[b] St. Luke xvii. 26, 27.

which show how fragile is this or that portion of the social fabric, and so suggest how much nearer to ruin the whole may be than we generally suppose. But it is so easy to put out of account that which does not obtrude itself on sight ; to make no allowance for the unforeseen ; to assume that the apparent is the real, and that the real is always permanent. And so men drift on until something happens that startles the world out of its dream of security ; and as an old régime breaks up and disappears beneath the waves of revolution, or a throne that has been raised on a million bayonets is humbled to the dust, a voice sounds from above for those who have ears to hear, which foretells a more universal and final doom : " It is done ! "

## III.

Still more difficult do men find it to accustom themselves to the conviction that one day this earthly home in which we live will itself be the scene of a vast physical convulsion. In the short Epistle which tells us so much about the future, St. Peter says that " the day of the Lord will come as a thief in the night ; in which the heavens shall pass away with a great noise, and the elements shall melt with fervent heat, the earth also and the works that are therein shall be burned up." [a] The course of nature— the phrase itself helps to disguise the truth—the course of nature seems so ascertained and, within certain limits, so unvarying, that the mind recoils from the thought that one day all this ordered sequence of movement and life, of growth and decay, will suddenly cease, buried in the ruins of a vast catastrophe. The difficulty really resides in the reluctant imagination ; but Imagination always looks much

[a] 2 St. Pet. iii. 10.

more respectable when she gives herself the airs of Reason
—especially of scientific Reason—and so talks about the
reign and perpetuity of physical law.   Law, it seems,
will effectually prohibit the occurrence of any such catastrophe ; it could, we are told, only be anticipated, even by
an Apostle, in an unscientific age.   Now, let us observe
that such a catastrophe need not imply the utter cessa-
tion of what we call law, but only the suspension of some
lower law or laws through the imperial intervention of a
higher one.   We see this suspension of lower by higher
laws constantly going on around us ;  indeed, it is an almost
necessary accompaniment of man's activity on the surface
of this planet.   You and I never lift our arms without so
far suspending and defying the ordinary operation of the
law of gravitation ; and constantly, in our industrial activities, in our railroads and steamboats, we hold powerful
laws in check by inviting the assistance of other laws,
until some fine day the repressed law escapes for a moment
from our control, and crashes in upon us with a terrible
revenge.   St. Peter, when arguing against the scoffers of
his time, who maintained that because all things continued
as they were from the beginning, therefore the promise of
Christ's coming had become worthless, points to the Flood
" whereby the world that then was, perished." [a]   Yet
this catastrophe was brought about by the operation of
existing laws.   And if this was so, is it inconceivable that
He, in Whose Hands and Whose workmanship we are,
should have other and more imperative laws in His illimitable universe than those which immediately surround our
puny life ; moral laws which have their roots in the necessities of His Eternal Being, and not mere physical laws,
which He has made to be what they are according to His
good pleasure ?   Is it inconceivable that a day shall come

[a] 2 St. Pet. iii. 3–6.

when these highest and royal laws should override the
lower, bursting in upon them with the decisive authority
of the Perfect and Supreme Will, and utterly wrecking
that fair natural order of things which seems to us so
stable and so beautiful?

Ah! there are occurrences from time to time in this
our earthly home which may suggest to us the possibilities
of a greater and more world-embracing catastrophe than
any we have yet witnessed. Earthquakes are not things
of remote antiquity. Even your children will have heard
something of the mighty convulsions by which a fair
island off the coast of Naples was made, not long since,
utterly desolate;[a] by which, in the Eastern Archipelago,
the very surface of the globe was changed, tracts of
country covered by large populations being submerged
beneath the sea, while new islands and promontories were
thrown up from its depths.[b] Nay, this very year, as the
wonted benevolence of the Mansion House may remind
us, the tremendous subterranean forces which are ever at
work beneath the thin crust of our globe have burst up
to the surface with savage impetuosity, at one moment in

[a] The earthquake at Ischia took place on Saturday, July 28, 1883.
The town of Casamicciola was almost entirely destroyed. In fifteen
seconds all was over. Some 3000 persons were said to have been killed by
the falling buildings.

[b] "All previous natural catastrophes seem to grow pale before the
tremendous disaster that befell the island of Java on the 26th of August,
1883. Torrents of fire on land and huge waterspouts at sea were the
prelude to the entire disappearance, about midnight, of a large tract of
country with a whole chain of mountains. On the following night one
volcano was split into five distinct peaks, and on the succeeding morning
sixteen new volcanic islands had appeared in the sea between Java and
Sumatra. A large part of the town of Batavia was wasted, first by the
streams of lava, and then by the advancing waves; several other towns
were completely destroyed; and all the lighthouses on the Sunda Strait
have disappeared. The total loss of life is estimated at from 80,000 to
100,000" (*Guardian*, September 5, 1883).

Greece,[a] and at another at Charlestown,[b] as if to warn us
that a broad belt of insurrectionary fire runs along under
the very countries which are the home of our most
advanced civilization, and that where man's empire over
nature seems to be most completely assured and established, it is, perhaps, most frail and insecure. In
presence of a great earthquake, how powerless is man ;
how utterly do his wonted resources fail him ; how tragi-
cally does his very knowledge add only to his weakness
and confusion, by making him only better able to comprehend his utter impotence, his inability to escape from
or to arrest his doom! And do not such occurrences
suggest to us a greater and more overwhelming scene,
when not this or that portion only of the globe will
be laid desolate ; when, after a scene of final and universal ruin, the words will be heard from out the Throne,
"It is done "?

## IV.

These are the elements involved in the Christian representation of the Second Coming of Christ ; the end of all
human probations, the final dissolution of the organized or
social life of man, the destruction of man's present home
on the surface of this globe. There is, then, nothing in
them violently contrary to experience ; nothing more than
an extension of facts of which we have experience. Indi-

[a] On August 27, 1886, an earthquake was felt throughout Greece,
occasioning a loss of life which was estimated at 300, and injuries, which
were not fatal, to 600 persons. Its greatest violence was in the south-west
of the Morea.

[b] On August 27 and 28, 1886, some shocks were felt at Charlestown,
and in other parts of South Carolina and Eastern Georgia. The centre of
the disturbance was Charlestown, which was almost destroyed. On the
31st occurred the most destructive earthquake on record in the United
States. It affected twenty-two states, from the Gulf of Mexico to the
Great Lakes, and from the Atlantic to the Mississippi.

vidual life abounds with the presages and presentiments of
death. The aggregate life of man, human society, con-
tains within itself many a solvent which threatens its ruin.
And the planet which we inhabit is an encrusted ball of
fire, which may one day pour out over its fair surface the
destructive lava which already surges and boils beneath
our feet. And when all is over, what will remain? "He
said unto me, It is done. I am Alpha and Omega, the
Beginning and the End." God, the Almighty, the All-
wise, the Compassionate; God, the Infinite, the Immeasur-
able, the Eternal; Father, Son, and Spirit in undivided
Essence, remains. Before anything was made, He was as
He is; He will be as He is when all this present order
of existence shall have passed away. "The beginning!"
It is from Him that the planet on which we dwell, the
society of which we form a part, the souls and bodies
which are ourselves, draw their being. "The end!" It is
for Him that all exists; His good pleasure is the reason
and warrant that any being exists that is not Himself;
and when the creatures of His Hand vanish, He still is.
He sits above the waterflood of human life, remaining
a King for ever.[a] He sits above it; and its busy labours,
its boisterous agitations, its insurgent passions, its mad-
ness and its scorn, its frivolity and its insolence, its forgetfulness of Himself, its defiance of Himself, its loud-voiced,
foolish blasphemies against Himself, die away upon the
ear, and, except that they are recorded in His Book, are
as though they had never been, while He remains. He is
Omega as well as Alpha; He is the End as well as the
Beginning. He will have the last word, after all. He is
not merely a spectator; He is a Judge, the most instructed
and the most equitable. He will have the last word; the
word of mercy and the word of justice.

[a] Ps. xxix. 9.

There are two principal reflections which you should
try to take home with you.

One is the insignificance of our present life. We
understand this when we look back on it. We most of
us spend our time in looking forward; and anticipation,
like a magnifying-glass, makes earthly objects look much
larger than they really are. We only understand their
true littleness when we have handled, and have passed
them. That success in literature, that new measure of
social consideration, that fortune, that professional decoration, that opportunity for indulgence,—how big did it
loom in the distance while as yet it was future! And now
you have attained your wish, and look back on it; and lo!
it fills neither the heart nor the eye. " It is done ! " So
with long tracts of time. We look forward eagerly to a
coming year; we have plans, and schemes, and ambitions,
and cares in view which light it up with interest. We
look back when it has passed; and little or nothing
remains but the mark which it has left upon our
characters.

It is natural that, so long as they can, those who believe
in no future life should exaggerate the worth of this. It
is, indeed, their all; and when, before their eyes, it begins
to break up and disappear, they have no resource but
despair. But we Christians have a hope, sure and steadfast,[a] of a future which is infinitely greater, and which can
assure to an immortal spirit, through union with Him
Who is the true End of its existence, a satisfaction which
is here impossible. For us, the instability and perishable-
ness of all human things are but a foil to the Eternal Life
of God. When a calamity befalls him or his, a pious
Moslem will exclaim, " God alone is great ! " And we
Christians do well to think over all that disappoints us

[a] Heb. vi. 19.

here in the light of the Prophet's description of that day, when all will be seen to be insignificent save God.

> " Enter into the rock, and hide thee in the dust,
> For fear of the Lord, and for the glory of His Majesty.
> The lofty looks of man shall be humbled,
> And the haughtiness of men shall be bowed down,
> And the Lord Alone shall be exalted in that day.
> For the day of the Lord of Hosts shall be
> Upon every one that is proud and lofty,
> And upon every one that is lifted up ;
> And he shall be brought low :
> And upon all the cedars of Lebanon, that are high and lifted up,
> And upon all the oaks of Bashan,
> And upon all the high mountains,
> And upon all the hills that are lifted up,
> And upon every high tower,
> And upon every fenced wall,
> And upon all the ships of Tarshish,
> And upon all pictures of desire.
> And the loftiness of man shall be bowed down,
> And the haughtiness of men shall be made low :
> And the Lord of Hosts shall be exalted in that day." [n]

The other reflection is the immense importance of life. Yes, this life, so brief, so transient, so insignificant, so made up of trifles, of petty incidents, of unimportant duties, is the scene upon which, in the case of every one of us, issues are decided the importance of which it is impossible to exaggerate—issues immense, lasting, irreversible. It is this conviction which in Christian eyes invests every life with interest and dignity, and makes the career of the poorest and the humblest as important, when looked at from this lofty point of view, as that of the greatest in the land. It is this conviction which supplies the answer to the secularist criticism upon Christian ideas of life, that they direct our attention so engrossingly to the world beyond the grave as to unfit us for the duties of

[n] Isa. ii. 10-17.

this. No; this is not the legitimate or natural effect of Christian faith. If it refuses to regard this state of being as other than insignificant in itself, it never can think of it as of less than the highest importance in its consequences. Here, under the gloomy skies of our northern home, we may be training for that world which needs no sun, since the Lamb is the Light thereof.[a] Here, within the narrow bounds of a few years of time, we decide, by using God's grace or by neglecting it, what we are to be for ever. And when the short space allotted to us has passed, we too shall hear, each of us, the voice, in judgment or in mercy, "It is done. I am Alpha and Omega; the Beginning and the End."

May we learn to keep well in view both the insignificance of life and its transcendent greatness; its greatness in its capacities and prospects, its insignificance in itself! And may He Who has made us for Himself, enable us, by His grace, to resolve this very Advent that we will begin to live in good earnest for Him, Who once came among us that He might redeem us by His Blood, and Who will come again to judge us, and the vast, unnumbered company of the quick and the dead!

[a] Rev. xxi. 23.

# SERMON XLV.

## PREMATURE JUDGMENTS.

### (THIRD SUNDAY IN ADVENT.)

1 Cor. iv. 5.

*Therefore judge nothing before the time, until the Lord come.*

THE Church of Corinth, almost in its earliest days, and unfortunately for its highest interests, was turned into a school of ill-natured criticism. There were several parties in it, each claiming the authority and sanction of great names; one even, with less reverence than audacity, claiming the Most Holy Name of all. "One saith, I am of Paul; and another, I of Apollos; and I of Cephas; and I of Christ." [n] Each party was occupied in finding what fault it dared or could with the names appealed to by the others; and thus three of the parties, or some of them, taunted those who clung especially to the name of St. Paul with the suggestion that their much-loved Apostle was not "faithful." He might be an active preacher and organizer; he might be a person of great versatility and resource, a great letter-writter, an ingenious disputant. This they were not prepared to deny. But he had one capital defect: he was not "faithful." He

[n] 1 Cor. i. 12.

was wanting in that directness and sincerity of purpose which is indispensable in a public servant of Christ.

Now, St. Paul deals with this charge in that paragraph of his Letter to the Corinthian Church which is selected for to-day's Epistle.[a] People had better, he says, think of himself and of all the Apostles, not in their personal capacity, but as being by office ministers of Christ and stewards of His Sacraments. No doubt a steward must be before all things faithful. But whether the Corinthians or any other men think him, Paul, faithful or not, matters little, he says, to himself; since he does not even venture himself to decide whether he is or is not faithful. His conscience, indeed, reminds him of nothing that obliges him to think himself unfaithful; but, then, he remembers that this does not of itself prove him to be faithful, since he does not see very far, and he is judged by One Who knows more than he knows; Who, in fact, knows all. And, therefore, the Corinthians, too, had better give up their habit of thus judging either him or other men. Let them "judge nothing before the time, until the Lord come."

This precept against judging others often occurs in the Bible; it is prominent in the teaching of our Lord. "Judge not, that ye be not judged. For with what judgment ye judge, ye shall be judged : and with what measure ye mete, it shall be measured to you again."[b] And St. Paul himself warns the Romans, "Therefore thou art inexcusable, O man, whosoever thou art that judgest;"[c] and he asks, "Who art thou that judgest another man's servant? to his own master he standeth or falleth;"[d] and he presently adds, "Let us not therefore judge one another any more : but judge rather this, that no one put

---

[a] 1 Cor. iv. 1–5.      [b] St. Matt. vii. 1.
[c] Rom. ii. 1.      [d] *Ib.* xiv. 4.

a stumbling-block or an occasion to fall in his brother's way."[a] These are only samples of passages which will occur to your memories.

## I.

Now, what is the exact force and import of the precept? Is it meant that we are to form and express no judgment whatever upon human conduct; upon anything that we see and hear of in the world around us?

This, it would seem, cannot possibly be meant, and for more reasons than one. The first reason is, that, if we think at all, many judgments, of the mind, if not of the lips, are inevitable. What is the process that is going on with every human being, every day from morning to night? Is it not something of this kind? Observation is perpetually collecting facts and bringing them under the notice of Reason. Reason sits at home, at the centre of the soul, holding in her hands a twofold rule or law; the law of truth and the law of right. As Observation comes in from its excursions, laden with its stock of news, and penetrates thus laden into the chamber of Reason, Reason judges each particular; by the law of right, if it be a question of conduct; by the law of truth, if it be a question of faith or opinion. In a very great number of cases the laws of truth and right, as held by the individual Reason, are very imperfect laws indeed; still Reason does the best she can with them, and goes on, as I say, sitting in her own court, judging and revising judgments from morning until night. Probably two-thirds of the sentences we utter, when closely examined, turn out to be judgments of some kind; and if our mental or moral natures are healthy, judgments of some kind issue from us as naturally as flour does from a working

[a] Rom. xiv. 13.

corn-mill. How can it be otherwise? God has given to
every man a law or sense of right. As a consequence,
every action done by others produces upon us a certain
impression, which, when we put it into words, is a judgment. When we hear of a monstrous fraud, of a great
act of profligacy, or of a great act of cruelty, we are
affected in one way; when we hear of some self-sacrificing
or generous deed, of some conspicuous instance of devotion
to duty, we are affected in another: we condemn or we
approve, as the case may be. Woe to us, if we do not
thus condemn or approve; for this would mean that our
moral nature was drugged or dead! Woe to a society
which feels no indignation at evil and wrong-doing, and
no enthusiasm for good; for it is in a fair way to go
utterly to pieces! Woe to a man who has no eye for the
lights and shadows of the moral world; to whom virtue is
much the same as vice; who sees between them only a
difference of physical tendency, or a difference of sentiment or taste;—he, too, is on his road to ruin! "Woe to
them," cries Isaiah, "that call evil good, and good evil;
that put darkness for light, and light for darkness; that
put bitter for sweet, and sweet for bitter!" [a] If the moral
sense is alive, if the moral nature is sound, it must judge;
not with a parade of declamation against the vices of
other days or other classes than our own, but with the
short, sharp, resolute expression of antipathy to that
which is in contradiction to its governing law. Not to
do this is to capitulate to the forces of evil; it is to
cancel the law of right within us. In the same way
God has given us a law or sense of truth. As to what is
true, some of us are, probably through no merits of our
own, better informed than others; we are, for instance,
instructed Christians and instructed Churchmen, who

[a] Isa. v. 20.

know and believe the whole body of truth taught by our
Lord and His Apostles.  If this is so, many opinions we
hear around us, contradicting in various senses and degrees the body of truth which we hold to with the full
strength of our understandings, cannot but provoke judgments.  We approve of agreement; we disapprove of dis-
agreement with that which we hold for truth.  Not to do
so is to cease to hold truth as true; it is to hold it to be
nothing better than probable opinion.  In our days men
sometimes think it good-natured to treat truth and falsehood as at bottom much the same thing; but this cannot
be done for long with impunity.  In the first age of
Christianity it was not so.  "Ye have an unction from the
Holy One," wrote St. John to the first Christians, "and
ye know all things.  I have not written to you because
ye know not the truth, but because ye know it, and that
no lie is of the truth.  Who is a liar but he that denieth
that Jesus is the Christ?  He is antichrist, that denieth
the Father and the Son."[a]  This direct language of St.
John would jar upon the ear of a generation which thinks
that something is to be said for every falsehood, and
something to be urged against every truth ; but it is the
natural language of those to whom religious truth is a
real thing, and not a passing sentiment or fancy.  The
law of truth within us necessarily leads to our forming
judgments no less than does the law of right.

Nor is this all.  For, in the second place, as, indeed,
you will have already reflected, Holy Scripture stimulates
and trains the judicial faculty within us, making its activity keener and wider than would have been possible
without it.  The servants of God in the Bible are intended
to rouse us to admire and imitate them ; and what is this
but a judgment of one kind ?  The sinners in the Bible,

<hr />

[a] 1 St. John ii. 20–22.

from Cain to Judas Iscariot, are intended to create in us
moral repulsion, not for their persons, but for their crimes ;
and what is this but an inward and emphatic judgment
of another kind? And as the Jewish Law, by its higher
standard, makes the judicial faculty in man more active
than it was in the case of the heathen ; so Christianity,
with a higher standard still, makes it yet more active in
the Christian than in the Jew. Thus, a Jew might give
his wife a writing of divorcement for various causes : our
Lord says that this was permitted only for the hardness
of men's hearts; and He withdraws the permission.
Eminent Jews, like David, were polygamists : our Lord
proclaimed anew the original law of one husband and one
wife. A Christian cannot help condemning acts—I do
not say agents—that violate the law of Christ; not to do
so is to renounce that law as a rule of thought and conduct.
Perhaps, by the exhortations appended to his Epistles,
St. Paul has done more than any other writer in the New
Testament to rouse and guide the Christian judgment. A
Christian ought, according to the Epistle to the Hebrews,
to have his moral senses exercised to discern between
good and evil.[a] The most serious charge brought by the
Apostle against the Church of Corinth was that the
Corinthians had not taken to heart a notorious case of
incest which had occurred among them. " Ye are puffed
up, and have not rather mourned, that he that hath done
this deed might be taken away from among you." [b] Evidently the Apostle wished the faculty of moral judgment
to be active at Corinth, if it was to issue in such practical
consequences as this. Human society has always found
it necessary to lay upon some of its members the duty of
judging others. Every day of term causes are heard and
judged in our law-courts " before the time." Is this to

[a] Heb. v. 14.          [b] 1 Cor. v. 2.

contravene the teaching of St. Paul? Is it not clear that, without some such officer as a judge, associated human life would be impossible? Differences will arise, crimes will be committed, human nature being what it is, even when it has been renewed and blessed by Christ; and unless differences are adjusted and crimes are punished, human society will go to pieces. No; a judge, so far from being an unchristian functionary, is the organ, within narrow limits, of the judgment of the human and Christian conscience. Within narrow limits, I say, because he can only deal with human actions so far as they do or do not traverse the law which, wisely or less wisely, society has made in order to protect itself. What these actions are in themselves, what they are before God, what He is thinking about them now, and how He will deal with them hereafter; of all this a human judge, at least as a judge, knows nothing. He has no pretensions to be a moral inquisitor; his duty is to administer the law of the land. In this last capacity he is, most assuredly, not traversing the precepts of the Gospel, unless the law of this or that country, in this or that particular, should unhappily be opposed to them.

## II.

What, then, is the Apostle's exact meaning when he bids the Corinthians judge nothing before the time?

The point is, what does he mean by "nothing"? what is the class of judgments no one of which is permitted to a Christian?

Some of the Corinthians were saying that the Apostle was not faithful or sincere. If they had merely said that he did not teach the truth, he would have argued the matter out with them, as he did with the Judaizers in

Galatia. As it was, they undertook to decide what was
the character and worth of his motives. And therefore
he bids them "judge nothing;" that is, nothing of this
purely internal character, "before the time, until the Lord
come." Our Lord would drag bad motives from their
obscurity, "bringing to light the hidden things of darkness." Our Lord would show, in the full light of day, the
motives upon which all before His Throne had really acted,
"making manifest the counsels of the hearts."[a] It is, then,
the judgment of that which does not meet the eye—of
characters as distinct from acts—which is forbidden us by
our Lord and His Apostle. If we witness an act of theft,
we must say that it is an act of theft, and that Almighty
God will punish it. If we are asked to say what is the
moral condition of the thief before God, the answer is
by no means so easy; there are serious reasons for our
hesitating to give one at all. This thief may be already,
like his penitent predecessor of old, preparing for death
and with a promise of Paradise sounding in his ears.[b]

One reason which makes it difficult for all of us to
judge the characters, as distinct from the acts, of other
men equitably is this; we are seldom, if ever, without a
strong bias ourselves. We have, as the phrase goes, our
likes and dislikes; and only those who have a very strong
sense of justice try to keep these tendencies well in hand
before they speak or act in relation to others. We, perhaps, flatter ourselves that we only really dislike that
which is evil, or which we believe to be so. Goodness
often comes to us in a very unattractive garb, with a
rough manner and a coarse address; we think too much
of the garb to do justice to that which it shrouds. Evil
comes to us dressed up in the best possible taste, with
the tone and distinction of good society everywhere

[a] 1 Cor. iv. 5.          [b] St. Luke xxiii. 40–43.

apparent in its movement and expression; and we shut
our eyes to its real character for the sake of its outward
charm. Are we sure that we always welcome virtue, even
when it is not presented to us disagreeably? Just let us
reflect that, whether we know it or not, each of us has a
weak side, as we call it; a tendency to some one kind of
sin. If we watch ourselves, we are pretty sure to discover that this tendency exerts a subtle influence on our
judgments of others. We do not heartily welcome virtues
which we instinctively feel condemn ourselves. If our
tendency be to vanity, we find it hard to do justice to the
humble; if to sloth or sensuality, we disparage the ascetic;
if to untruthfulness, we make fun of the scrupulously
accurate; if to uncharitableness, we vote those who say
the best they can of their neighbours dull company. We
assume, without exactly knowing what we do, that the
virtues which cost us little or nothing to practise are the
most important virtues, and that the vices which contradict them ought to be judged with the greatest severity.
We think little of, or at any rate less of, those portions
of the Divine Law which we find it hard to obey, or
perhaps do not obey; we are disposed to treat violations
of them in others with great tenderness. Who does not
see that a bias like this disqualifies us for honest, equitable judgment of character, and that it warns us not to
judge character before the time, until the Lord come?

Another reason which makes a true judgment of the
real moral condition of a fellow-creature so difficult, is our
necessary ignorance of all his circumstances. If circumstances do not decide our actions—and they certainly do
not, the human will being what it is—they do, nevertheless, influence us very seriously.[a] Natural temperament is
sometimes a protection, sometimes a temptation; home is
sometimes a temple of holiness, sometimes a very furnace

[a] Sanderson, *De Oblig. Consc.*, Pr. ii. Wks. iv. 30.

of evil; education may be a training for Heaven, it may
also be a training which would make Heaven odious if it
were attainable. The balance of passions in one man's
physical frame; the balance of natural qualities in the
understanding and heart of another; the grace which
has been given, or which has not been given; the friends
who have been near us, at critical times in our lives, to
give our career a good or, it may be, a fatal turn, by a
word in season, or a sneer, or an innuendo never since
then forgotten;—all these things enter into the serious
question, How far do circumstances excuse or exaggerate
our guilt; how far do they account for or enhance what
there is of good in us? Who of us would dare, with
his eyes open, to attempt an answer in the case of any
human being whom we know? One Eye only can take a
full and equitable account of circumstances. He knew
what had been the circumstances of the penitent thief,
when He said, "This day shalt thou be with Me in
Paradise." [a] He knew what had been the circumstances
of Judas, when He said, "It were good for that man if he
had never been born." [b] As for us, we do not know, we
only guess at, the real sum of circumstances, inward and
outward, of any human life; and therefore we had better
"judge nothing before the time, until the Lord come."

A third reason is that we see only the outside of life
and character in those whom we judge, and whom we
think, perhaps, we know most intimately. This consideration tells in two directions. Sometimes, under the most
unpromising appearances, there is a fund of hidden good.
We all of us have known people with a manner so rude
as to be almost brutal, whom we have afterwards discovered to have very tender hearts. And persons are
to be found in London who have a reputation for stingi-

[a] St. Luke xxiii. 43.   [b] St. Mark xiv. 21.

ness, but who really save up their money that they may give it to the poor without letting the world know what they do. In the same way we may have met people whose conversation strikes us as uniformly frivolous, or at least as wanting in seriousness, and yet it may be that this is the effect of a profoundly serious, but shy, reserved nature, bent on concealing from any human eye the severe, self-scrutinizing, self-repressing life within.

On the other hand, outward appearances may be uniformly fair, while concealing some secret evil that is eating out the very heart of the soul, like an organic disease which is at work upon the constitution long before it declares itself. Nay, every man who is trying to serve God must know and deplore the contrast between his real self and the favourable reputation which he enjoys among his friends, and must experience something like relief when, now and then, he gets abused, even unjustly, since in this way the balance is partly redressed. We cannot anticipate God's judgments in either direction; He alone knows His elect; He alone knows who will finally be parted from Him for ever. He looked of old on a pagan, and He said, "Lo, I have not found such great faith, no, not in Israel." [a] He looked on some of those who had the greatest reputation for goodness in His day, and He pronounced them "whited sepulchres, which indeed appear beautiful outward, but within are full of dead men's bones, and of all uncleanness." [b] He said that the first on earth would often be the last hereafter, and the last first. [c]

You may here remind me of our Lord's words, "By their fruits ye shall know them." [d] Yes! but know whom, or what? Is our Lord speaking of the human character, and telling us that a man's acts are always the clue to

[a] St. Matt. viii. 10.    [b] *Ib.* xxiii. 27.
[c] *Ib.* xix. 30.    [d] *Ib.* vii. 20.

his inmost self? No; He is speaking of false prophets, and He tells us that the goodness or badness of human actions is a guide to the worth of the systems which produce them. He is giving us a test of doctrines. As for character, it is by no means always or adequately to be measured by acts. The Pharisee's good acts were more numerous than those of the publican; but the publican's inward disposition justified him before God.[a]

Once more, there is the soul of every action; the intention with which it is done. It is the intention which gives to our acts their real meaning, their moral worth. Apart from its intention, an act is merely the product of an animated machine. We cannot say that an action is really good, though it may be good in its outward form and drift, until we know something of the purpose with which the agent went to work.[b] Thus many actions in themselves excellent are corrupted by a bad motive. Prayer is a good action; so is fasting; so is almsgiving. But we remember what our Lord said of those who prayed, or gave alms, or fasted, to be seen of men.[c] Let us ask ourselves what was our motive in coming to church this very afternoon. There is only one motive which Almighty God would accept; a desire to serve Him, and to approach nearer to Him. Was that motive ours? If we take two-thirds of the acts on which we pride ourselves to pieces, and ask ourselves quite honestly why we did them, what will the answer be? This, surely, is a very serious question; since a bad motive destroys the acceptableness of an act, however excellent in itself, before God. On the other hand, certainly, a good motive cannot transform an act, in itself bad, into a good act. A lie remains a lie, even if we tell it with a pious motive. Murder is murder, even though its object be to rid the world of a tyrant or an assassin. All that a good motive can do is to soften the character of a bad act in certain circumstances. St. Paul says that he obtained mercy for the acts of cruelty and oppression of which he was guilty in his old unconverted days, because he had persecuted the Church in the good faith of ignorance, believing himself to be thus doing God service.[a]

What a mysterious, unknown world is that of the intentions with which men act! Human law is justly shy of this undiscovered region; it touches the fringe of it, but reluctantly, now and then, as when it essays to distinguish manslaughter from murder. But what do we really know about it? And, in our ignorance, how can we possibly undertake to judge the inward life of others before the time?

On two occasions, indeed, St. Paul might seem to have violated the spirit, if not the letter, of his own precept. When, on the occasion of his last visit to Jerusalem, he was pleading his cause before the Jewish council, the High Priest, Ananias, illegally commanded him to be smitten on the mouth. St. Paul hereupon addressed him as a "whited wall,"[b] that is, a hypocrite; since he professed anxiety for the law which he was actually breaking. If St. Paul subsequently apologized[c] for not recognizing the High Priest, he did not apologize for so describing a person who had acted as the High Priest had acted. So when, at an earlier date, Elymas the sorcerer, at Paphos, was doing what he could to prevent the conversion of Sergius Paulus, and withal enjoyed a reputation for goodness to which the Apostle knew he was not entitled, St. Paul addressed him as "full of all subtilty and wickedness, a child of the devil, an enemy of all righteousness."[d]

---

[a] 1 Tim. i. 13; Acts xxvi. 9; cf. iii. 17.
[b] Acts xxiii. 1-3.  [c] *Ib.* 5.  [d] *Ib.* xiii. 10.

The acts both of the High Priest and of Elymas had afforded the Apostle grounds for his language; and yet, if we had been in his position on either occasion, such language about individuals would have been wrong in us. The truth is that the Apostle was acting under the influence of a high inspiration, which discovered to him the real character of the men with whom he was dealing, but which it would be altogether contrary to humility and good sense in you or me to assume that we possessed. If our Lord said to His hearers, "Ye hypocrites!"[a] as He did more than once, Christians at least believe that He saw the men through and through whom He thus addressed; He saw them so perfectly, that there was not a trace of injustice in the description. And if at times this power of discerning spirits[b] was imparted to His servants, it is clear that they were not, in exercising it, on the one hand forgetful of their own teaching, or on the other hand examples for us to imitate.

### III.

"Until the Lord come!" Yes! only when He comes will there be a judgment at once adequate and universal. Well is it for us that we have not to trust to any of the phrases which are sometimes proffered us as substitutes for the Last Judgment. The judgment of conscience! Yes, but whose conscience? What probability is there that the wrong-doer's conscience will do justice to his victim; and how would it profit his dead victim, if it did? The judgment of posterity! Lazarus would have deemed the judgment of posterity a poor exchange for Abraham's bosom; and how would you or I, if we were wronged in this life, be bettered by the judgment of posterity? Pos-

---

[a] St. Matt. xvi. 3; St. Mark vii. 6; St. Luke xi. 44.   [b] 1 Cor. xii. 10.

terity, the chances are, will know nothing whatever about
us.  Posterity forgets all in the generations that precede
it, save the few names of historic eminence that float upon
the surface of the mighty past.  With these it does busy
itself; and it may be that hereafter some such now living
will receive a measure of justice which is denied them by
contemporary opinion, while others, who are much on the
lips of men, will be consigned to relative insignificance.
Posterity does judge the few eminences of a past age ;
and our days have seen various attempts to rehabilitate a
Tiberius, an Alexander VI., a Richard III., a Henry VIII.,
an Oliver Cromwell.  But whether posterity is right or
wrong, what does it matter to those most concerned?
They hear nothing of its favourable or unfavourable
verdicts; they have long since passed before a higher
tribunal than that of the modern literary world which
thus absolves or condemns them.  And what about the
millions of whom posterity never hears, but who have no
less need of a claim on justice than the few names that
survive in literature?  Surely it is well that we may
look forward to something better than the judgment of
the human beings who will take our places here.

"Until the Lord come!"  Yes!  He can do that which
we cannot do.  He can judge men as they are.  He has
been appointed to judge the world in righteousness, because He is what He is, the Sinless Man, and withal infinitely more.  There is no warp in His perfect Humanity,
whether of thought, or temper, or physical passion, that
can affect the balance of His judgment; there is no sin
or weakness to which He has a subtle inclination, or of
which He will ever exaggerate the evil.  Nor is He
ignorant of any circumstances that excuse or enhance the
guilt of each who stands before His Throne; He has had
His eye all along upon each one of us, as of old upon the

woman of Samaria, up to the moment when she met Him
at the well of Jacob.[a]  And He can form not merely an
outward but an inward estimate of us; for now, on the
Throne of Heaven, no less than in the days of His earthly
life, He knows what is in man.[b]  He has no need to make
guesses about us; He sees us as we are.  He is never mis-
led by appearances; He has searched us out and known
us, and He understands our thoughts long before.[c]  And
therefore, when He does come, His judgment will be
neither superficial nor inequitable; it will carry its own
certificate of justice to the inmost conscience of those
whom it condemns.  "He will bring to light the hidden
things of darkness, and make manifest the counsels of the
hearts."[d]  In view of this judgment we may well shrink
from judging before the time that which really lies
beyond our ken; the inner condition of those about us.
To climb up upon the Throne of the Judge of quick and
dead is something worse than a waste of time; it were
better to act on His own warning by judging ourselves,
as unsparingly as we have been tempted to judge others,
that we may not be judged.[e]  We have the consolation
of knowing that He Who did not abhor the Virgin's
womb, and Who overcame the sharpness of death, will
also come to be our Judge.  "There is mercy with Thee,
O Lord; therefore shalt Thou be feared;"[f]  "We therefore pray Thee, help Thy servants whom Thou hast
redeemed with Thy Precious Blood."

[a] St. John iv. 7-26.  [b] *Ib.* ii. 25.  [c] Ps. cxxxix. 1.
[d] 1 Cor. iv. 5.  [e] St. Matt. vii. 1.  [f] Ps. cxxx. 4.

# SERMON XLVI.

## THE DIVINE SERVANT.

(FOURTH SUNDAY IN ADVENT.)

St. Luke xxii. 27.

*I am among you as he that serveth.*

WHEN, in His love and condescension, our Lord Jesus Christ came among us, nearly nineteen centuries ago, He brought with Him a new ideal and standard of what human life should be. It differed in many respects from the standard which was accepted by the Jews; it differed, of course, still more widely and deeply from that which was generally accepted by the heathen. And· in nothing was this latter difference more marked than in the encouragement which our Divine Saviour gave to a life of service, and the high honour which He put upon it.

## I.

In the old pagan days it was generally held that the best and happiest thing for a man was to do as little work as possible, and to be waited upon by all around him. This idea prevailed very largely throughout the ancient world; but its greatest sway was in the East. In the opinion of an Oriental, the happiest of human beings was a despot of the Babylonian or Persian type.

His throne was an isolated social pinnacle, around which multitudes of men fawned and trembled, and he was only approached with prostrations of the most abject character. His word, though expressing but a passing whim, was absolute law, before which the greatest as well as the lowest of his subjects bowed their heads. Every duty that could make life irksome was discharged for him by an array of slaves, silent, obsequious, accomplished, active; everything that could irritate or disturb him was, so far as possible, kept out of the reach of his eye and ear; and thus his life was spent in a ceaseless round of serene pomposities, in which the monotony of undisputed command was only varied by the sensual indulgences which it placed at his disposal. This was, nay, it still is, through large districts of Asia, the prevalent idea of happiness; nor was it much otherwise when our Lord was on the earth, and for some centuries afterwards, among the subjects of Imperial Rome. Millions of men looked up to the reigning Cæsar, to a Tiberius, to a Nero, to a Domitian, as to the happiest of mortals, who had, presumably, unbounded wealth, unbounded power, and, above all, nothing to do, or at least no more to do than he had a mind for. Such happiness was indeed, in the popular opinion, more than human in its compass; and when the Cæsars betook themselves to claiming the honours of divinity, and had temples, and altars, and statues erected to promote their worship, their obsequious subjects, instead of resenting the absurdity and blasphemy of the proceeding, found it quite natural to acquiesce in or even to anticipate it. What could be nearer divinity, in the judgment of those toiling millions—largely slaves—than a human being who had so much power, so much money, and, above all, so much leisure?

Israel was an Asiatic people; but in Israel the reve-

lation of the One True God kept the exaggerations which
were natural to the Asiatic temperament more or less in
check. A people which had upon its heart and conscience the impress, the awe-inspiring impress, of the
Everlasting and Infinite Creator, could not readily bend
before ideals of human happiness which appeared un-
questionable to Babylonians or Persians.

The Jewish kings, however disloyal at times to the
religion of Sinai, were never as a class kings of the
thoroughly absolutist type; they were themselves subjects
of a Being Whose infinite superiority they could never
wholly forget; they were servants of God as well as rulers
of their people. Of all the Jewish kings Solomon is, perhaps, most like an ordinary Eastern monarch. And yet
Solomon's life, notwithstanding its parade of wealth and
luxury, and of worse things towards its close, was mainly
a life of service. For, in truth, the Mosaic Law was
remarkable as a consecration of labour; and the prophets
again and again insisted upon aspects of the Will of God
and of human duty which were entirely opposed to the
ideas on which was built the throne of an Assyrian king.
Especially in the last period of his long ministry, Isaiah's
prediction of the promised Messiah, not as an unoccupied
Sovereign of man, but as the Servant of God, toiling, misunderstood, insulted, suffering, yet eventually triumphant,
was an inspired picture which could not but leave its mark
on the mind of Israel.[b] Still, whether the reason was
traceable to their captivity in Babylon, or to their subse-
quent contact with the Syrian kings in the Maccabæan
period, Israel was often haunted by the Eastern ideal,
which, nevertheless, it did not wholly accept. Our Lord
implies this when He asked His hearers whether, when
they went into the wilderness to see St. John the Baptist,

---

[a] Bersier, vol. vii. p. 215.          [b] Isa. xlix.–liv.

they had expected to find a man clothed with soft raiment,[a] like the well-dressed and leisurely officials who hang about the ante-chambers of an Eastern Sultan. His hearers were still beset by the notion that there was something especially blessed in being thus altogether provided for, and having nothing to do. But it was upon the Gentile world that our Lord had His Eye, at least mainly, when insisting on the blessedness of service. It was of the kings of the Gentiles exercising lordship over them,[b] and representing immunity from obedience and work, that our Lord was thinking when He pointed to the Son of Man, "Who came not to be ministered unto, but to minister."[c] It was to a world which deemed obedience and labour to be degrading as well as unwelcome that He pointed the implied contrast, "I am among you as he that serveth."

## II.

Yes, He came holding up what was practically a new idea of what the best human life should be—the idea of life voluntarily devoted to service.

What do we mean by service? We mean generally two things; obedience and occupation. There is much occupation that is in no sense service; it is self-chosen, motiveless, frivolous. And there is obedience which does not involve occupation, or at least active occupation; it is the constrained obedience of a prisoner in his cell, or the unproductive obedience of mutes at a funeral. True service means work, and work performed, not at a man's own discretion, but under orders of some kind; at the least, under an imperative sense of duty. And in this sense our Lord led a life of service.

[a] St. Matt. xi. 8.    [b] *Ib.* xx. 25.    [c] *Ib.* 28.    Cf. Bersier, *ubi supra.*

Now, Holy Scripture speaks of this aspect of His appearance among us as involving a contrast, almost a violent contrast, with His pre-existent state. " Being in the Form of God, He did not look upon His equality with God as a prize to be eagerly retained in His grasp,[a] but He took on Him the form of a servant.[b] He folded it round His Eternal Person; He assumed a Body of Flesh and Blood, a Human Soul, that in this created Nature He might work and obey, rendering to the Father a true and perfect service on behalf of His brethren. His Incarnation meant, as we knew, much else; but, among other things, it meant a capacity for service.

And this feature of our Lord's Life is stamped upon it from His early youth. As a Boy of twelve He went down with His mother and St. Joseph to Nazareth, and was subject to them.[c] We can picture Him, even as a young Child, running day by day by His Mother's side from the Holy Home, which was some way up the hill, on the slope of which Nazareth is built, down to the fountain which still flows in the valley; and watching her fill her pitchers with water; and helping her, as He grew in years, to carry her burden up to their humble dwelling. We can see Him, as a young Man, working in the carpenter's shop hard by with His foster-father, St. Joseph; doing the rougher work, no doubt; sent on messages to customers, carrying the timbers, sharpening the tools, fastening pieces of wood together in a rude way; and leaving it to the older workmen to put the finishing touch to what He had begun. And when He entered on His ministry, His whole later life was marked by the character of service. Consider His teaching. While, on the one hand, the truths which He taught were so profound and sublime that even the reluctant intelligence of His keener con-

---

[a] οὐχ ἁρπαγμὸν ἡγήσατο.  [b] Phil. ii. 6.  [c] St. Luke ii. 51.

temporaries proclaimed that "never man spake like this
Man,"[a] His method of instruction was accommodated to
the narrow minds, the vulgar prejudices, the moral obtuse-
ness, the slow and gross understandings of the peasants
who followed and listened to Him.   If we imagine Bacon
or Newton spending their whole lives in a village Sunday
school, and teaching very young children in words of
one syllable, we should only get a very distant and faint
idea of the intellectual interval that parted our Divine
Lord from the disciples who understood Him best.   His
parables, His explanations of His parables, His repetitions
again and again of what He had said already, His patient
refutation of arguments which must have appeared to
Him infinitely silly—in short, His whole bearing as a
Teacher face to face with His disciples and with the Jews
—bears the strong constant imprint of service.   So, too,
it was with His actions.   He never moved about Palestine on the principle of a traveller who had no ties, and
was free to go where He liked.   Every movement, every
action, was dictated by the exigencies of a rule—the rule
of obedience to the Father's Will.[b]   He did not invite or
seek success ;  He did not look out for audiences or neighbourhoods which might do Him, as we speak, some sort
of justice ;  He spent those three years within a territory
scarcely larger than the largest of English counties, and
in a ministry which seldom or never won for Him any
considerable return of appreciation or gratitude.   'What a
waste!' many a man might be tempted to exclaim, in an
age when, as in ours, publicity is taken to be the test of
excellence.   'What a waste of power, of capacity for effect-
ing enormous results, on a theatre too insignificant to
permit them!'   What a waste indeed; unless it had been
more than justified by that note of moral beauty which

[a] St. John vii. 46.          [b] St. Luke ii. 49.

amply compensates for what we call failure—the note of service.

On one day, as you will remember, when the end was close at hand, He exhibited this inner law of His life in outward characters, so that all might read it. He literally served His disciples after the menial fashion of an Oriental slave. "Jesus knowing that the Father had given all things into His Hands, and that He was come from God, and went to God; He riseth from supper, and laid aside His garments; and took a towel, and girded Himself. After that He poureth water into a basin, and began to wash the disciples' feet, and to wipe them with the towel wherewith He was girded." [a] What a spectacle is here! Here is One before Whom the highest of creatures is insignificant, demeaning Himself as though He were the lowest and the last of all; washing one by one the feet of His wondering, sometimes reluctant, Apostles; washing, among the rest, the feet of Judas! Never, surely, was the possible dignity, I had almost said the majesty, of service illustrated so forcibly as in that humble chamber in Jerusalem, unless it was when, a few hours later, the Servant of His brethren became obedient unto death; and, ere He died, took on Him a burden which cost Him, the All-holy, more to carry than we sinners can conceive; the burden of "the sins of the whole world." [b] "He bare our sins in His own Body on the tree;" [c] as though He were Himself the representative sinner, the typical criminal of the whole race. He did not flinch from the hateful burden till He had thoroughly discharged His appointed task, His unshared, unrivalled, incomparable service; He did not lay it down until He could pronounce that no further service of this high order remained or was needed; until He could exclaim, "It is finished!" [d]

[a] St. John xiii. 3–5.　　　　[b] 1 St. John ii. 2.

[c] 1 St. Pet. ii. 24.　　　　[d] St. John xix. 30.

# III.

Let us ask ourselves, brethren, why our Lord has done so much for mankind in proposing a life of service as the true life of man. Service is thus necessary, in some shape, for all of us, because it involves the constant repression of those features of our nature which constantly tend to drag it down and degrade it. That acute observer of human nature, Aristotle, remarked more than two thousand years ago, that all our faulty tendencies range themselves under the two heads of temper and desire; bad temper or ill-regulated desire. When the one element is not predominant in an undisciplined character, you will find in some shape the other; and sometimes the one and sometimes the other, at different periods, in the life of the same man. Now, service, that is, the voluntary undertaking of work in obedience to a Higher Will, is a corrective to each of these tendencies; and first of all of temper, in its ordinary and every-day form of self-assertion, or pride. The man who serves heartily cannot indulge self-assertion; he represses self, if he tries to perform his service well. Each effort, each minute, each five minutes, each hour, each day of service, has the effect of keeping self down; of bidding it submit to a higher and more righteous Will. And this process, steadily persevered in, ultimately represses self, if not altogether, yet very considerably.[a] And what a substantial blessing is this to human nature, to human character! Be sure that self-assertion, if unchecked, is pitiless, when any obstacle to its gratification comes in its way. Cain cannot pardon Abel for the acceptance of his sacrifice;[b] the brethren of Joseph cannot forgive those presentiments of a greatness which will eclipse their own;[c] Saul will not tolerate

[a] Cf. Pusey, *Par. Serm.*, i. serm. 23, "The Will of God the Cure of Self-Will."  [b] Gen. v. 3-5.  [c] *Ib.* xxxvii. 5-11.

David's endowments and popularity so near his throne;[a] Haman would fain revel in the extermination of a whole people, because forsooth a single courtier has failed in the etiquette of some public homage to which he conceives himself entitled.[b] With us, indeed, outrageous self-assertion is kept in order by law. No Nero can fire London for the pleasure of contemplating the sight; no Attila or Timour can ravage the world for the pure satisfaction of seeing dynasties, kingdoms, cities, races, crumble away, or shrink from before him in abject terror. But the same brutal willingness to sacrifice everything to self is there, even though cramped and confined within very narrow limits; it still has the power of diffusing pure wretchedness in a circle, petty or wide, as the case may be. The self-asserting man delights in making an equal or an inferior feel the full weight of his petty importance; he enjoys the pleasure of command in the exact ratio of the pain or discomfort which he sees to be caused by obedience. Thus sooner or later self-assertion becomes tyranny, and tyranny, sooner rather than later, means some revolt which involves the ruin of order. The tyrant in the state, in the family, in the office, in the workshop, is the man bent on the assertion of self; and, despite the moments of gratification, such a tyrant is more miserable than his subjects. For the governing appetite of his character can never be adequately gratified; it is in conflict with the nature of things, with the laws of social life, with the Divine Will. And when it is repressed, curbed, crushed by voluntary work in obedience to a Higher Will, a benefit of the first order has been conferred on human nature, on human society.

In like manner, work voluntarily undertaken in obedience to a Higher Will corrects ill-regulated desire. Distinct

---

[a] 1 Sam. xviii.          [b] Esth. iii. 5, 6.

from gross sins, is the slothful, easy, enervated, self-pleasing temper, which is the soil that fosters them. The New Testament calls this district of human nature concupiscence,[a] that is to say, misdirected desire; desire which was meant to centre in God, the Eternal Beauty, but which, through a bad warp, does in fact attach itself to created objects, and generally to some object attractive to the senses. This evil can only be radically cured by making God once more the Object of desire ; that is, by a true love of God. And a true love of God will express itself in service ; the service of men as well as of God. For, as the Apostle argues, " he that loveth not his brother whom he hath seen, how can he love God Whom he hath not seen?"[b] Service keeps ill-regulated desire at bay, and it concentrates the soul's higher desire, or love, more and more perfectly upon its One legitimate Object. Besides this, it braces character; and this is what is wanted if a man is to escape from the enervation of the life of sensuous and effeminate ease.

Look at that young man ; he has been well brought up, perhaps even in a religious atmosphere, and yet all the vigour of his temperament is gone ; it is undermined and sapped by the enervating influence of a life of pleasure. Perhaps he bears a noble name ; but what will he do with it ? What will he do with the old castle, which some rude but vigorous ancestor won for his stock ? He breathes an atmosphere now which vitiates all that he touches and is. He delights only in the literature, the art, the companionships, which reflect the soft, nerveless, sensual character that vegetates rather than lives within him ; that feels when it ought to think, and talks when it ought to resolve or to act. Without any true interest in one serious study, how will he be able to kill time ? Ah ! we well may ask. He will occupy himself with all that ministers to the life of sense; the balls, the theatres, the gossip, the clubs, which feed his diseased nature with congenial nutriment. But what will he do that costs him anything? Nothing. What will he do for the comfort or honour of his family? Nothing. What for the credit of his order, or for the glory of his country? Nothing. What for the real good of mankind, or for the interests and promotion of religion? Nothing. These things mean effort; and he is as incapable of effort as one of those creatures, half vegetable, half animal, that stick to the rocks or the seashore, and only open their fat flabby mouths to eat whatever may be floated into them by the waves. Not that such characters are only to be found among the more prosperous classes of society. Human nature is much the same at either end of the social scale, whether in its regenerate or unregenerate state. And many a man who might find work ready to his hand, but who spends his time lounging about the streets and the public-houses, till want and desperation drive him, perhaps, into violent courses, is not less a Sybarite at heart, though there be more to be said in excuse for him than for .his wealthy compeer. When such types of character as these are common, the ruin of a great country is not far off. And that which defers it is the resolute adoption by her better citizens of a life of service; of work dictated by a sense of obedience or duty; in a word, of a life modelled upon the Supreme Example which has been given us by our Lord and Saviour.

## IV.

It is then, rightly, the glory of our Lord and of His Religion and Church to have proclaimed that the true life of man is a life of service. But this glory has been

made a subject of reproach by a not inconsiderable school
of modern writers. Yes! it is said, Jesus Christ told us
that He was among us as one that serveth; and He has
imprinted only too successfully the temper of servility
on the Christian world. His Apostles are true, in this
matter, to the servile spirit of their Master. They preach
the subjection of every soul to the higher powers,[a] even
when a Nero is on the throne. They will not interfere
even with slavery; it is part of the established order of
things. The world, they held, may come to an end any
day; and there was no object in promoting changes which
might be the last events in history. Hence Christianity
has always been in favour of passive submission to wrong;
of contented acquiescence in the indefensible; of resignation which, if it adorns individual character, only does so
at the heavy cost of protecting any antiquated social abuse
that retards the progress of the race.[b]

Now, it is obvious to remark that the bearing of our
Lord and His Apostles, in circumstances of difficulty
and danger, ought of itself to have made this criticism
impossible. Servility is the last charge that can be
brought against the fearless Preacher Who confronted
mobs, ignorant and ferocious, and scribes and Pharisees,
less ignorant but more ferocious, with the invincible
calmness that befits the possession of Truth. Indeed,
another infidel criticism on His work is that He was a
reckless incendiary, Who led a revolt against the old laws
and institutions of His country, and was justly punished by
their appointed guardians. And if St. Paul is classed by
some moderns among those who have misused their influence to induce men to submit to established evils without complaint or resistance, he was, as we know, described
in his own day, by those who most earnestly opposed him,

---

[a] Rom. xiii. 1.      [b] J. C. Morison, *The Service of Man*, p. 187.

as one of a band who had "turned the world upside
down." [a] The incompatible criticisms may be left to
balance or to eliminate each other; the fact being that
the service enjoined by our Lord and practised by His
Apostles was in no sense servile. It was voluntary service
—the service of God and man—the motive of which was
the love of God. Certainly the Apostles did not undertake to reform the government of the Roman Empire, or
to do away with slavery, by preaching revolution and a
social war. Had this been their object, they might have
given trouble, at least at the close of the Apostolic age,
to the Roman authorities; there was a deep sense of
wrong among Christians, as we may read between the
lines of the Epistle to the Hebrews, or even of the Epistle
to the Romans. But the Apostolic preaching was, "Let
every soul be subject;" [b] "Let every man abide in the
same calling wherein he was called." [c] They might have
appealed to what they taught concerning justice, and the
fundamental equality of all human beings before God;
they might have met violence with violence, blood with
blood, even if they were eventually crushed. They pre-
ferred the power of conscience to the power of the sword,
silence and patience to retaliation; they won the day, not
as soldiers on battle-fields, but as martyrs on the blood-
stained floors of amphitheatres; and they conquered by
suffering.

What is it, brethren, that prevents the service of our
fellow-men from degenerating into servility? It is the
consideration that in this service, in all service, a Christian should aim, before all else, at serving God. As
St. Paul says of the Christian slave, when performing
menial duties for his heathen master, he is to do it, not
with eye-service, as a men-pleaser, but in singleness of

[a] Acts xvii. 6.          [b] Rom. xiii. 1.          [c] 1 Cor. vii. 20.

times, is a man who administers a property which is not his own. This, we may be very sure, was the occupation of Eliezer of Damascus,[a] the oldest steward known to history; the steward of the house of Abraham. Eliezer brought with him, as it would seem, from the ancient Syrian city, the experience and knowledge which enabled him to preserve and to add to the flocks and herds and movable utensils of the wandering patriarch. But Eliezer had no sort of joint proprietorship in the possessions of Abraham; he was probably a slave, or at any rate an unpaid servant. He found his reward in the supply of his own daily needs which was thus secured to him; and still more in the trust reposed in him by his master, and in the frequent and intimate intercourse which it implied. And so it has been with stewards ever since down to our own day. The steward's relation to a property is distinguished, on the one hand, from that of those who have nothing to do with the property, because the steward has everything to do with it that he can do for its advantage; and on the other from that of the owner of the property, because the steward is in no sense an owner of it, but only an adminis- trator; his duty towards it is dependent on the will of another, and it may terminate at any moment. You remember how Shakespeare marks the ancient difference between the King of England and any who acted for or under him :—

> " Take on you the charge
> And kingly government of this your land :
> Not as protector, steward, substitute,
> Or lowly factor for another's gain."[b]

And as, with the progress of years, the nature of property has become inevitably more complex than it was in simpler times, the duty of taking care of it has been more

[a] Gen. xv. 2.  [b] *Richard III.*, act iii. sc. 7.

and more largely delegated by its real owners to others who represent them ; and great estates and great commercial companies, indeed every considerable accumulation of wealth, is almost, as a matter of course, committed to the care of some person or persons, who in fact are stewards. The steward, whatever he may be called, is at least as familiar a personage in the modern as he was in the ancient world.

Now, what is the central idea of such an office as a steward's ? It is before all things a trust. It represents, in human affairs, a venture which the owner of a property makes upon the strength of his estimate of the character of the man to whom he delegates the care of the property ; it is an assumption—it may be a warranted, it may be a precarious or unsound assumption—that the risk is a justifiable one, and that a generous confidence will not be abused. We know how fully this confidence was justified in the case of the ancient steward to whom reference has been already made. The difficult and delicate mission to Padan-Aram, in quest of a wife for Isaac among the kinsfolk of Abraham, was carried out by Eliezer with a loyal faithfulness which contributes one of its most beautiful episodes to the Book of Genesis.[a] We know how this confidence was abused by the steward in the parable,[b] who may not have been an imaginary person, but an actual administrator of an estate in ancient Palestine. And we have not to tax our memories very greatly in order to recall examples of a great abuse of a great trust, resulting in the misery and ruin of hundreds of persons who had placed their little properties in the keeping of some one who had no sense of the sacredness and obligations of his position. Of this let us be sure, that as no greater honour, because no more practical proof of good opinion, can be

[a] Gen. xxiv. 2–67.  [b] St. Luke xvi. 1–7.

done by one man to another than is done when trust or
confidence is practically reposed in him ; so no greater
wrong can be done, nothing more calculated to destroy all
good understanding, and, indeed, all permanent social relations between man and man, than a breach of trust.  To
repose trust in another is an act of generosity ; and to
betray that trust, when so reposed, is an act of baseness
proportioned to the nature and greatness of the trust
reposed.

This is the first idea attaching to a steward's office ; it
is a trust.  And a second is, that for its discharge an
account must at some time be rendered to some one.  This
accountability of the steward to some one lies in the
nature of things.  A steward with no account of his work
to render is, morally as well as socially, inconceivable.
The liability to give an account can only be avoided
where nothing has been received from another, and where,
consequently, there is no trust.  Strictly speaking, one
Being only, He from Whom all else proceed, and Who
owes nothing to any besides Himself, is not liable to give
an account of His administration.  The being who merely
takes oversight of, and does what he can with that which
is not originally and properly his own, must at some time
or other, in some way or other, to some one or other, give
an account.  Upon no subject is the verdict of the conscience of man, when moderately healthy, more unvarying
or more peremptory in its judgment, than that every office
of the nature of a trust must be ultimately accounted for.
The human conscience—our human elementary sense of
justice—had not to wait for the Gospel to know that every
steward must, sooner or later, give an account of his
stewardship.

But if an account is to be given, it must be given
to somebody ; it cannot be given to a product of the

imagination, to an abstract idea, to an unborn posterity. In this metropolis of business there is no need to insist on so obvious a truth; every account that is kept for others must be audited by somebody; every trustee is liable to answer for mismanagement of his trust in a court of law. Is it otherwise in the moral and spiritual world? We are accountable, you suggest, to public opinion. But public opinion is guided by a very variable standard, and, as regards the private actions and still more the motives of men, it sees a very little way. We are accountable, then, to our own consciences. Yes, but what if our consciences are corrupt judges; what if conscience has been bribed by the truant passions, or silenced by the rebellious will? If our accountability, as human beings, for our thoughts, words, and acts in the various relations of life is to be something more real than a phrase of literature, there must be a Judge Who knows too much to make mistakes about our characters, and Who is too just, when trying us, to do anything but right.

Perhaps the deepest of all differences between man and man is that which divides the man who does in his secret heart believe that he is a steward who has an account to give, from the man who does not. With the one man there is a present motive of almost incalculable power entering into the recesses and secrets of his life; he is constantly asking himself, How will this look at the Day of Judgment? What is the Eternal Judge thinking of it now? What a view of the destiny of Christians is implied in that one sentence of St. Paul's, "Every one of us shall give account of himself to God"![a] What an estimate of the real condition of the heathen world, lying in its polished ungodliness all around him, escapes in these words of St. Peter, "They shall give account to Him that

[a] Rom. xiv. 12.

is ready to judge the quick and the dead"!ᵃ What a deep, if unusual, idea of the work of the ministers of Christ is that Apostolic saying, "They watch for your souls as they that must give an account"!ᵇ Everywhere in the New Testament this belief in man's accountability meets us; not an abstract accountability to some vague unknown power, but the clear and certain fact that we shall have to account, each one of us, one day, to a living Judge. And where this conviction is wanting, how enormous is the difference in the whole range of thought and action! If man has no account to give, no wrong that he does has lasting consequences; if man has no account to give, no wrong that is done to him, and that is unpunished by human law, will ever be punished; if man has no account to give, life is a hideous chaos, or a game of chance, in which the horrible and the grotesque alternately bury out of sight the last vestiges of a moral order; if man has no account to give, the old Epicurean rule, in all its profound degradation, may have much to say for itself: "Let us eat and drink; for to-morrow we die."ᶜ

## II.

Such, then, is the office of a steward. He is a trustee, as distinct from an owner; he acts authoritatively, yet only for another; in the property which he administers, he has no interest beyond those obligations of duty and honour which bid him do the best he can for it; his duties are terminable, and he has an account to render. And human life is a stewardship; we are all of us, though in different senses, stewards. None of us is an owner in his own right; none is so insignificant that his work will

---

ᵃ 1 St. Pet. iv. 5.  ᵇ Heb. xiii. 17.  1 Cor. xv. 32.

not be noticed; none so highly placed that there is not One higher Who will review his work. But life, in its many aspects, is also an almost infinitely varied steward-ship; we are stewards, whether as men or as Christians, not less in the order of nature than in the order of grace.

Now, the stewardship of which nine men out of ten think, when they honestly admit to themselves that they are stewards at all, is their real or personal estate ; the total capital or income, be it great or small, which they happen to possess by a legal title. It may be a fortune which touches upon millions; it may be the scanty and precarious earnings of a shop-boy or a needlewoman. In either case it is a property; it is rightfully, and by the operation of Divine Providence, placed at and secured to the disposal of one human being, and cannot be violently taken from him without violation, I do not say of the legal enactments of man, but of the Moral Law of God. Unless property is a real thing, recognized as such by the Moral Ruler of the world, the eighth commandment has no meaning; and this broad truth is not to be set aside because particular properties or classes of property may have, morally rather than legally, defective titles. If we say that every owner of property is in God's sight a steward of that property, we do not deny that his rights in it, as against those of any other man, are real and absolute; only this absolute and real character thus attaching to property as a right maintained against the claim of other men does not affect its character when placed in the light of the rights of God. My brethren, what are the causes to which it is due that you or I own any property whatever that we happen to own? It has been left us by will. But what cause or causes brought about the legacy, or made it possible that there should be

any legacy at all? It was earned by a father or a grand-
father, and has come to us by inheritance. Here, again,
our parents are not the last term in an ascending series;
and their enterprise and energy were not originally their
own. Or it has been accumulated by ourselves; it is the
fruit of the toil of our hands, or of the toil of our brains; it
has the best known title to property. Be it so; but who
gave us the hands or the brains with which to earn it?
While these titles to property hold good as against all
human claims to take it violently from us, they point back
to an original Owner of the one universal estate, Who has
allowed or enabled us to settle upon it as His tenants;
they point back to the rights of that Supreme Proprietor
Whose stewards we are.

And therefore, depend upon it, sooner or later, He will
say, "Give an account of thy stewardship. What hast
thou done with that which I entrusted to thy keeping,
but which perhaps thou thinkest of habitually as thine
own?" My brethren, let us try to answer that question
here and now. Has it been spent conscientiously, or as
the passion or freak of the moment might suggest? Has
the larger part of it been lavished upon self, or a fixed
proportion upon others? Has God, His known Will, His
Church, the support and extension of His Kingdom, had
any recognized share in its disposal? Has it gone mainly
or altogether in luxuries which pamper the body, but at
least do nothing for the mind or the spirit? Has Dives
fared sumptuously upon it every day, while Lazarus has
lain at his gate full of sores, and desiring to be fed with
the crumbs that fell from his table?[a] Has little or nothing
been done with it towards redressing those inequalities of
condition which are permitted mainly that they may elicit
a generosity and self-sacrifice that would be impossible if

[a] St. Luke xvi. 20, 21.

all shared an equal lot? My brethren, suffer me to use
plainness of speech in this matter. You to whom God
has given wealth would naturally and rightly protect it
against theories which are, no doubt, in the last resort, as
subversive of all social well-being and order as they are
surely at issue with the moral teaching of the Bible. But
if you would do this, you must remember that the responsibilities of property are even more certain than its rights;
that those who, legally speaking, do not share it with you
may have, morally speaking, in a proportion which your
sense of justice should be eager to recognize, a valid claim
on your consideration which your conscience may not
refuse to entertain; you must remember that the old rule
still holds, "If thou hast much, give plenteously; if thou
hast little, do thy diligence gladly to give of that little," [a]
or else, be sure, there may be, even here, some rude
summons to account for the stewardship which you have
abused. Property only becomes insecure when a considerable portion of it is held by people who think only
of themselves. The best insurance against anti-social
doctrines, which treat property as robbery, is such a
wise and generous use of it, for the glory of God and
the good of others, as Christian justice would always
prescribe.

Or the estate on which we are stewards is more interesting and precious than this; it is situated in the
world of the mind; in the region where knowledge, and
speculation, and imagination, and taste have their place
and sway. This fair district is the resort of men for whom
mere accumulations of wealth have no charms. Here,
at least, they claim to be owners, and to reign; here, as
artists, as historians, as philosophers, as poets, as men of

[a] Tobit. iv. 8.

hard fact, or as men of cultivated fancy, they live as in an earthly paradise, in which no supremacy is owned save that of the faculties which have made it the beautiful and fascinating home that it is.

And yet in this world of art and literature, not less truly than among houses and lands and investments, man is a steward. It is not—whatever he may think— really his; it is not his in the last resort, whatever he may have had to do with creating it. All the industry which has amassed its varied treasures; all the keen intelligence which has sorted out and analyzed and arranged them; all the imagination which, with almost infinite versatility and resource, has played on and around them for centuries;—all is from Another. "Every good gift and every perfect gift is from above, and cometh down from the Father of Lights."[a] Whether they have been made the most or the least of, whether they have been devoted to unworthy or to noble ends, whether they have been debased or abused, He is the Author of the gifts which have laid out the world of taste and thought and knowledge ; and each contributor to that world, and each student or loiterer in it, is only a steward; the trustee of faculties and endowments which, however intimately his own when we distinguish him from other men, are not his own when we look higher, and place them in the light of the rights of God.

"Give an account of thy stewardship." The real Author and Owner of all the gifts of mind sometimes utters this command to His stewards before the hour of death. He withdraws the higher mental life of man, but leaves him still with the animal life, intact and vigorous. Go to a lunatic asylum, that most pitiable assortment of all the possibilities of human degradation, and mark there, at least

[a] St. James i. 17.

among some of the sufferers, those who have abused the
stewardship of intelligence.  Be it far from us to attempt
to determine in single cases, or, still worse, to proclaim
aloud, what we suppose to be the secrets of the just judgments of God.  We are not always told by a Prophet why
some Nebuchadnezzar is driven from the haunts of men.
Of those who fill our lunatic asylums some are the victims of
profligacy, and others should command a sincere compas-
sion, since they suffer from inherited disease.  But others,
too, there are, or have been, who in the days of mental
strength and buoyancy have forgotten the Author of their
powers, have exulted in their consciousness of intellectual
might, and have used it without regard to the honour
of God or the true well-being of man; and of these some
have lived to show that the ruin of the finest mind may
be hideous and repulsive in the very ratio of its original
strength and beauty, when the presiding gift of ordered
reason is withdrawn.

Or the estate of which we are stewards is yet more valu-
able than these; it is the Creed which we believe, the hopes
which we cherish, the religion in which we find happiness
and peace as Christians.  With this treasure which He
has withheld from others, God has entrusted us Christians,
in whatever measure, for the good of our fellow-men.  All
other gifts are little enough in comparison with this.  The
knowledge of the Author and End of our existence; of
the Infinite, Everlasting God, Father, Son, and Spirit, ever
Blessed; the knowledge of the Mediator, Jesus Christ, both
God and Man, in union with Whom we have real access to
God, and through Whose acts and sufferings in our behalf
our acceptance with God is secured; the knowledge of what
those great words, life, death, sin, repentance, time, eternity,
really mean; the knowledge which may make us " wise

unto salvation, through faith which is in Christ Jesus;"[a]—
this is, indeed, the gift of gifts. "This is life eternal, that
they may know Thee the only true God, and Jesus Christ,
Whom Thou hast sent."[b] Of this estate of Revealed
Truth, the ministers of Christ are in a special sense
stewards. A Bishop, to use the Apostle's words, is to be
blameless as a steward of God;[c] and men are to account of
the ministers of Christ as also stewards of the mysteries
of God;[d] that is, as stewards of the Sacraments as well as
of the once hidden, now partially revealed, truths of the
Gospel. But every believing Christian is also a steward
of the faith which he believes. He has to make the most
of it, to explain it, to apply it; to make it, as years go
on, increasingly blessed to himself, and to impress it, as
his opportunities shall suggest, on the thoughts and lives
of others.

It might seem to need no proof that of this treasure of
Revealed Truth we are stewards, not owners; that it is
not ours unconditionally and for ever, treat it as we may.
Religion too, is a loan, a trust; it is not an inalienable
property. There was a well-known personage who used
to speak of his religion as he might speak of his family,
of his estate, of his seat in Parliament, of his coat of arms;
it went to make up the whole which constituted his respectability. To be sure, that you cannot do without religion
is the very common sense of life. But to treat the knowledge of the Infinite and the Eternal as though it were
a decoration of a social position, would surely be impossible for any man who had ever got beyond the region of
phrases into real and spiritual contact with truth.

More common it is to meet with men who treat their
faith as though it were a mental toy; who are never tired

_____

| | |
|---|---|
| [a] 2 Tim. iii. 15. | [b] St. John xvii. 3. |
| [c] Titus i. 7. | [d] 1 Cor. iv. 1. |

of discussing its speculative or its controversial bearings; and who forget that it relates throughout to a living Person, and is chiefly to be prized because it enables us to think about Him, and so to commune with Him, as He is. They who make this mistake may be summoned before they think to part with the stewardship which they have abused. The loss of faith which we hear of from time to time is not always to be explained by the formidable character of any objections which are urged against Revealed Religion; it may be the result of forgetfulness that faith is a stewardship; that the faith which is not a practical force in life is in a fair way to be forfeited; and that the believer as such, no less than the possessor of property or the possessor of mind, has an account to give.

Then, a product of these joint estates is the estate of influence; that subtle, inevitable attraction towards good or evil, which every man exerts upon the lives of those around him. That is a property which most assuredly cannot be purchased by money. It escapes those who would try to grasp it; it comes unbidden, undesired, perhaps unwelcome, to those who dread the responsibilities it entails. But there it is, a possession of which, whether we will or not, we are in various degrees stewards; and the question is, What use are we making of it? How is it telling upon friends, acquaintances, servants, correspondents, upon those who see much of us, or upon those who know us only from afar;—are we helping them upwards or downwards, to Heaven or to hell? Surely a momentous question for all of us, since of this stewardship events may summon us before the end comes to give an account. We can hardly dismiss from our thoughts the chief magistrate of a great people, who two days since had to

resign the reins of government, because, while possessing many titles to the respect and good opinion of his
countrymen, he had not known how to make a good use
of the stewardship of influence.[a]

And a last estate, of which we are but stewards, is health
and life. This bodily frame, so fearfully and wonderfully
made,[b] of such subtle and delicate texture that the wonder
is it should bear the wear and tear of time and work, and
last as long as for many of us it does,—of this, too, we
are not owners, but stewards. It is, most assuredly, no
creation of our own, this body; and He Who gave it us
will in any case one day withdraw His gift. Yet how
many a man thinks in his secret heart that, if he owns
nothing else, he does at least own, as its absolute master
might own, the fabric of flesh and bones, of nerves and
veins, in which his animal life resides; that with this at
least he may rightfully do whatsoever he wills; even
abuse, and ruin, and irretrievably degrade, and even kill
it; that here no question of another's right can possibly
occur; that he is here a master, and not a steward!

Piteous forgetfulness! in a man who believes that he has
a Creator, and that that Creator has His rights. Piteous
ingratitude! in a Christian who should remember that he
is not his own, but is bought with a price, and that therefore he should glorify God in his body no less than in his
spirit, since both are God's.[c] Piteous illusion! the solemn
moment for dissipating which is ever hurrying on apace.
The Author of health and life has His own time for
bidding us give an account of this solemn stewardship;
often, too, when it is least expected. There are inscrip-

[a] M. Grévy resigned the Presidency of the French Republic, December 3, 1887.

[b] Ps. cxxxix. 13.　　　　　　　　　　[c] 1 Cor. vi. 20.

tions upon tombstones in any large cemetery which tell a
story that none can misread.  Of late all English hearts
have been turned to one, intimately related to our own
Royal Family,[a] who, with exceptional endowments of
physical strength and mental vigour and elevated character, and standing on the highest steps of the most
powerful throne in Europe, which at any hour for a long
while since he might have been called to fill, is stricken
down by that Unseen Power Whose visitations, however
inscrutable, are always loving and just.  In many a poor
cottage, amid unnoticed tears, some true and noble though
humble life has bent low before the same awful summons; but there are sorrows, as there are sins and virtues,
which command the attention of the world.  Certainly
it is not always in judgment that the Voice is uttered,
" Give an account of thy stewardship."

The solemn summons which God addresses to different
men from time to time on this side the grave, point to
an account beyond, to a judgment that shall be universal and final.  As St. Paul said at Athens eighteen
centuries ago, " God hath appointed a day, in which He
will judge the world in righteousness by that Man Whom
He hath ordained ; whereof He hath given assurance unto
all men, in that He hath raised Him from the dead." [b]

Each earlier summons to any soul, " Give an account of
thy stewardship," suggests that solemn moment "when
the Son of man shall come in His glory, and all His Holy
Angels with Him, and then shall He sit on the throne of
His glory: before Him shall be gathered all nations: and
He shall separate them one from another, as a shepherd

---

[a] The Imperial Crown Prince of Germany, who lived to become the
Emperor Frederick III., and died after a reign of three months, June 15,
1888.

[b] Acts xvii. 31.

divideth the sheep from the goats." [a]   And the principle
of this separation will be the use or the abuse of the
stewardship which each has received.   " Then shall the
King say unto them on His right hand, Come, ye blessed
of My Father, inherit the kingdom prepared for you from
the foundation of the world : for I was an hungred, and
ye gave Me meat : I was thirsty, and ye gave Me drink :
I was a stranger, and ye took Me in : naked, and ye
clothed Me : sick, and in prison, and ye visited Me. . . .
Then shall the King say unto them on the left hand
Depart, ye cursed, into everlasting fire, prepared for the
devil and his angels : for I was an hungred, and ye gave
Me no meat : I was thirsty, and ye gave Me no drink : I
was a stranger, and ye took Me not in : naked, and ye
clothed Me not : sick, and in prison, and ye visited Me
not." [b]

May we, by God's grace, lay to heart these solemn
warnings of our Most Merciful Redeemer, remembering
that though, in this sphere of sense, Heaven and earth
may pass away, yet most assuredly these His words will
not pass away.[c]

[a] St. Matt. xxv. 32, 33.      [b] *Ib.* 34-43.      [c] *Ib.* xxiv. 35.

# SERMON XLVIII.

## THE ONE APPROACH TO THE FATHER.

### (THIRD SUNDAY IN ADVENT.)

St. John xiv. 6.

*No man cometh unto the Father, but by Me.*

PERHAPS in no other of His recorded words does our Lord state more clearly or more imperatively than in these the real nature of His claim upon the attention and homage of the world: "No man cometh unto the Father, but by Me."

## I.

He implies that there is a need, common to all human beings at all times, greater and more urgent than any other. It is the need of coming to the Father.

He Who has made all men for Himself, has so ordered His work that the powers and faculties of man can only find at once their full exercise and their true harmony when they rest in Him. As the Highest Truth, He satisfies the intellect of His creature, which, amidst its many observations, is constantly seeking the Absolutely True. As the Highest Beauty, He takes captive the heart which He has so fashioned, that it can find complete expansion and delight in no beauty of form or mind beneath His

Throne.  As the Eternal Rule of Right, Whose moral laws are but the expression of His essential Nature, He secures to the created will which obeys Him that strength and directness of purpose in which its excellence consists. Parted from Him, the Father of our spirits, human nature is at best a magnificent wreck ; keen intelligence with a sore and unsatisfied heart, or with a truant and feeble will; warm affections, with nothing on which the understanding can rest, or which the will may obey ; vigorous purpose, but with no such discernment of an Object in which thought and affection can be lastingly satisfied, as to save it from enterprises which only plunge man deeper into unhappiness and error.   And, at a distance from Christ, man is also, in different degrees of remoteness, distant from God.  Just as in a fair region which has been desolated by an earthquake we may see, side by side with the ruined edifice, or the burnt-up soil, or the deep fissure, not a few traces of the beauty which had been so cruelly marred ; so human nature without Christ, and at its worst, ever bears about it traits and relics of an ancient excellence side by side with proofs of some catastrophe to which it owes its present ruin.   That remote event which Christian Faith speaks of as the Fall of Man is less distinctly proclaimed in the pages of Revelation than it is attested by the actual facts of human life ; since in practice men themselves treat their own nature not as a thing of ideal excellence, but as a restless and disturbing force. Against this nature, they themselves, in the interests of their own well-being as members of society, must perforce take the precautions of law and police.   And the secret whisper of the human heart echoes the verdict of man's action as a social or political being.  If there is any one of the masters of the Roman world in whom Englishmen have an interest, it is the warlike Emperor Septimius Severus,

since, years after he had been invested with the purple,
he would have passed through London on his way to his
Scottish campaign; and, as you would remember, he died
at York. Severus ruled the Roman Empire before it had
yet seriously entered on its decline; and he had risen to
that great eminence from a humble station by a com-
bination of determination, ability, and unscrupulousness,
which enabled him to crush his rivals, to gratify all his
personal wishes and ambitions, and to secure for his
children the succession to the imperial throne. Yet
there is a remarkable saying of his which is worth
remembering: "Omnia fui et nihil expedit;" "I have
been everything by turns, and nothing is of any good."[a] It
is a heathen echo of the experience of the kingly Preacher:
" Vanity of vanities; all is vanity."[b] It is a witness to the
heart-sickness of man, when all that this world can give
is entirely at his disposal, while he is separated from his
highest Good, the true Satisfaction of his being—separated
from God.

"No man cometh unto the Father, but by Me." How
does our Lord effect man's return to the Father? Partly,
no doubt, by His teaching, but also and still more by His
Person. He does not merely encourage us to return by
proclaiming that God is Love as well as, or rather because
He is also, Justice; He says also, "I am the Way."[c]
Here we see the force of that remarkable saying, that
Christ is Christianity. Plato is not Platonism; Platonism
might have been taught though its author had never lived.
Mohammed is not Islam; the Koran itself would warn us
against any such confusion between the teacher of its
doctrine and the substance of the doctrine itself. But

---

[a] *Hist. August. Spart. Sever.*, c. 18, quoted by Gibbon, *Decline and Fall*,
i. 236, ed. 1862.

[b] Eccles. xii. 8.        [c] St. John xiv. 6.

Christ Himself is Christianity; His teaching is inextricably bound up with His Person; and it is not merely because He taught what He did, but because He is what He is, that through Him we can come to the Father. His proclamation of Himself would be intolerable, if He were not more than man; but as God and Man in One Person, He spans the abyss which had yawned between earth and Heaven; He touches on the one hand the awful Purity of the Everlasting Father, and on the other, though without share in its defilements and ruin, the ruined and defiled race which He came to save. And thus does He remove the one cause which created and which maintains the separation of man from God. By a Death which crowned a Life perfectly conformed to the Divine Will, and invested with incalculable value through association with His Divine Nature, He made for human sin a perfect atonement, which all may claim to share, if they will, by union with Himself; and He conquers sin, not only for us, but in us, by those gifts of grace, involving real oneness with Himself the Conqueror, which His Spirit secures to us, even to the end of time. And thus, since He is God as well as Man, we too may approach, nay, be united with, that Being in Whom alone our weak and distracted nature can recover its repose and strength.

My brethren, I cannot doubt that many of you will confirm what I am saying from your own experience. "Unto you that believe He is precious."[a] That sense of union with Him, awe-inspiring, but unspeakably blessed and incommunicable,—what soul that has known it can fail to understand how He is for it the Way to the Father? In hours of sorrow, in hours of anxiety, in the desolation of bereavement, perhaps in the prospect of death, it has been by clinging to Him that you have found that strength

[a] I St. Pet. ii. 7

and peace which has enabled you to await the joy that
cometh in the morning.[a]    And why?    Because in union
with Him you are already united to the Universal Father;
the End and Satisfaction of your being.

"No man cometh unto the Father, but by Me."    The
saying has a negative as well as a positive aspect, an
excluding as well as an assertive force.    Not only does
Christ reconduct man to the Father, but He alone can
do so.    He does not say what many a modern teacher
would fain make Him say: "Others have led man, others
will lead man out of his errors and degradations back to
God; and I can do so too, only somewhat better than
they."    He does not put forward His Religion as the
elder or fairer sister among a number of competing
creeds, no one of which is without some token of a Divine
authentication.    This is what many, if they could, would
have Him say; only He does not say it.    "No man
cometh unto the Father, but by Me."    True it is that, as
St. Peter teaches, "in every nation he that feareth God,
and worketh righteousness, is accepted of Him;"[b] but
then, this fear of God, this working righteousness, is such
that it involves the acceptance of the one Mediator, so
soon as He is known.    His claim on the world is not
merely relative; it is absolute.    He dares to monopolize
the opening of the road to Heaven.    He alone holds in His
Heart and Hand the secret of man's happiness and greatness.    As His Word only is infallible, so only His Blood
has cleansing power; and His grace alone can restore
the ruined nature which He would save.    And thus His
Apostles knew what He meant when they too proclaimed,
"Neither is there salvation in any other: for there is
none other name under Heaven given among men, whereby
we can be saved."[c]

[a] Ps. xxx. 5.        [b] Acts x. 35.        [c] *Ib.* iv. 12.

## II.

This is the fundamental conviction which justifies and invigorates missionary enterprise. If, when Christians have been free to do their best for their Master's cause, missionary enterprise has at any time slackened or been abandoned, it has been because the real nature of the claim of Christ has been lost sight of. Missionary enterprise is at once wasteful and impertinent if the Christian religion, instead of being necessary to every child of Adam, is only suited to the Western world at particular stages of its civilization. And if all religions are partly true and partly false, and the choice between them is to be settled, not by recognizing any universal necessity of man, or any decisive proof of a real mandate from God, but by considering what the "genius," as it is called, of a particular people has contented itself with in past times, then Christianity has been mistaken in a vital matter and from the very first. The cultivated centres of Greek life had, each of them, its favourite object of worship, surrounded with everything that popular enthusiasm and the devotion of generations and the perfection of art could supply. Ephesus had its world-famed Temple of Artemis or Diana; and Athens had been for centuries the city of Pallas Minerva; and Corinth rejoiced in the impure worship of Aphrodite. But St. Paul did not consider these local manifestations of the religious genius of paganism any reason against opening a Christian Mission in each one of these centres of elegant or degrading illusion; and if we have not lost part and lot in the spirit of St. Paul, we shall not deem the antiquity and vast empire of Buddhism, or the more aggressive although more modern religion of the false prophet Mohammed, any reason which should deter us from doing what we may to rescue the races—some of them more highly endowed by nature than ourselves—from the tyranny and darkness of these and other errors.  Be the genius of these people what it may, we, like St. Paul, are " debtors both to the Greeks and to the Barbarians; " [a] we owe them the Gospel. We owe it in some cases to races endowed with natural qualities finer and more varied than our own ; we owe it to their honest strivings after light ; we owe it to their unspeakable degradations; but especially do we owe it to the Work of that living and gracious Saviour Who, without any claim or merit of ours, has " called us out of darkness into His marvellous light," [b] and has bidden us " go into all the world and preach the Gospel to every creature." [c]

### III.

But here there are objections which, unless I am mistaken, will present themselves to some minds, at any rate, at the present day.

If, it will be said, Christianity is so great a blessing, so much greater a blessing than any other to mankind, may it not be trusted to recommend itself without the machinery and apparatus of Missions ? Man is not slow to understand his true interest in everyday and earthly matters.  Railways and telegraphs make their way in all directions without being heralded by missionaries devoted to the honour of electricity and steam ; and if Christ has really enabled men to attain the great end of their existence by reconciling them to the Universal Father, may not men with an enlightened sense of self-interest be trusted to find this out, and to avail themselves eagerly of so incomparable a privilege ?

[a] Rom. i. 14.    [b] 1 St. Pet. ii. 9.    [c] St. Mark xvi. 15.

No, brethren; this language, if sincere, is not the language of Christian wisdom. There is one point, of the greatest importance, which marks the difference between the blessing of Christianity and any earthly blessings or advantages whatever. It is that Christianity, if it is to bless us here and hereafter, requires us to conquer and renounce a great deal to which our fallen human nature is admittedly prone. It is not necessary to give up theft, or adultery, or evil speaking in order to reap the full advantages of railroads, steamships, and electric telegraphs: material progress encounters no obstacles to its extension in the passions of fallen man. And there are false religions in the world which can flatter and bribe these passions without compromising themselves. The harem of a Mohammedan prince or caliph involves no dishonour or disloyalty to Islam. With Christianity it is otherwise. Christianity requires a putting off "the old man, which is corrupt according to the deceitful lusts," [a] and a renewal, not merely in outward conduct, but in the spirit of men's minds. It bids us put on "the new man, which after God is created in righteousness and true holiness." [b] With such a demand, Christianity makes enemies in human nature; it cannot help making them. And, therefore, the greatness of the blessings which it offers are not able of themselves to outweigh the prejudice which it inevitably creates. If the herald of Christ proclaims "peace on earth, good will among men," [c] achieved by the reconciliation of God and man, fallen human nature mutters half-aloud, "I hate him; for he doth not prophesy good concerning me, but evil." [d] And therefore Christianity, though the dispenser of the greatest of all blessings, always has met, always will meet, with secret

[a] Eph. iv. 22.  
[b] *Ib.* 24.  
[c] St. Luke ii. 14.  
[d] 1 Kings xxii. 8.

or avowed resistance; and sacrifices of time and money, ay, and of life itself, will be necessary, if it is to be a match for the obstacles which its very excellence creates.

But it is further urged that missionary work, like charity, should begin at home. " Look at your great cities "—so an anonymous correspondent wrote to me a few days ago—" look at London, before you busy yourselves about the needs of distant populations. Consider the hundreds of thousands around your own gates, for whom the Unseen has practically no existence, who never enter any place of worship; consider the drunkenness, the profligacy, the crime of every description, which baffles the efforts of all Christians of every kind; consider the poverty and distress which cry out to all who bear the Christian name to do something to relieve, or—better still, if they can—to prevent it. Look at home, at any rate, before you go abroad, and earn a right to recommend the blessings of Christianity in distant lands by doing something more for a people which still so greatly needs higher Christian influences and education, although it has been Christian by profession for much more than a thousand years."

Now, without discussing how far there is or is not an element of exaggeration in some current pictures of our social and religious condition in England, it might be pointed out that the first efforts of the great Missionary Society for which I am pleading [a] are directed to the colonies and dependencies of Great Britain, and so are designed to benefit, and do very greatly benefit, that large body politic of which, after all, we here in London, and in England, only form a part, though it be the most important part. But I do not dwell on this, because the obligation lying on all Christians to make known our

[a] The Society for the Propagation of the Gospel.

Blessed Master's Name is certainly not limited by the frontiers of any empire, ancient or modern. Our Lord did not say to His Apostles, "Go ye into all the provinces of the Roman Empire and make disciples of all the subjects of the Cæsar." A religion issuing from the mind and heart of the Universal Father must be adapted to the needs of every one of His rational creatures, and to say that there are any races, at any stage of their development, for which it is not adapted, or for which it is less adapted than some false creed that would fain supplant it, is to deny by implication that our Lord is what He claims to be—the Saviour of the world. No! the Gospel is due to, as it is needed by, every human being. But are those who object to Christian Missions, because they would have us address ourselves to Christian duties nearer home, always and entirely sincere? What do we hear when the Church is taking their advice, and is enabled to restore Christian faith and life in a particular English town, or district, or diocese to something like a primitive standard of fervour and excellence? Are we not gravely cautioned against thinking too much of such success while two-thirds of the human family are not Christians at all? If we ask our critics to help Missions to the heathen, they plead their absorbing interest in the condition of our home populations. If we ask them to strengthen the hands of the Bishop of Bedford, and of the band of devoted clergy and laity who work with him for the physical and social as well as the spiritual well-being of the people at the East End of London, they observe that the world is much vaster than London, and that Christianity has as yet done nothing for the larger part of it. To such criticisms we cannot well afford to listen, since time flies, and our Master's bidding is plain and imperative.

Some of you would remember an occurrence which

took place during the Second Punic War, at the most
critical period of the long struggle between Rome and
Carthage for the empire of the Western world; it has
often been referred to, as showing how from early days
the Roman people possessed what is called the instinct
of empire. When the victorious Carthaginian general
Hannibal was in the heart of Italy, and threatening the
very existence of Rome, the senate despatched a fleet and
army to Spain, that they might strike a blow in the rear
of the conqueror by laying siege to Saguntum; and this
bold venture, which could be so ill afforded at the time, was,
as you know, abundantly justified by the result. Every
heathen land is the Saguntum of the Christian Church;
and if it be true that some spiritual Hannibal is ravaging
populations which have long owned her sway, or is even
threatening her ruin in this or that of her ancient homes,
still she owes the Gospel of salvation to all the world.
She remembers the instruction, "If they persecute you
in one city, flee to another;" [a] for she too, in a nobler sense
than Rome, has the instinct of world-wide empire, since
she looks forward to a day when "the earth shall be filled
with the knowledge of the Lord, as the waters cover the
sea." [b]

Assuredly, unless our hearts are really interested in
the extension of the Kingdom of Christ, we are not
likely to be much interested in the average missionary.
There are, of course, missionaries and missionaries; and
we need not assume that every man who bears the title
is all that it should convey. But a man who has given
the best years of his life to spreading the Faith among
some heathen people comes back to England. He has
been cut off from the main currents of higher English
thought; he knows nothing of the recent phases of our

[a] St. Matt. x. 23.          [b] Isa. xi. 9.

politics except from a stray newspaper which has reached
him now and then; nothing of our popular literature;
nothing of that varied and singular conglomerate of
information and conjecture, of knowledge and gossip, of
high aspiration and base enterprise, which from week to
week and month to month engages popular attention at
home, and familiarity with which is a certificate of general
popularity. From all this he has been banished. He has
put his whole mind and heart into the work of bringing
some very degraded human beings to the knowledge and
love of their Saviour. Of this work his heart is full, and
whether he gets up to speak at a missionary meeting, or
enters into society, he can talk of this, but not of much
else. And, too often, what is our verdict on him? "A
good man, no doubt; a very good man, but very dull."
A verdict which might have been passed, in certain
quarters among us, upon St. John or St. Paul. And this
idea of a missionary, as good but dull, extends itself in
too many minds to the whole subject of Missions; makes
them an unwelcome subject even when inevitable; chills
our hearts, and closes our hands, when, if ever, we should
be prodigal of sympathy and generosity.

Ah! there is a pathetic nobility about a missionary's
life which a Christian should be able to understand. A
young man, in whose mind the generous aspirations after
work and sacrifice, which are kindled by the love of our
Divine Redeemer, have not yet been killed out by the
cynicism which too often is mistaken for the wisdom of
later years, has caught sight of the glory which attaches
to the life of an Apostle, and has desired to share it.
Combining something of the enterprise of a discoverer and
the courage of a soldier with the assured convictions of a
Christian, he devotes his opening manhood to the missionary work of the Church of God. On the day of his

ordination, or of his departure, he is upheld by the strength of a great enthusiasm which is shared by the relatives and fellow-Christians who crowd around him, supporting him so strenuously by their sympathy and their prayers. It seems in these bright moments as though nothing could be difficult; as though failure were impossible; as though the convictions and hopes which glow within his soul and the souls of others must carry all before them; as though, like the walls of Jericho at Joshua's trumpet-blast, the old fortresses of heathen error must crumble immediately at the summons of the soldier of Christ.

This is his youthful enthusiasm. Then comes the stern reality. He lands in Africa, or India, or China, or Japan; he notes the glance, half-pitying, half-contemptuous, with which some countryman, who has come out before him to make a fortune by whatever means, recognizes the arrival of a missionary.[a] Sick at heart, he turns to the heathen. He hopes to find satisfaction in his work among the savages whom he comes to enlighten and to save. How is he to get at them? He scarcely knows, if he does know, the grammar of their language, much less its vocabulary; and with this poor and awkward instrument of intercourse, which raises a smile on their faces as he essays to use it, he hopes, forsooth, to change their most fundamental convictions and their whole manner of life. The task is not impossible; it has been, and is at this moment being achieved, by many a devoted worker in the missionary field; but it is a task of enormous difficulty. And then, just as he is beginning to surmount it, the climate, which is hostile to any European constitution, begins to tell upon him, and he is laid low by fever —a fever which may or may not be fatal. There, at a distance from the comforts of home, with its loved voices

---

[a] This passage is a reminiscence of a speech of Bishop Wilberforce.

and the services of his relations, he lies in the solitude of his hut, perhaps tended by some kindly savage, perhaps untended by any human hands, but resting only on the Arm of God. It is not necessary to point to those missionaries who, in our own and in other days, have attained to the highest distinction of shedding their blood for Christ; it is enough to say that any missionary who is moderately true to the spirit of his vocation belongs to the moral aristocracy of the Church of Christ; he is enrolled in our Lord's own guard of honour. And those of us who take the easier path in ministerial or Christian life, and stay at home, should be the first to recognize his high distinction.

It is sometimes said that England best does her duty to heathen lands by conferring on them the blessings of civilization; good laws, equal justice, social order, and all those material improvements in human life which European science and industry have so largely multiplied during the present century. Certainly it is no duty or wish of mine to depreciate these great advantages; but, unhappily, our civilization is accompanied by an alloy of evil which we cannot ignore. We cannot forget what has often been the moral meaning of the sale of a British drug among a pagan population, or the arrival of a British ship's company at a pagan port, or the enrichment of a British capitalist or company in a pagan district. There is no need further to lift the veil. All who have looked into this matter must know and own that England owes to more pagan lands than one, not merely that glorious Gospel, which is the birthright of the whole world, but also some sort of moral reparation for evil which those who bear her name and are protected by her flag have too often carried with them to add to the darkness and misery of the heathen. And how can this debt of justice be better discharged than by teaching our

creditors to know and to love the Sun of Righteousness;
by assuring them that it was not in obedience to His
rule and law, but in despite and defiance of it, that the
wrong was done of which they rightly complain; and
that He now offers to them that truth which has conferred on the Western civilization, which they both
admire and fear, whatever of real strength and excellence there is in it? There are, no doubt, heathens
and Moslems who look wistfully at our European life
and manners, and would fain copy and share them, but
without our Christian Faith. Not a fortnight since a
distinguished Moslem was reported to have expressed
himself in this sense: "We will have your benevolence,
your charity, your justice and truth, your science of
health, your railroads, telegraphs, and manufactures; we
will have what is good for us, but not your Christian
dogmas—your Trinity, your Divinity of Jesus, and the
rest of it." [a]  It was as if the Jews of old had said to our
Lord, "Heal our sick, cleanse our lepers, raise our dead,
cast out the devils which beset us, feed on our hillsides
the four thousand, the five thousand, famishing peasants
who crowd around Thee; but do not insult our most
cherished prejudices by such moral teaching as that of Thy
Sermon on the Mount." As if it were possible for Christians to omit from the Gospel the truth of the Divinity of
Jesus, in order to make it easier to build a hospital or to
lay down a new railway, say in Persia! Why, it is this
truth of the Divinity of our Lord which is the very motive-
power of our interest in the heathen world; it is because
He is Divine as well as human that "through Him we have
access by one Spirit unto the Father." [b]  Be silent about

[a] Abridged from the *Pall Mall Gazette*, November 30, 1887. The
Persian Minister on Dogma, by 'a Broad Church Clergyman.'
[b] Eph. ii. 18.

this, and what would be the real worth of the philanthropy and the railroads—unless, indeed, this world is our all, and the world beyond the grave a creation of fancy? Be silent about this, and you may get a certain measure of applause from unbelievers who have no mind for the faith which justifies before God; but do not flatter yourselves that you are treading in the steps of St. Paul and St. John. Be silent about this, and your converts—if those whom you attract could deserve the name—when they had learnt from you the ways of civilized Europe without the Faith of Christendom, might expect to hear the Divine Master repeating that ancient reproach, "Ye seek Me . . . because ye did eat of the loaves."[a]

I ask you, then, my brethren, to give to-day your generous support to the Society for the Propagation of the Gospel in Foreign Parts, the oldest association for missionary work in the Church of England. Incorporated under King William III., it has since his time counted among its advocates and supporters almost every single name that has been held in honour in the English Church. With a history that now approaches the completion of its second century, it has necessarily done more than any other body for the expansion of our portion of the Kingdom of Christ; and if of late its claims have been somewhat lost sight of, this is largely because, in things human, all recent enterprise is generally more attractive, if not always more effective, than that which dates its origin from an earlier time. But it is not creditable to us as a Church that this great Society should be straitened in its resources; it is not for the honour of our Lord that so tried a means of propagating His Gospel should be lost sight of. Think for a moment what has been achieved. In Australia, New Zealand, and Canada it has nurtured

[a] St. John vi. 26.

twenty-four Dioceses, until they have become self-support-
ing ; and now Australia and New Zealand are sending
Missions of their own to Melanesia, and New South Wales
is organizing a Mission to New Guinea. And it is largely
due to the action of this Society that the Church in India
is becoming more and more every year what we must
earnestly desire it to be ; a Church whose pastors and
people are natives of India. Out of six hundred and forty
clergymen in India, two hundred and seventy are Indians ;
and next Sunday Bishop Caldwell will ordain twelve natives
of India to the Diaconate, as in December last year he
ordained fifteen. Meanwhile, apart from the difficult task
of adequately supplying Missions for which the Society
is already responsible, there is the duty of responding to
new invitations; the duty of "lifting up our eyes and
looking on the fields that are white already to harvest." [a]
Japan is welcoming with increasing cordiality the religion
which she once persecuted so bitterly; and its Bishop
is making ready to resign some portion of his wide
charge to an Episcopal colleague. Other lands claim
our attention with even more pressing importunity. On
January 1, 1886, the world learnt that Burmah, a territory larger than the United Kingdom, had been annexed
to the Empire of the Queen ; but such an annexation
surely implies new and vastly increased responsibilities
for English Christians, which this Society is most anxious,
but as yet, from lack of means, very little able to discharge. It is not often, my brethren, that we ask you
to contribute to any cause whatever at the close of
the regular Sunday services in St. Paul's. It has been
felt that one great object of a Church maintained on such
a scale as this is, that, as a rule, it should offer to the
people of London the opportunities of Christian worship

[a] St. John iv. 35.

and Christian teaching "without money and without price."[a] If to-day is an exception to this rule, it is because, in our judgment, there is an exceptional necessity; and you will not, as we hope, be wanting to an effort which must command the sympathy of every man and woman who sincerely believes that through our Lord Jesus Christ alone is there real approach to the Father of spirits.

[a] Isa. lv. 1.

# SERMON XLIX.

## THE SUDDENNESS OF CHRIST'S COMING.

### (FOURTH SUNDAY IN ADVENT.)

#### REV. III. 11.

*Behold, I come quickly.*

THESE words, which have just been read to us in the
Second Lesson, occur in our Lord's message from
Heaven to the Bishop, or, in St. John's language, the
Angel of the Church of Philadelphia. It is not improb-
able that this Bishop was no other than the Demetrius
who is mentioned in St. John's Third Epistle as having a
"good report of all men, and of the truth itself;"[a] and
if this is the case, we have before us a holy man who,
probably, was not a very resolute one, and was placed in
a position of much difficulty. Great as is the place occupied by the "Angels" of the Seven Asiatic Churches,
they would have appeared to their heathen fellow-citizens
very insignificant people, of whom no account was to be
taken by the elegant and wealthy society that surrounded
them. Assisted by one or two Presbyters and Deacons, a
Bishop of that Apostolic time ministered to and governed
a small congregation of Christians, gathered out of the

---

[a] 3 St. John 12; cf. *Apost. Const.*, vii. 47.

back streets of those generally splendid cities, in which Greek art and life went hand in hand with the luxury and the superstitions of Asia. Such a Bishop had, as a rule, two kinds of difficulties to contend with. There was a fermentation of thought on the frontiers of the Apostolic Church, in which Jewish and heathen ingredients were constantly producing one or another form of so-called Gnostic error, one phase of which is described in the Epistle to the Colossians, and another in the Epistles to Timothy and Titus; and this was a constant subject of anxiety to those primitive rulers of the Churches of the Lesser Asia. Thus the deeds of the Nicolaitanes at Ephesus,[a] the doctrine of Balaam at Pergamos,[b] the " woman Jezebel, which calleth herself a prophetess,"[c] at Thyatira, were samples of the trouble in question; and at Philadelphia there was what is described as " a synagogue of Satan,"[d] the proceedings of which would have been watched by the Bishop with natural and serious misgiving.

Besides these dangers from within, there was the constant danger of popular violence, or official persecution from without. Each Jewish synagogue, and still more each heathen temple, was the centre of a strong anti-Christian fanaticism which might at any moment rouse passions too violent to be appeased with anything short of bloodshed. Thus at Pergamos Christ's faithful martyr Antipas had already been slain,[e] the pagan vehemence of the population being such that the place is described as the seat or throne of Satan.[f]

Philadelphia was a comparatively modern city, but it had been almost entirely destroyed by an earthquake somewhat more than half a century before St. John wrote; and an impoverished and superstitious population would

---

[a] Rev. ii. 6.     [b] *Ib.* 14.     [c] *Ib.* 20
[d] *Ib.* iii. 9.     [e] *Ib.* ii. 12, 13.     [f] *Ib.* 13.

be likely to see in the Christian Church a legitimate and inviting object of assault. Bishop Demetrius, if it was he, had hitherto made head against the anxieties around him. Hitherto he had kept the Word, and had not denied the Name, of Christ;[a] and he had the promise which past faithfulness always commands; while at the same time, since no such promise suspends man's freedom to rebel or to obey, he is warned of the urgent duty of perseverance. "Because thou hast kept the Word of My patience, I also will keep thee from the hour of temptation, which shall come upon all the world, to try them that dwell upon the earth. Behold, I come quickly : hold that fast which thou hast, that no man take thy crown."[b]

## I.

"Behold, I come quickly." If our Lord's words are understood of His Second Coming, it is obvious to reflect that the good Bishop of Philadelphia died without witnessing their fulfilment. Nay, he has been in his grave for some eighteen centuries, or nearly so, and our Lord has not yet come to judgment. The event has shown that the predictions of our Lord at the close of His ministry[c] referred only remotely to His Second Coming, and immediately to the destruction of Jerusalem; and the generation that heard Him did not pass away until all that referred to that event had been fulfilled. But this saying of our Lord in the vision to St. John, "Behold, I come quickly," cannot have referred to the destruction of Jerusalem; and yet, if it meant the Second Advent, the Bishop of Philadelphia did not witness the fulfilment of it, and it is still unfulfilled.

---

[a] Rev. iii. 8.     [b] *Ib.* 10.     [c] St. Matt. xxiv.

St. Peter warned Christians not long before his death
that this delay would be used as an argument against
Christianity in later times. "There shall come in the
last days scoffers, walking after their own lusts, and
saying, Where is the promise of His coming? for since
the fathers fell asleep, all things continue as they were
from the beginning of the creation."[a] That this idea of
an unvarying order maintained uninterruptedly since the
creation is not accurate, St. Peter argues by pointing to
the Flood; and the Flood was a catastrophe of such a
kind as to imply that another catastrophe might, after
whatever lapse of time, succeed it.[b] But the "scoffers," of
whom St. Peter was thinking, would probably insist rather
on the indefinite postponement of Christ's coming than of
any intrinsic impossibility attaching to it; and this is met
by St. Peter in another way. What had to be remembered—so he would teach us—was that God necessarily
looks at time in a very different way from the way in
which man looks at it. Man sees only a little distance,
and he is impatient because his outlook is so limited; to
him it seems that an event will never arrive which has
been delayed for some centuries; and so that a judgment
long apprehended, but also long delayed, will not really
take place at all, but may well at once be classed among
the phantoms of a morbid and disordered brain. With
God it is altogether otherwise. Long and short periods
of time do not mean to Him what they do to us. A day
seems to us a short period of twenty-four hours; but it
may be regarded by the Supreme Intelligence, for Whom
time is not less capable of Infinite divisibility than is
matter, as a period of extended duration. "One day is
with the Lord as a thousand years."[c] Conversely, to us a
thousand years appears, to say the least, a large period

[a] 2 Pet. iii. 3, 4.    [b] *Ib.* 5–7.    [c] *Ib.* iii. 8.

in the history of the world; during such a period some thirty generations of men are born and die, and kingdoms and empires rise and fall; but with the Awful Mind that can embrace eternity, " a thousand years are but as one day." [a]

Let me beg your more particular attention to the point before us. It is not that one day and a thousand years are in themselves the same; or that duration of time is not a real thing, but only an illusive impression on thought. It is that when we speak of a long or a short period of time, those epithets, long and short, are only comparative; they mean the comparison of some given period of time with some other which we have before our minds. You and I think that a life of eighty years is a long life; but a man like Methuselah would have thought it a short one: he had a higher standard to judge by. In the same way, we English think five hundred years a considerable period in the duration of an empire; but it would have appeared, to say the least, much less considerable to an ancient Egyptian, who could look back to so great an antiquity for his country. A period appears to us long only until we compare it with another that is much longer; and the longest period of time that the human mind can possibly conceive must seem insignificant when it is compared with eternity. God, Who subsists throughout the unbegun, unending series of ages; God, Who is Himself without beginning of days or end of years; [b] God, Who does not live in eternity as we in time, but Who possesses it, since it is an attribute of His own; God, Who sees as with a present glance what we can only think of as an unmeasurable past and an unmeasurable future;—God must think of that very inconsiderable enclosure within His eternity, which we speak of as time, very differently from ourselves. To us ten thousand or twenty thousand years seem a very long period; to Him it may be little enough; by comparison with the standard of eternity, it may be as nothing. Yet, in reality, it is not nothing. God, Who sees all things as they are, sees that it is twenty thousand years; but, then, He forms a different estimate of its relative value from our estimate of it, because He has in His own eternity a standard of comparison which is not present to us. We see this truth more clearly if we reflect that to us men the passage of time seems slow or rapid, its periods long or short, according to our varying moods and tempers. When we are suffering acute pain of body, or very great anxiety of mind, time, as we say, hangs heavily; we count the minutes, the half-minutes, the quarter-minutes, the seconds; we seem to extend the duration of time by the suffering we compress into its constituent moments. On the other hand, when we are experiencing great pleasure, whether of mind or body, we become insensible to the flight of time; we pass into a state of consciousness which has no relation apparently to the succession of events. From this we may understand how the One Being, Who is the Fountain of all goodness, because He is in Himself infinitely blessed— blessed in contemplating His own perfections and the works of His Hands—would be as such insensible to the impression of time; how His perfect blessedness, which as such excludes all consciousness of the sequence of events, implies His grasping, possessing, nay, being Eternity. I say being Eternity, because Eternity implies a Being Who always is; and one only such Being there is Who always is, namely, the Eternal God.

Thus we see how differently God and man measure time. Man measures one portion of time by another; God measures all time by His own Eternity. If we men try to conceive of eternity, we pile up ages upon ages, millions of centuries on other millions, and still we are as far off as ever from reaching it. God lives in, He is Eternity; and from His Eternity He looks out upon the succession of ages by which His creatures measure their brief existence. It was in view of this that the Psalmist · exclaimed, "Behold, Thou hast made my days as it were a span long: and mine age is even as nothing in respect of Thee;"[a] "A thousand years in Thy sight are but as yesterday: seeing it is passed as a watch in the night."[b] And if God says, "Behold, I come quickly," we have to remember that God is speaking; that "quickly" is a relative term, which may mean one thing when man uses it, and another when it is uttered by the Eternal Being.

## II.

"Behold, I come quickly." The good Bishop of Philadelphia, Demetrius, probably felt that, as far as he was concerned, these words received their fulfilment when, his pastoral labours being completed, he laid him down to die. In death our Lord comes to each of us; He comes in mercy or in judgment to bring the present stage of existence to an end, and to open upon us another.

And there are two things about death which are full of meaning, and which do not admit of contradiction. The first is the certainty that it will come to each of us some day; the second is the utter uncertainty of the day on which it will come. "Behold, I come;" that admits of no doubt whatever. "Behold, I come quickly;" that introduces a question of date, which may, nay, must be, very different in different cases, but not very distant in any.

[a] Ps. xxxix. 6.     [b] Ib. xc. 4.

That we shall die, each one of us, some day, is quite
certain. The verdict of experience is too plain to admit of
discussion. All do die. One sentence of Revelation is not
questioned by those who question all else : "It is appointed
unto men once to die."[a] No charm, no elixir of life, no
discovery of science, has availed to do more than postpone
the event which is at last inevitable. Reason has nothing
to say against a certainty which she cannot help acknowledging; but in how many minds is this certainty, which
Reason cannot reject, sedulously kept out of the mental
sight, as though to forget it were the highest wisdom!
How much pains is taken to avoid the sight of anything
which reminds us of death; how much to avoid speaking
about it or hearing of it! What studied circumlocutions
do some of us employ rather than use the word which
describes that which awaits each one of us! In this we
are surely less well-advised than was that old Macedonian
monarch who, lest the cares of state and the blinding
flatteries which surround a throne should lead him to
forget his lot as a man, made it the business of one of his
slaves to remind him every morning that he had to die.
And our own Christian ancestors were in this matter
braver and truer to facts than we. A common subject
for paintings and verses three or four centuries ago was
what was weirdly called the "Dance of Death." There was
a famous representation of it in the cloister attached to
the old St. Paul's; and it was engraved in the margin of
Queen Elizabeth's Prayer-book. Death, as a skeleton
with a scythe, was represented as approaching men in
every rank of society, in every order of Church and state;
the monarch, the prelate, the man of learning, the man of
business, the squire, the physician, the lawyer, the minstrel,
the soldier, the hermit. Each estate was represented, so

[a] Heb. ix. 27.

that all beholders might be impressed with the fact that none would escape the visit of death. The rule of true thinking is that the first business of the mind should be to familiarize itself with facts. If this rule is to hold in the most important of all matters, then our first duty as men is to take full account of, to dwell upon, to base all our calculations on the certainty of death. The Lord of life and death says to each of us, "Behold, I come."

And as death is most certain, so the hour and manner of its approach is utterly uncertain. Few more curious chapters are there in the history of the human world than that of the efforts to diminish this uncertainty by such false and fanciful sciences as astrology. Astrology has had its day; the stars can tell nothing to you or me of the destiny that awaits us. But we moderns try to make up for the supposed loss by more searching examination of nature. We measure the strength of a constitution, the progress of a disease, all that is likely to retard, all that is likely to accelerate, man's descent into the grave with a patient and anxious accuracy of which our fathers dreamt not. Yet how often may it be said, even in the sphere of nature, that nothing is probable except the unforeseen! How often does some hidden mischief from within, or some unanticipated influence from without, burst in upon and baffle our nicest calculations! The invalids who have been invalids for years live on, as though they would never die. The young, the strong, the high-spirited, are hurried by some fatal accident, or some swift disease, away from our sight into the world of the departed. The lot of those who to the eye of man have an equal prospect of life is often, in fact, so different. It is now as our Lord described it: "Two men shall be in the field; the one shall be taken, and the other left. Two women shall be grinding at the mill; the one shall be taken, and the other left." [a]

When the end before us is so certain, and the date of its approach so utterly uncertain, man's true wisdom cannot be doubtful; it is a matter on which the most clear-sighted philosophy and the most fervid religion are agreed. It is to sit easily to the things of time; to keep the eye constantly fixed on that which will follow. It is day by day to untwine the bands and cords which the scenes and persons among whom we move here are constantly winding tightly around our hearts, that we may be ready, at a short notice, to quit them for the world in which all is real and lasting. Duty will not be done less thoroughly because consciously done on a passing scene; since if it is done rightly it will be done with an eye to the higher existence for which it is a preparation. "But this I say, brethren, the time is short: it remaineth, that both they that have wives be as though they had none; and they that weep, as though they wept not; and they that rejoice, as though they rejoiced not; and they that buy, as though they possessed not; and they that use this world, as not using it to the full: for the fashion of this world passeth away." [b] At Philadelphia, the memories were still fresh of the earthquake which a generation before had laid the city in ruins, and there was no saying at what moment an angry multitude might not attempt the extinction of the Christian Church in a tempest of fire and blood. We may be sure that the Bishop to whom the message was sent, "Behold, I come quickly," would have had in his mind those earlier words of the Divine Master, "Watch ye therefore; for ye know neither the day nor the hour at which the Son of Man cometh." [c] Beyond all question the words mean

---

[a] St. Matt. xxiv. 40, 41.     [b] 1 Cor. vii. 29-31.     [c] St. Matt. xxv. 13.

this : " Be ready for Christ's coming before He comes ;
prepare for death before you find, as you will find one
day, that you are already dying." Certainly there are
instances of death-bed repentance which, like that of the
penitent thief on the Cross,[a] compress into a few minutes
the work of years, and illustrate conspicuously the triumphant power of redeeming grace. But when modern
unbelief, concentrating its gaze on an entirely one-sided
conception of the Saviour of men, objects to us that a
religion which attributes saving efficacy to a death-bed
repentance is hostile to the general interests of morality,[b]
because it offers a way of escape from, and so a motive
for persevering in, a bad life, the answer is that the
objector mistakes the rare exception for the rule. The
rule is that men die as they have lived ; the rule is that
habit, which has been strong in life, is stronger than ever
when the mind is becoming overclouded and the strength
is failing ; the rule is that a Christian who would die
well must have lived well, by bearing in mind every day
of his life these words of his Lord, " Behold, I come
quickly."

### III.

" Behold, I come quickly." The expected coming of
Christ throws a flood of light upon human existence.
We are struck first of all with the insignificance of life.
Reference has already been made to the shortness of its
duration, which impressed the heathen as it struck the
Psalmist. And man's frailty is not less remarkable. Men,
cries the Psalmist, " fade away suddenly like the grass : in
the morning it is green, and groweth up ; but in the evening it is cut down, dried up, and withered."[c] To the same

---

[a] St. Luke xxii. 40-43.
[b] J. C. Morrison, *The Service of Man*, p. 94, *sqq.*      [c] Ps. xc. 5, 6.

purpose Isaiah, in the passage which Wise's beautiful
anthem has made so familiar to us: "The voice said,
Cry. And he said, What shall I cry? All flesh is grass,
and the goodliness thereof is as the flower of the field:
the grass withereth, the flower fadeth."[a]

And as life is short, so it is largely, for a great number
of persons, unhappy. "Man that is born of woman hath a
short time to live, and is full of misery."[b]  Much of the
disorder and unhappiness that is in the world is a product
of the undisciplined passions of men. But we have also
to think of the millions of human beings who have lived,
and live, under cruel and despotic governments, or without
any order or government at all, among scenes of violence
and bloodshed. Then, again, multitudes are born with
some imperfection of body, or still worse, of mind; and
we see them growing from infancy to manhood, and from
manhood to old age, insensible to all that is beautiful in
nature and life, and weighed down by the overwhelming
sense of a calamity from which there is no escape. And
even when man is in possession of all his faculties of
mind and body, how often is he obliged to pass his life in
occupations which are at once exacting and mechanical;
occupations which make scarcely any demand upon the
mind beyond that of attention to the movement of the
feet or the fingers; occupations which might almost or altogether be discharged by machinery, and which, taken by
themselves, appear unworthy of a being capable of appre-
hending truth and of growing in the apprehension of it,
and of enjoying a happiness proportioned to his own vast
desires![c]

"Behold, I come quickly." If Christ's coming means
anything, it means an introduction to the life which has

[a]  Isa. xl. 6, 7.  [b]  Job xiv. 1.
[c]  Speech of Mr. Gladstone about 1857, at Cuddesdon.

no end; to a world in which neither the moth nor rust of
time doth corrupt.[a]  It means, for all who will, succession
" to an inheritance, incorruptible, undefiled, and that fadeth
not away." [b]  The coming of our Lord means that all the
wrong-doing and passions of men which create so much
misery will have had their day.  It means an entrance,
actual or possible, upon a stage of existence in which
there will be no sorrow or crying, no pain or tears, no
weariness or monotony of life, since the former things will
have passed away.[c]  It means the exercise of man's highest
powers to the fullest extent of their capacity; the beginning of an existence in which thought and heart and will
will rest in ecstatic satisfaction on their One True Object,
and which will last for ever.

If a large number of human beings are disposed to look
almost exclusively on the darker side of life here, there
are others who regard it only as an opportunity for enjoyment, often of unlawful enjoyment.  The wealthy, certainly, have means of making it a succession of pleasurable
sensations; and the social reformer of our time is sometimes, like the old Roman Emperors, hard at work en-
deavouring to bring about a state of things in which these
pleasurable sensations shall be shared, if possible, by all
classes of the community.  And as the poor, who have
few such enjoyments, look at the homes and equipages of
the possessors of wealth, they think of their owners, often
very unjustly, as of people who must be supremely happy,
because they need do nothing, and can eat every day
until they can eat no more, and above all can enjoy
themselves as they like.

Nothing, probably, is more certain than that the pleasures of sense, at any rate when pursued beyond a certain limit, are so far from promoting happiness, that they

ᵃ St. Matt. vi. 20.    ᵇ 1 St. Pet. i. 4.    ᶜ Rev. xxi. 4.

actively destroy it.   They destroy the very organs and
faculties which are the instruments of the pleasurable
sensation; they tend steadily to destroy the physical
frame which is the seat of the sensation.   They cannot
be the true pleasures of a being like man, since they
exclude and are hostile to the nobler parts of his nature,
namely, the rational and moral parts of it.   They are
pleasures which belong to him in common with the lower
animals; only the lower animals appear to enjoy them in
a greater degree than he.   It surely is not for this purpose
that man is endowed with the splendid light of reason,
with the vast wealth of imagination, with the retentive
grasp of memory, with the imperial energy of will, with
the constant restless activity of desire and hope reaching
out from the actual and visible into the unseen and the
future.   How superfluous is the whole higher side of
man's nature if his real happiness lies in the pleasures
of sense![a]   True it is that a large number of men and
women in each generation do devote themselves with
extraordinary ardour to the pursuit of these pleasures;
so great a number, indeed, that they create a large body
of false sentiment, which holds that such pleasures are
the true happiness of man.   And in a city like Philadelphia, half Greek, half Asiatic, there would have been
a large number of people of this opinion; there were
customs, institutions, even worships, which, to the anguish
of the Bishop Demetrius, tended to foster it.

Now, this devotion to the pleasures of sense is an illusion which will vanish at the coming of Jesus Christ.
"Behold, I come quickly."   He would not be Himself if
His appearance could sanction that which He became
incarnate in order to destroy; if the votaries of these
things could find a place in His Everlasting Kingdom.

[a] W. E. Channing.

" As it was in the days of Noah, so shall it be also in the days of the Son of Man. They did eat, they drank, they bought, they sold, they were marrying, and giving in marriage, until the day came that Noah entered into the ark, and the flood came, and destroyed them all." [a]

Many men, however, who would not care to use wealth as a means of gratifying the senses, yet do value it as a means for gratifying ambition. They would not care to be gluttons or profligates; but they value the consideration and respect which are paid to high position. To be a peer rather than a commoner, a member of Parliament rather than a voter, an archbishop rather than a parish clergyman, seems to them desirable on account of the homage which the higher position exacts. In reality, the notion that any real satisfaction belongs to the higher position is a fiction of the imagination; and it is only a possible fiction until the coveted decoration is actually enjoyed, when the fiction is dissipated by contact with reality. Until a man reaches the desired place of honour, he conceives himself, by an inflation of the imagination, able somehow to extend himself over the whole sphere in which he would preside; but, having reached it, he knows that he is the same being, with the same very limited faculties, that he was before, and that he has at command no larger or surer avenues to the true satisfaction of his life than before were open to him.

No doubt there are ambitions and ambitions; there is the ambition which seeks harder service or more extended usefulness, side by side with the ambition which aims at greater personal dignity and power and ease. And men's motives are very mixed; so mixed that the best have often in them an alloy of selfishness, while the worst are not always without some ingredient of disinterestedness.

[a] St. Luke xvii. 26, 27.

But listen: "Behold, I come quickly." It is the coming of One Who has taken the measure of human life, and by the Incarnation and the Cross has put His own mark and certificate on real greatness. He "took on Him the form of a slave, and was made in the likeness of man."[a] "Ye know the grace of our Lord Jesus Christ, Who, when He was rich, yet for your sakes became poor, that ye through His poverty might be rich."[b]

There is yet another class; men who despise the pleasures of sense, and for whom the ambitions of public life have no attractions, but who devote themselves to knowledge and polite letters. That the pleasures of intellect are much higher than those of sense or those of public life, is indisputable; they are generally worthier of man; they are more refined in their own nature; they are more lasting. But, are they the true satisfaction of human life? Obviously they are denied, and always will be denied, to the great majority of human beings. In order to enjoy them, mental abilities of a certain kind, and at the least considerable opportunities for culture, are necessary; and this shows that they can never be shared except by a few. But if so, they cannot be the satisfaction of man as man. The cultivated class in the old heathen world did not feel this difficulty; they were content to believe that the highest good of man might be one which only a few men, themselves included, could possibly enjoy; but that larger humanity of the modern world, which is itself a creation of the Gospel, cannot admit the truth of any such supposition. And, further, the pleasures of intellect are very dependent on circumstances; they require leisure, the absence of serious anxiety, fairly good health, in order to be secured; the invalid, the unfortunate, the friendless, can hardly ever

[a] Phil. ii. 7.  [b] 2 Cor. viii. 9.

secure them. Nay, more; the increase of knowledge, apart from other things, means, as the Bible tells us, an increase of sorrow.[a] Knowledge by itself is not enjoyment; knowledge only promotes real enjoyment when it introduces us to some object which appeals to the affections; and the seat of true enjoyment or happiness is not in the intellect, but in the heart. Knowledge by itself, and without the guidance of religion, only opens to the mind vast and bewildering problems, which, whatever else may be said about them, do not make men happy.

"Behold, I come quickly." It is the Word of Him "in Whom are hidden all the treasures of wisdom and knowledge,"[b] Who has nothing to learn from the wisest of the sons of men, but Who has said to all of us, "Except ye be converted, and become as little children, ye cannot enter into the Kingdom of Heaven."[c]

Lastly, there are those to whom the service of God, manifested in His Blessed Son, is the main object of life; men who, living in this world, and doing their duty in it to the best of their power, because from a high and pure motive, yet are not of it; men who set their affections on things above, not on things of the earth,[d] and look forward to the day when He Who is their Life shall appear, in the humble hope that they too will then appear with Him in glory.[e]

For this they have been preparing. For this they have renounced the world, the flesh, and the devil; and have embraced, each according to his measure, the Cross of Christ; the Cross which means discipline no less truly than it means salvation. One such, as I have learned since entering this church, has just passed away; a man whose name was very prominent in controversy a few years

---

[a] Eccles. i. 18.    [b] Col. ii. 3.    [c] St. Matt. xviii. 3.

[d] Col. iii. 2.    [e] Ib. 4.

ago. He has been withdrawn of late by illness from his public duties, and his true character as a sincere servant of God and a devoted friend of the poor will probably be recognized by all good men now that he has gone.[a]

Such, no doubt, were many of the Christians gathered round the first Bishop of the Church of Philadelphia; such, probably, was Bishop Demetrius himself. But they had, as we have, one great problem before them. Would they persevere unto the end? Would they have a share, not only in the kingdom, but also in the patience of Jesus? Would they not be worn out by the ceaseless opposition of the heathen, the manifold temptations of the scenes amidst which they lived, and the hardest battle of all, that with their own truant hearts and undisciplined tempers? Would they not give up the contest before the crown was won? Ah! that was then, that is now, a most anxious question for every servant of our Lord Jesus Christ; and if there is any one conviction that can brace the will, and enable us to endure unto the end, it is the conviction that, whether in death or judgment, yet certainly at last, Christ's word to the Angel of Philadelphia will be fulfilled, "Behold, I come quickly: hold fast that thou hast, that no man take thy crown."[b]

May our Lord Jesus, Who shed His Precious Blood for us, of His mercy, so invigorate us by the conviction that He will one day come, that when at last He makes His word good, we may know Whom we have believed,[c] and may welcome Him with the words, ancient but always new, "Lo, this is our God; we have waited for Him: He will save us!"[d]

[a] Rev. A. H. Mackonochie died from exposure on a hillside near Glencoe, December 17, 1887.

[b] Rev. iii. 11.       [c] 2 Tim. i. 12.       [d] Isa. xxv. 9.